Out of the Cotton Fields (and into the Classroom)

A Memoir of A Long Row to Hoe

by

Horace G. Danner

OCCOQUAN
BOOKS
A RIVER OF KNOWLEDGE

Published by
Occoquan Books
Occoquan, Virginia 22125

Library of Congress Catalog Card Number: 99-90453

ISBN: 0-937600-03-2

Horace G. Danner is also the author of
Words from the Romance Languages
and coauthor of
A Thesaurus of Word Roots of the English Language,
A Thesaurus of Medical Word Roots,
Discover It! A Better Vocabulary, the Better Way,
The English Tree of Roots: and Words from around the World

All books are available from
Occoquan Books
P. O. Box 614
Occoquan, VA 22125
703-491-5283
email: danner@occoquanbooks.com
website: www.occoquanbooks.com

Dedication

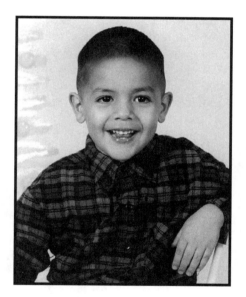

Julio Angel Segui-Rodriguez (Angelo)

A Note on the Structure of the Memoir

The memoir is largely chronological up until 1965, when I became the minister of music and education at Manassas Baptist Church, Manassas, Virginia. Then the memoir becomes quite topical, for working in the church; serving in Virginia National Guard and the Air Force Reserves; studying at University of Virginia, George Washington University, and American University; writing *Words from the Romance Languages*; working for The MITRE Corporation; teaching in the Fairfax County and Fauquier County public schools and at Northern Virginia Community College, Montgomery College, the District of Columbia Prison and at University of Maryland University College, all become intertwined to such an extent that I felt it best to write about one topic at a time. Thus, an incident mentioned in one topic often overlaps with that of another episode.

Toward the end of the memoir, I relate anecdotes of teaching at the National War College, teaching piano, and my mid-winter excursion to Puerto Rico.

Acknowledgments

As with every book, no matter how small, there are many people to thank for helping make it a reality. This memoir is certainly no exception. The teachers and family members who have been most influential in my education are, of course, named in the memoir itself.

Over the years, many people have asked what possessed me, who had rarely gotten out of the cotton fields of southeastern Alabama, to finish high school and go to college, eventually earning a Ph.D. from American University, Washington, D.C. I have never been able to give a ready answer, possibly because I didn't have all the answers myself. I eventually wrote the memoir in an attempt to find the answers.

Three persons suggested that I write my memoir, as each felt it would be an inspiration to young people as well as adults. For their motivation and prodding, I wish to thank each of the following: Peter Funk, writer of "It Pays to Increase Your Word Power," *Reader's Digest*; James E. Lyons, President, University Press of America, Lanham, Maryland; and Jeptha V. Greer, Executive Director, Council for Exceptional Children, Reston, Virginia. To all three of these gentlemen, I am deeply appreciative for their encouragement.

I am further indebted to colleagues, students, the United States Air Force, Disabled American Veterans (DAV), and the Veterans Administration (VA), all of whom played a significant role in my education and in the writing of the memoir. As far as colleagues and students, there are too many to list, and in the Air Force, the DAV and the VA, they are mostly unknown to me.

I am especially grateful to Joyce McDowell; she has the uncanny ability to capture the essence of several paragraphs into appropriate headings. Joyce also edited several of the initial versions.

And last, Roger Noël, my long-time writing partner, was most helpful in bringing certain irregularities to my attention.

My sincerest thanks to all of them. I should add, however, that after their readings, I have added many episodes. Consequently, any errors in the text I must claim as my own.

Thanks also to Ric Clark and others who helped publish this book.

It is my wish that the memoir will encourage students facing struggles to have renewed hope. It is also my desire that teachers will be lifted up by their tireless efforts and little pay to continue encouraging their students, as my teachers encouraged me. I would also encourage you to write your own memoir.

TENNESSEE

TENNESSEE RIVER

ALABAMA

GEORGIA

MISSISSIPPI

•BIRMINGHAM

BLACK WARRIOR RIVER

•TUSCALOOSA

TOMBIGBEE RIVER

ALABAMA RIVER

MONTGOMERY

TROY •

EUFAULA•

BARBOUR CO.

PEA RIVER

•OZARK

DOTHAN •

FLORIDA

MOBILE RIVER

•MOBILE

GULF OF MEXICO

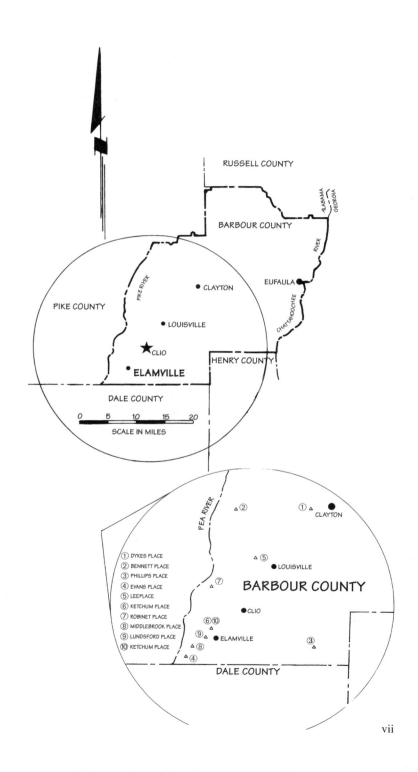

RUSSELL COUNTY

BARBOUR COUNTY

ALABAMA
GEORGIA

RIVER

PIKE RIVER

● CLAYTON

EUFAULA ●

PIKE COUNTY

● LOUISVILLE

CHATTAHOOCHEE

★ CLIO

HENRY COUNTY

● ELAMVILLE

DALE COUNTY

0   5   10   15   20
SCALE IN MILES

PEA RIVER

△ ②   ① △
                      ● CLAYTON

① DYKES PLACE
② BENNETT PLACE   △ ⑤
③ PHILLIPS PLACE   ● LOUISVILLE
④ EVANS PLACE
⑤ LEE PLACE   ⑦
⑥ KETCHUM PLACE   △   BARBOUR COUNTY
⑦ ROBINET PLACE
⑧ MIDDLEBROOK PLACE
⑨ LUNDSFORD PLACE   ● CLIO
⑩ KETCHUM PLACE   ⑥⑩
                     △
                 ⑨ △ ● ELAMVILLE   ③
                 △ ⑧   △
                 △ ④
                      DALE COUNTY

vii

Out of the Cotton Fields
(and into the Classroom)

A Long Row To Hoe

School was a haven for me, a light in my day, my vision at night. Not only was it a place which I looked forward to attending each day, it was also where I received encouragement and support. But getting an education wasn't always easy, because in the early years, I was often barefoot, destitute, and hungry. Hunger was a constant adversary and companion for my first nine years of school, dogging my steps, invading my thoughts, and stalking my actions. And it was hard to study at home since I often didn't have a lamp to read by. Graduating from high school, to use a Southern expression, would be a long row to hoe.

I was the youngest of ten children—the seventh son of the seventh son. I was born on a Saturday, February 4, 1933, when Daddy was 42 years old, and Mama, 44. Of German descent, Daddy was named James Nelson Danner (known as Nelse); my mother, Hettie Mae Dykes, was mostly English with some Scottish and Irish blood. Though my mother's name was Hettie Mae, I never heard Daddy call her anything but Sook. Both sets of my grandparents had already died by the time I was born, or at least before I knew them. Daddy smoked; pulling a thin cigarette leaf from a packet, he rolled his own limp cigarette from a can of Prince Albert tobacco.

To pay Dr. Robert Olon Norton of Louisville for delivering me, Daddy shaved cypress logs into roof shingles, inasmuch as I came along at the depths of the Great Depression, when in our family, there was no money and little hope of earning any. I was born at home, as were my nine siblings, but it was our own home; or at least, it belonged to my maternal grandfather, William Penn Dykes, who had always farmed just outside Louisville. Shortly after I was born, however, the Federal Land Bank foreclosed on the property. When Grandpa Dykes lost the farm, we moved about seven miles due west to the Bennett Place.[1] The Bennett Place was within walking distance of Pea River—not the mighty Tennessee, the broad Alabama, the rushing Tombigbee, the majestic Black Warrior, the lazy Choctowhatchee (all colorful names of riv-

---

[1] In the Deep South, *Place* refers to the houses and land owned by a landlord but occupied by a tenant farmer or sharecropper, and is usually designated by the last name of the landowner.

ers in Alabama)—but the sparkling Pea,[2] except after a heavy rain; then, it was the muddy Pea. My earliest memories are of the river, and of my father's love affair with its bountiful supply of channel cat, bream, and eels. The river coursed in and out of our lives for most of the eighteen years I lived at home.

When we moved to the Bennett Place, there were five boys still living at home: Olon, Loyce, Ralph, Bennie, and I. About the only thing I remember about living at the Bennett Place was Daddy once going fishing before I got up and catching a bream, which he told Mama to fry for my breakfast. But I do recall Mama recounting that a Mrs. Mills, who lived about a mile from us, once came to our house, ostensibly to borrow a cup of flour, and then said that while she was there, she would also need a cup of sugar, an egg, as well as other ingredients to bake her husband a birthday cake, a luxury Mama couldn't afford even for her own family. It was also at the Bennett Place that I first heard of Effie, but I'll tell more about her later.

While my father was the seventh son, he was the ninth of twelve children, the only one who drank excessively, and the only one who was a sharecropper. Only recently did I learn he descended from a long line of prosperous landowners, and that my great-grandfather, Thomas Marion Danner, had received a vast tract of land for his valiant leadership in the Creek Indian War, 1813-1814. But alcohol had become Daddy's master early in life, even though some of my older siblings said he wasn't a particularly heavy drinker when they were growing up.

Twenty-five years spanned the age difference between my oldest brother and me. Most of us had Anglo-Saxon names, as the following, starting with the oldest, indicate: William Lovick, Lalar Irene, Vallie Leona, James Franklin, Ellie Mae, Olon Webster (a namesake of Dr. Norton, who delivered most of the Danner children), Edgar Loyce, Jesse Ralph, Bennie Harold, and me, Horace Gerald.

I don't know what possessed my parents to name me Horace. Maybe, the reason was vengeance for my not being born a girl; there had been six boys ahead of me—including four directly older, and it seems everyone thought it was time for a girl to help Mama around the house. So intent were my mother and three sisters on my being born a girl, they refused to let my shoulder-

---

[2] *Pea River* is a calque, or literal translation, of the Creek Indian *Talak* (Pea) and *Hatchee* (River). The original name was Talakhatchee, similar in spelling to Choctawhatchee, another river in South Alabama.

length, curly locks be shorn until I was around four. My father only reinforced the idea that his youngest son was supposed to have been a girl. Often, when my older brothers were leaving for the cotton or peanut fields, he would tell me to stay home and help my mother. Other times, when I wasn't working the way he thought a boy my age should, he would order me back to the house. Or, I was the water boy, fetching water from the well or from a nearby spring for my brothers and him. Through the years, his favorite expression to me was "Make haste, Fiddler." Until I was well into high school, I thought the two words were one— m'KASTE. But I knew from the tone of his voice exactly what he meant: no dillydallying around looking for Indian arrowheads, once quite abundant in our area, or looking at birds and admiring wildflowers along the way.

Another word that was used throughout my childhood was "fawty," as a fawty pecan, a fawty peanut, or a fawty peach, that is, one that is defective, blemished, or imperfect. I'm not sure when I finally realized that "fawty" was a dialectal form of "faulty."

My father always called me Fiddler. My sisters, who were already married when I was born, called me Horace Gerald. Ralph and Loyce called me Skeezix, a character in "Gasoline Alley," a comic strip popular at the time. They continued to call me Skeezix even after I had little Skeezixes of my own. To just about everyone else, I was simply Horace, though I must admit that my mother often called me Baby, at least before I started school.

I have often thought of starting a website called "For Men Named Horace," and printing the comments made when these men introduce themselves. As I've done so over the years, the other person has often said one of two things: "What had you rather be called?" or "What do other people call you?" If I can count on the accuracy of the Internet, I am the only person in the entire United States—and probably the planet—named Horace Gerald Danner—that is, other than my firstborn. And it wasn't my idea to name Jerry after me—that blame can be laid directly on his mother. Since I was stuck with the name, I wanted to be the first person by the name of Horace G. Danner to write a book. Alas, in checking the Library of Congress catalog when I wrote my first book, *Words from the Romance Languages*, I found that there was another Horace G. Danner, who wrote a mathematics book, but his middle name was not Gerald. A first cousin was H. G. Danner, but the initials stood for Homer Glenn.

As soon as I knew what a dictionary was and how to use it, I looked up my first name. I didn't expect to find it, for I assumed the dictionary contained only the names of common objects and concepts. But I found that Horace was a Roman poet, and I would later learn that he wrote odes and satires. He was also noted for his sayings, one of which is *Naturam expellas furca, tamen usque recurret*: "You may drive out Nature with a pitchfork, but she will always come back." Another is *Dulce est desipere in loco*: "It is pleasant to act foolishly in the right place." Horace is also credited with the phrase *carpe diem*, or "seize the day," the theme of the movie *Dead Poets Society*; the theme is also expressed rather succinctly in Robert Herrick's 17th-century poem, "To Virgins, To Make Most of Time," the first verse of which reads, "Gather ye rosebuds while ye may,/ Old time is still a-flying;/ And this same flower that smiles today/ Tomorrow will be dying."

Since my academic pursuit is classical etymology, where I delve into the Greek and Latin roots of English, many of my colleagues have asked if my parents were professors or academicians and had anticipated my ultimate career and, therefore, named me after the poet. Once, when one of my colleagues saw a photo of Daddy dressed in a suit, he declared that my father reminded him of a physics professor he once had at Stanford. Daddy did have the mien of a professional. No doubt it was his young handsomeness that made him an attractive suitor to my petite mother, who at 18 years of age, regarded her 17-year-old, broad-shouldered, 6-foot beau as a grown man.

Through the years, Daddy's youngest sister, Aunt Bessie Preston, would tell me that the seventh son of the seventh son was destined to be someone special, and I've tried to live up to her expectations. Excepting myself, only Bennie, my next-older brother, would go beyond grade school, graduating from high school two years ahead of me. The other eight had to drop out of school and work in the fields, planting, chopping, and picking cotton as well as planting, hoeing, and stacking peanuts. I am extremely grateful to my older brothers and sisters for their sacrifices; all of them could have excelled in school had they been afforded the opportunity.

[3] As I was writing this section about WPA and NYA, it occurred to me that I hadn't visited the Franklin Delano Roosevelt Memorial in Washington, D.C., even though it's only about 15 miles from Occoquan, Virginia, where I live. So, I went to visit the memorial and could

Beginning around 1937, after the crop was in, my father often did "public work" during the winter for the WPA (Work Projects Administration), which was part of President Roosevelt's New Deal.[3] WPA was one of a number of efforts to pull the nation out of the Great Depression. Though the New Deal's many programs cost the government more than it received in taxes, it was still a boon for us. We began to see some actual money for a change. About the time I started school, Daddy was working for the WPA more than he was on the farm, leaving the work to Olon, Loyce, and Ralph. Daddy was now covered under Social Security, another New Deal innovation. When he was out of a job, I remember him saying that he was going to "collect his pennies," which were usually spent on another bottle.

My father was never violent when he drank; rather, he would lie down on the bed and pass out. Intermittently, he would stir and call out, "Fiddler, Fiddler, come see me; I'm a-dying." I became rather inured to his ritual of calling me, and tried to ignore it and continue playing outside. But once, he simply called and called, till I had no choice but to go in and see him. I knelt on the floor by his bedside, and finally reached up and touched him. He was warm, and I knew he would be all right the next day. When I touched him, he aroused slightly and told me to go back outside and play. I feel that touching my father was a defining point in my life; for many years afterward, I sought the warmth and closeness of a care-providing adult male.

When Daddy would pass out, Mama would start looking for the bottle. When she found it, she would hide it, as if by doing so, she would make him forget that he had bought one. But the next morning, he would tell Mama to fix him a toddy—a raw egg mixed with liquor—to help him get over his hangover. Mama would tell him she couldn't since she didn't have anything to fix it with. But Daddy knew better, and he would then tell her in no uncertain terms to make him one.

It didn't take long for Olon and Loyce to become disenchanted with doing most of the work on the farm, and around 1938, both of them enrolled in the NYA (National Youth Administration), another program originated by President Roosevelt to put low-income youth to work. When they returned home on the weekends, they told fabulous tales of having all the food they could eat, in-

hardly contain my emotions, seeing the statues of men in soup lines as well as those of destitute farmers. I returned the following week, simply to ponder his many sayings inscribed on the granite blocks, especially "The only thing we have to fear is fear itself."

cluding fresh fruit and nuts. One of the projects that the NYA completed in Clio, the commercial center of southern Barbour County, was planting rose gardens at both the elementary and high schools. Loyce and Olon said the project superintendent told them they were entitled to pick a rose at any time they wanted, to give to their girlfriends. When I started school, the gardens of full-blown roses were still being maintained.

It wasn't long until the Supreme Court declared most of the public work projects created by President Roosevelt to be unconstitutional. After the NYA disbanded, Olon and Loyce ventured to Birmingham, where they found work in the coal and ore mines. They both had good reason to leave the farm because Daddy took the money they earned and spent it on whiskey, or so I've been told on good authority.

In only a few weeks, Olon returned home, saying he wouldn't live in Birmingham and work in the mines even if Tennessee Coal and Iron (TCI) made him the president of the company. He immediately began farming, married Estelle Hartzog, and started raising a large family. Following in Daddy's footsteps, he later became a brick mason, and eventually a construction contractor, though Olon said he picked up the mason trade on his own. Not long before Olon died, he told me Daddy never taught him anything, not even how to drink. And only a few months before Loyce died, he echoed the same sentiments about Daddy. Except for a brief time in Detroit in a defense factory and then his two and a half years in the Army during World War II, Loyce would stay with TCI until he retired.

On Loyce's first visit back to South Alabama after going to Birmingham, he opened an account at Davis' Store, located about a mile from us, in order for us to buy the basic necessities inasmuch as we couldn't always count on Daddy. I would often be sent to the store for some item with the instructions to put it on Loyce's account. Once I went to the store for Mama and told Mr. Davis to charge it. I was never so ashamed as when he said that he was afraid we were charging more than Loyce could ever pay. I am not sure if Loyce ever knew how much we charged, and we moved out of the area shortly afterward. I understand that Mr. Davis wrote off the remaining debt as uncollectable.

My Oases

Both my parents could read, though my mother somewhat halt-ingly; however, I was never read to at home because we had no books or magazines in the house except for a Bible. My father read *The Montgomery Advertiser*, and from time to time, I saw Mama reading from the Bible, but she never read it aloud to me.

My oldest sister, Lalar Irene, made up for the deficiency some-what. Though she may not have been named after Irene, the Greek goddess of peace, Lalar was the essence of tranquility. Married with two children of her own, she lived only a short dis-tance from us. She would gather both of them, Eldridge and Doris; their cousins, James and Sybil; and me together to read *Snow White and the Seven Dwarfs*, *Little Red Riding Hood*, *Goldilocks*, *Jack and the Beanstalk*, and dozens of other fairy tales. I looked forward to these sessions, for Lalar was an excellent reader, burst-ing with excitement and animation. The tales of the tortoise and the hare and of the goose that laid the golden egg were two of my favorites. Years later, when I studied the fable as a literary genre, I found that I knew most of Aesop's fables, thanks to Lalar.

In addition to the fairy tales and fables that Lalar either read or told, Vallie had taught me at least a dozen nursery rhymes, such as "Little Boy Blue." Some of the others were "The Three Little Pigs," "Little Bo Peep," "Jack and Jill," and "Hickory Dickory Dock." So, by the time I started school, I had acquired quite a rep-ertoire of children's stories, even if it wasn't Mama and Daddy who read them, or told them, to me.

When I was around five, I received a rather harsh lesson in race relations. Isaac Jefferson, a black boy the same age as I, lived across the brook from us. Isaac's father, Zeb, kept us both enter-tained, often for an hour at a time, performing magic tricks. Though Isaac soon became bored with his father's pulling nick-els from behind our ears, I never ceased to be enthralled. As the grand finale, Zeb would give each of us a nickel he magically pro-duced, for us to spend when the rolling store came by.

The rolling store—a store on wheels—was constructed on an open flatbed truck with an enclosed body, with shelves installed along the sides to display the wares. Farmers would usually buy a month's supply of staples when they went into Clio to buy fertilizer or a plow part; and the rolling store carried those items that a housewife might need in between the monthly visits to town, such as coffee, flour, sugar, black pepper, salt, and, of course, for us children, bubble gum, candy bars, suckers, and cinnamon balls. One could also trade an egg for a candy bar. Since we always had plenty of eggs, I was assured of a weekly Baby Ruth or an all-day sucker. But the nickels Zeb occasionally gave Isaac and me meant an extra treat. Isaac and I also scoured the neighborhood for scrap iron, which we could sell for a half a cent a pound when the scrap truck made its occasional rounds. Though we might not get more than five or ten cents for our effort, it was still enough to buy even more treats. I had always thought the rolling store was strictly a country convenience, and possibly only in southeastern Alabama, for I have never heard anyone in other parts of the state or country refer to it. However, *The Washington Post* recently ran an article that said "stores on wheels" are a big event in the housing projects in Washington; the modern "rolling store" carries everything from Pampers to Popsicles.

Isaac and I also caught tadpoles where we had dammed up the stream between our two homes. And we set all sorts of traps to catch bluebirds and redbirds, luring them with grains of corn and oats. After one of our many unsuccessful attempts, Daddy said, "Don't you fellas know that a bird in the hand is worth two in the bush?" He told us we should devote our time to an activity we could accomplish. Since Isaac and I had already planned to live together with our wives and children, we thought about planting a garden to support our future families, which we had planned on starting in a matter of weeks, though neither one of us had a girlfriend. Chuckling about our still-far-fetched plans, Daddy plowed us a couple of rows alongside the vegetable garden where Isaac and I set out to plant corn and beans.

Quite a dancer, Isaac tried to teach me some of his intricate dance steps. I just didn't have his rhythm. A lady who lived close by once saw the two of us together, playing, dancing, and just having a good time. She promptly asked my mother if I didn't have anyone better to play with than a little nigger boy. It wasn't the first time I had heard this opprobrious term, but I just didn't see how it could be applied to an innocent five-year-old boy—just like me, except for the color of our skins. But Mama apparently thought that anyone who was important, had an education, and was religious besides must be right, and said I shouldn't be seen playing with Isaac anymore, not around the house anyway. Surely this was the type of attitude Dr. Martin Luther King, Jr. was alluding to when he made his famous "I Have a Dream" speech. In the speech at the Lincoln Memorial, in Washington, D.C., he said that he had a dream when one day little white boys and little black boys of Alabama and Mississippi could play and walk hand in hand together.

Though Isaac couldn't go with me to my church, I had gone with him several times to his, the New Jerusalem Baptist Church. The hymns, many of which were the same ones as I had heard in my church, were sung in such a manner that I didn't understand the words. The worshippers also clapped their hands, often stamped their feet, and shouted Hallelujah, Amen. It wasn't long before I lost my reserve and clapped along with Isaac. I was especially intrigued with the unique swing style of piano-playing, one which I've never been able to replicate.

I hated leaving Isaac behind when I started to school. It was twenty years before schools were integrated in the South, and Isaac would have to trudge at least five miles to school, since there was no bus service for blacks. It wasn't long, however, before Isaac's family moved to Chicago. I've often wondered what became of my young friend. If he's still living, he would be 70 at this writing.

It was around the time I started to school that I first learned of the military. Mabel Key, the daughter of one of our neighbors, returned home on leave from the Navy, dressed in her sparkling white nurse's uniform, with the rank of Lieutenant Junior Grade. She was beautiful, and her uniform made her even more so. She served throughout the war. By the time the war was over, we had moved several times, and I never saw her again. But her uniform made an indelible impression upon me.

Entering Low School in Clio, Alabama

In September 1939, I entered first grade at Clio Low School in Clio, Alabama, a cotton and peanut town with a population of about 1,000, located some fifty miles north of the Florida border, thirty miles west of the Georgia line, and roughly fifty miles southeast of Montgomery, the capital—and the first capital of the Confederacy. *Clio* is pronounced KLY oh, not KLEE oh, as those from other parts of the state and country are prone to call it. The town may not have been named after Clio, the muse of history in Greek mythology, but it took pride in its past, as well as its present and, on the surface, its future. For example, the schools were well maintained and staffed with many state-certified teachers. And the town itself was a bustling community of thriving and well-stocked stores, two banks, a barber shop, a beauty salon, a butcher shop, a bottling plant, a train depot, a cotton gin, a boutique called "Ye Olde Shoppe," two large peanut warehouses, a hotel, a mule stable, two automotive garages, and a church each of the Baptist, Methodist, and Presbyterian denominations. (I never met a person of the Jewish or Catholic faith until I went to college.) We also had a doctor, Dr. Tillman, and a dentist, Dr. Reynolds. Clio's clean-swept streets were lined with colonnaded homes bedecked with japonicas as well as the showy state flower, the camellia. Of course, those nice homes belonged to bankers and absentee land-lords who rarely saw the poverty and deprivation endured by their tenant farmers and sharecroppers, though in only one instance in all my 17 years at home did I perceive we were ever mistreated by a landlord.

Starting school was extremely exciting for me. First of all, I had my first pair of store-bought overalls, as shown in my first-grade picture. With a cotton sack strapped over her shoulders, Mama, together with Bennie and me, gleaned the peanuts that had been left in the field after the harvest. Mama would then sell them in order to buy us school clothes. Even in the dead of winter, she scrubbed our clothes outside in washtubs and a washpot. After drying the clothes on the line in the fresh country air, she then starched and pressed them with a flatiron, heated on the stove during the warm months or on the hearth during the winter. Mama made sure we were Sunday-clean when we went to school. She was able to do this despite the fact that we usually couldn't afford good store-bought soap. The only store-bought soap we used at our house was a bar of Octagon. Extremely harsh and abrasive, Octagon was fine for washing floors and possibly clothes, but not when used as a bath soap.

There was a time when we actually made the soap that Mama

often used for washing. Daddy had built a wooden bin where we emptied the ashes from the fireplace and the stove. The bottom of the bin was equipped so that when boiling water was poured over the ashes, the alkali liquid, called potash, or lye, drained into containers. The liquid was then poured into an outdoor iron kettle—called a wash pot—and mixed with bacon drippings and hog fat. Soap-making was usually done in conjunction with a hogkilling when there would be plenty of otherwise useless fat to mix with the potash. As the scraps disintegrated and the water evaporated, the mixture thickened so that eventually it could be poured into wooden containers with separators to make bars of soap. The lye soap cleaned quite well, but it had a terrible odor.

I wasn't the child prodigy who learned to read before going to school, probably because of the lack of reading material in our home, but I was eager to learn. Bennie taught me my ABCs, and I had begun asking him how to spell particular words. Once, when I misspelled a word, Bennie said that every syllable must have a vowel in it. At the time, I had no idea what either a syllable or a vowel was.

The most exciting thing on the first day of school was that we rode on a brand-new, yellow school bus. It was a GMC with a Bluebird body. I knew that the school system was getting new buses, because Olon and Loyce had gone by train with a group of men from Barbour County all the way to Gary, Indiana, to drive the new buses back to Clio. There was one thing that bothered me about the school bus, and that was the words "Emergency Exit" over the rear door. Remembering what Bennie had taught me about sounding out words, I concluded that *emergency* was pronounced *emmer jensy*. A sixth-grader on the bus corrected my pronunciation, and I suddenly recognized the word. Daddy had used it when Ellie Mae, my youngest sister, had come to our house for her first baby to be born. He'd said that sending for the doctor was an "emergency." I looked back at the school bus door, wondering what a school bus door had to do with having a baby.[4]

Across the street from the low school stood the ivy-walled upper school, Barbour County High, in front of which proudly waved the flags of the United States and the State of Alabama. Seeing those flags on the first day of school, I began to get an inkling of a grander world than the one to which I was accustomed.

[4] In psychology, the term for linking one concept to another is called *concatenation*, literally "linking together," and is a viable learning tool. It helps, however, if the links are on the same chain.

1st Grade

It wasn't until the second grade that I learned that each of the 48 stars represented one of the states, with no one star being larger or smaller than the others, and that each of the stripes represented one of the 13 original colonies. I learned early on that Alabama's motto, *Audemus jura nostra defendere,* was Latin for "We dare to defend our rights." Latin, in fact, was then taught in high school, but by the time I became a student there, the school had lost its only Latin teacher to the war. Although Clio wasn't the seat of Barbour County, the high school was the first one in the county to be state-funded, and was thus named Barbour County High School.

Of my myriad memories of entering first grade that fall, the most vivid is the sandspurs, foot-high, spindly, tumbleweed-type plants that grow in the sandy soil of the Gulf Coastal Plain of southeastern Alabama. These plants produce small prickly balls that fall into the sand around mid-August, just before school starts. The same shade as sand, the spur balls are difficult to see. They're also extremely painful, and badly chafe one's bare feet. Since I didn't have shoes at the time school started, I was continually pricked by the spurs, especially on the sandy playground during recess.

After paying the landlord his share of the crop, Daddy bought me a pair of ill-fitting shoes that caused blisters more painful than the sandspurs. On a brighter side, however, there was a very pretty and charming girl in my class, Mary Ann, the only sister of George C. Wallace, who later was elected governor of Alabama. Although Mary Ann came from what I perceived as a very wealthy family, she treated me as though I belonged to her own social group.

There were three first-grade classes in the fall of 1939, and I was fortunate to be assigned to Miss Lula Andrews' room. Miss Andrews had already taught for almost two decades, beginning in 1922, and would continue for 30 more years. She would show words to the class, such as *Dick* and *Jane, cat* and *dog,* and we repeated them after her. Years later, I learned this method of teaching reading was called the sight word approach; at the time, phonics wasn't a part of the Alabama curriculum, or at least not in Clio Low School. Apparently, phonics had been taught in previous years, as I remember Bennie sounding out words. At any rate, it wasn't long before Mary Ann and I were at the head of the class, reading "See Spot run" in our primers. The parents of Dick and Jane who played with Spot were called *Mother* and *Father*. From the beginning, I learned that primers don't always reflect the real world, since I called my parents *Mama* and *Daddy*.

One of my most vivid memories of Miss Andrews is her correcting both my speech and my actions. Once, when I finished a worksheet ahead of time, I jumped out of my seat like a jack-in-the-box and blurted out, "Miss Andrews, look, look, I'm done!" Firmly but gently, she said she would have to stick a fork in me to see if I was *done* enough to eat. She admonished me to remain in my seat, raise my hand, and say quietly—if I must at all—"Miss Andrews, I am finished."

Another memory from first grade was the lunches served at the school. My favorite was beef-vegetable soup, saltine crackers, and peanut butter cookies. I suppose the lunchroom was state or federally funded, for none of us had to pay. Mary Ann didn't eat lunch at school though; either she went home or her maid brought little sandwiches, like hors d'oeuvres, with the crust of the bread neatly sliced off. What a waste, I thought to myself. We never threw any food away at our house.

The lunchroom staff served us first graders in our rooms. I told one of the ladies who came to pick up the trays that the peanut butter cookies were the best I'd ever tasted, and that I was sure my mother would like to add the recipe to her collection. The lady was so pleased with the compliment, she returned in a few minutes with the scaled-down recipe along with special instructions to pass along to my mother. She also told me to tell Mama what a polite and cute little boy she had for a son. The truth of the matter was I'd never before eaten peanut butter cookies and Mama didn't have any recipe collection. It was just an example of my many made-up stories. Although Mama never baked frosted cakes, she occasionally made the best rolled gingerbread cakes I've ever tasted. She didn't need a recipe for these. As I recall, it was a tablespoon of ginger and a half bowl of self-rising flour, adding an egg, and then molasses, to obtain the desired consistency. And, oh, she could make the most scrumptious blackberry and huckleberry cobblers!

When school recessed for Thanksgiving, the principal talked to all the students about the significance of the holiday. He then wished us a happy Thanksgiving and told us not to eat too much turkey. Frankly, I had never seen a turkey and didn't know anyone who even raised them. I knew that the holiday would pass at our house as just another Thursday. Our family never celebrated any event, except the Danner Family Reunion, held the third Sunday in June to commemorate Daddy's birthday, June 21.

Since I enjoyed school tremendously, especially learning to read, I couldn't wait to get home to tell Mama and Daddy all I had learned. I soon found that my schooling appeared to be of little consequence to either of them. Daddy, I think, felt cheated that I had a bent for learning and wasn't much of a field worker, and Mama was probably too busy trying to prepare three meals for our large family.

Even if Mama didn't appear to be very excited about what I had learned, I knew that she would have a baked sweet potato in the oven when I got home. One of the best things about growing up on a farm in the Deep South was the potatoes, not the kind usually found in stores today, but those so sweet the syrup oozed through the skin. When dabbed with freshly churned butter, there was no better eating—and nothing more satisfying. During the winter, the potatoes were protected with pine needles and covered over with a mound of dirt, called a hill, to keep them from freezing. Alabama, whose sobriquet is "Heart of Dixie," is indeed the heart of the Deep South, but the weather can become quite chilly in winter, usually with a freeze in February, even in Lower Alabama (or, L.A., as south of Montgomery is often called). North of Montgomery, there had even been occasional reports of snow, though I had no idea what it was, other than someone saying it came down as white flakes instead of drops like rain.

In later years, Lalar, my oldest sister, would tell me I had a justifiable reason for not being robust and aggressive like my older brothers. She said that I may have even been born a little odd inasmuch as Mama was worn out from already having carried so many babies—ten in 25 years; also, because of the Depression, she said Mama didn't have the proper nutrition before I was born, especially since she was already past normal childbearing years. Or, Lalar said, my oddity might have been caused by Mama getting bit by a rattlesnake when she was picking blackberries, in the summer she was carrying me. At any rate, Lalar said I was born lacking something—exactly what, she wasn't sure. I've never quite figured out why I was so unsettling to her. Doesn't every little boy like to dance, sing, and make up wild stories? And does anyone really enjoy working in the cotton fields under a scorching South Alabama sun? I must say, however, that in my teens, Lalar once said if she had a boy who had musical talent and wanted to play the piano, she would find some way to get him one on which to practice. That boosted my self-esteem, because, in many ways, I had often felt I was not a real Danner boy.

When I was in first grade, the school sponsored a dog show, with the dogs performing tricks, such as jumping through hoops and climbing ladders. The students were given a preview of the show, with the actual program being the next day. Admission was ten cents. Though I knew better than to ask Daddy for the money, I asked anyway, for he sometimes had change in his pocket, now that he was working for the WPA. As expected, he said rather peremptorily that I didn't need to see any dog show. As I was leaving for school the next morning, my 14-year-old brother, Ralph, dug into his pocket and found a dime, which he gave to me. The dog show was the last paid school event I would attend for the next ten years.

I have often wondered how Ralph might have had even so much as a dime. About a year before Ralph died, I asked him, and he said it was for digging up a pine stump for Foy Knight, a wealthy farmer who lived a half mile up the road. I had always assumed it was for one of his many whittling creations. For as long as I can remember, Ralph could carve anything from a piece of wood, even from peach seeds. He would take a peach seed and begin whittling; after a day or two, he would produce, for example, a monkey or a basket of flowers. In later years, I asked him how he could whittle an object so perfectly. He said it was easy, just whittle away the part that doesn't belong to the desired object. In later years, Ralph's elaborate nameplates of exotic woods would grace the desks of presidents, generals, members of Congress, governors, and country music artists.

In the first grade, I had neither paste nor crayons as did the other boys and girls, and I often didn't have a pencil or a tablet. Mary Ann, like many other students from well-to-do families, had not only paper and pencils, but also watercolors and other art supplies. However, that particular year the Nu-Icey Bottling Company of Clio gave free pencils and writing tablets to all the students in school. When the packages of supplies arrived, the principal sent gargantuan sixth-graders around to each of the rooms, giving a pencil, a tablet, and a ruler to each student. To this day, I am grateful for those supplies brilliantly inscribed in red against a white background, "Compliments of The Coca-Cola Company."

One day there was a knock at Miss Andrews' door, and there stood my father, all six feet, two inches of him. He handed the teacher a small paper sack, politely asking Miss Andrews to give it to his boy. He had brought a jar of paste and a box of crayons. Quite frankly, I was surprised as well as embarrassed that he had come to my room, for he was usually drinking. It didn't take but a glimpse of Daddy at the door to confirm my fear. But I was so happy to get the supplies, I didn't complain to him.

One of the downsides of starting school was discovering that other children received gifts at Christmas and on their birthdays. I knew I had a birthday, but I had no idea it was anything to celebrate or that for another child it could be an occasion for a party and gifts. No one ever said that February 4 was the least bit special, and, of course, I never had a birthday cake. The Christmas songs we sang in school said Santa Claus brought gifts to children who had been good, for he made a list and checked it twice to find out who'd been naughty or nice. After hearing the other children tell what they were expecting from Santa, I too began to pore over the Sears, Roebuck catalog, circling fancy cowboy outfits and shiny, sleek Schwinn bicycles, absolutely certain I would find my wishes fulfilled on Christmas morning.

From the time I can remember until about the first or second grade, we had an entire crate of oranges at Christmas, bought at Mr. Rex Davis' store. With his sharp pocketknife, Daddy could peel an orange the quickest and the neatest I've ever seen. And on Christmas Eve night, Daddy helped me hang one of Mama's old stockings on the mantel before I went to bed; even so, I wondered how Santa could fit a bicycle in it. Besides, Daddy kept a roaring fire in the fireplace, too hot for Santa to be sliding down the chimney to the hearth, I thought. The next morning, I found a tangerine, an apple, a cluster of raisins, and some Brazil nuts in my stocking. On the hearth was also an American Flyer red wagon—but, to my dismay and utter disappointment, no cowboy outfit or bicycle. I later learned that my sister Vallie had been saving for the wagon in order that I have something special.

By the second grade, I was onto the Santa thing, but still filled with high hopes, I hung a stocking on the mantel. Just like the year before, on Christmas morning, there was a tangerine, an apple, a cluster of raisins, and some nuts in the stocking. I thought that I had been as good as any happy-go-lucky boy my age could be, so I emboldened myself to tell my father, "If you didn't spend everything you make on whiskey, we could all get something special for Christmas." I didn't make it past *whiskey*, when he spun around and said, "What's that, Boy?" I was too scared to answer. He had never physically abused me, but the mere sound of his voice told me I was completely out of line. Not until the summer before I was to enter the eighth grade did I say anything more to him about his drinking. And never again did I bother to hang up a stocking, or expect to receive anything more from Santa. And I *didn't* receive anything more for the rest of the time I lived at home. In later years, I would've been happy to receive simply a cluster of raisins.

Music, Dancing, and Warts

My education was also influenced by my oldest brother, Lovick, and his wife, Lessie Shehane. Being crowded for room, Lovick and Lessie let us keep their hand-wound RCA Victrola phonograph player—with a picture of Nipper listening to his master's voice—and over a dozen 78-rpm records for about a year. For hours at a time, I listened to gospel songs, Irish ballads, and country music. A hyperactive youngster, I naturally started dancing to the music, even trying some of Isaac's fancy steps. Once, when a neighbor visited our home, Mama told me to wind up the Victrola and show her one of my dances. Since it didn't make any difference to me—or to Mama—what kind of music I was dancing to, I started swinging around the room to a religious song. The neighbor was aghast, and warned Mama that my desecration of religious music was nothing short of blasphemy. She called upon my poor mother to renounce her sin of bringing up an ungodly child—forgetting, no doubt, that the Bible says to dance and sing for joy.

Lessie, of full-blooded Irish descent, regaled us with stories that kept us entranced until she had finished, which could be hours, or until we were all completely exhausted. If anyone expressed impatience with her long-winded stories, she would reply in an Irish dialect, "At me own behest, prithee. I'm a-hurrying, but I mustn't—and shan't—leave out the good part." Her imaginative stories intertwined ghosts, goblins, witches, and the bogeyman, together with miracles and religion. Her ghosts and witches were as real to her as life itself because "I seed it with me own eyes, I did, for shore." She believed there really was a pot of gold at the end of the rainbow. True to the Irish tradition, she could blend realism and fantasy, mesmerizing her audience by modulating her voice from a whisper to a shout. I thought surely the shout would be the climax, only to find that part of the story segued into the next episode, and the next, and the next. As the stories were told closer to midnight, they became even darker and spookier, so scary that I was afraid I might not live to see the light of another day.

Once, when Lovick and Lessie were visiting, I had an awful seed wart on the back side of my left thumb. While Lessie was telling one of her stories of bone-crushing panthers, blood-thirsty vampires, fire-eating dragons, hooded haints (haunts), hainted houses, wailing banshees, bogeymen, goblins, and witches, she espied the wart. With a toss of her long blond hair and with those flashing blue eyes, she asked, "Honey, you like that old ugly wart?" Of course, I told her I hated it, that I kept hitting and snagging it, whereupon she declared that by tomorrow night, the wart would be gone. She then steeled those sparkling blue eyes on the wart and intoned:

> *Wart of toad, seed of Satan*
> *Ugly thang, fit fer hatin'*
> *Critter of dark, afeered of light*
> *Fade away by tomorrow night.*

In a spookish whisper, this latter-day Druid then said we would have to find an "Arsh" potato, make a slit in it, take a straw from the kitchen broom, singe the straw with a hot arn (iron), touch the wart with the straw three times—for the Father, the Son, and the Holy Ghost—slip the straw into the slit in the potato, and then bury the potato with the straw in it next to a red zinnia—not just any flower or any zinnia, but a red zinnia. Lessie then blindfolded me as she led me out into the overcast and gloomy moonlit night to the flower garden, where Mama grew her zinnias and verbena. By the next night, the wart was gone, never to return. And the zinnia plant wilted and died. And 'tis a fact, fer I seed it with me own eyes!

Lessie was Lovick's second wife; his first wife, Effie, who bore his son, Webster, was in the "pen." I was never told that directly; I learned it by overhearing snippets from older members of the family. A lot of my thinking went into trying to figure out what kind of pen poor Effie—whom I had never known—was in, and who might have put her in a pen and who was feeding her. I knew that on the farm we had hog pens and cow pens. We slopped the hogs and fed hay to the cows, but I'd never known of a person being in a pen.

Though no one seems to know for sure why Effie was in the pen, I've heard it was because of her stealing a Model T Ford. Forty years later, when Webster died after retiring from the Army, Effie was out of prison and wanted to come to her son's funeral. But Michael, Webster's son, said that Lessie had been the only mother Webster ever knew, and that Effie had no business attending. Lessie, indeed, was a good mother and a godsend to a boy who'd never known anything but a hard life. On at least one occasion, I witnessed Lovick unmercifully whipping Webster for no good reason. (In fact, is there ever any good reason for whipping a child?) He would have whipped me too, he said, but he knew he'd have to answer to Daddy. Webster had an ally in his stepmother, however; Lessie once told Lovick the next time he took a notion to whip Webster, he would have to whip her first. As much as Lovick loved Lessie, Webster would never have to worry about being mistreated at the hands of his father again. Much to the joy of the extended family, the two later reconciled their differences.

Some of my education had nothing to do with books and learning to read, but with manners and social etiquette. In my own home, a two-room, tin-roofed shack beside a cotton field, we had no two plates that were part of the same set, and our eating utensils were of no particular design. But my sister Vallie, twenty-one years my senior and just younger than Lalar, had married a prosperous landowner.

Vallie and her husband Adoniram (or, Addie) lived in "the big house," about a mile from us. Addie owned the land we lived on and farmed; it had been in his family since that part of Alabama was wrested from the Creeks. Although Vallie and Addie had no children together, each summer for several years, they hosted two pre-teenage orphans from the Alabama Baptist Children's Home, in Troy. The boys were in paradise on the farm, for Vallie delighted in baking their favorite cookies and taking them swimming. The boys were well-fed and well-treated at the orphanage; however, Vallie thought that when they left at the end of the summer, they were always a little ruddier and healthier. She continued to follow their lives for many years, as they joined the military or went to college, got married, got divorced, had children, and on and on. Twenty years later, I ran into one of them, Charlie Beard, when I was in the seminary; I was pleased that he had matured into a very fine young man.

Vallie had refined her speech, and had learned to cook and bake well (her baking specialties were Parker House rolls, jellyrolls, and sugar cookies, which Mama with her English and Scottish-Irish background called tea cakes). She was known for her chocolate fudge, divinity, and pecan pralines. I have tried many times to make candied sweet potatoes like Vallie made. She also made carrots delicious by candying them. Vallie had learned in home demonstration meetings about nutritious foods, such as carrots, but she said sometimes it's necessary to cultivate a taste for them. An excellent seamstress, she made most of the shirts I wore, using the fabric from 50-pound flour sacks.

One of the many things that set Vallie's cooking apart from ours was that she used celery, something we cotton and peanut farmers had never seen, much less used. Vallie always had several fresh stalks in a jar of water on the back porch. And there was always a bowl of lemons on the kitchen counter, just waiting to be made into lemonade for all the neighborhood kids who congregated at her house. And Vallie was in the midst of them, savoring all their stories. On one occasion, a boy mentioned that his family had found bedbugs between their mattresses. Even Vallie chuckled when I told the group that I bet the bedbugs weren't as big as ours.

Vallie made sure I was in Sunday School every week at nearby Salem Baptist Church, where she and her husband worshipped. So that I would look like a boy when I went to church, she reluctantly sheared my shoulder-length curls. She continued giving me subsequent trimmings until I was in my teens, when I began to shave. She said she didn't cut men's hair. When I needed a haircut in later years, I would ask Mr. Steve Holland, the barber in Clio, to let me sweep up the clippings in the shop in return for his services. Otherwise, I would have had to come up with a whopping 25 cents. A cousin, Roy Ketchum, often barbered at Holland's Barber Shop on Saturday, and he would sometimes cut my hair for free, knowing the financial situation of my family.

After church, several families would gather outside and begin inviting each other to their homes for Sunday dinner. It was quite amusing to listen to their interchanges. One would typically start out by saying, "Y'all come on over now for dinner. We got plenty of fried chicken, roastnears,[5] butter beans, and fresh collards." The other family might respond, "Now, Lawdy, Lawdy, you never did pay us back for our last visit." Then the other might say, "Well, now, we surely were at your house. Remember, we were the judges for the taffy-pulling contest." Responding, they would typically say, "Now a taffy-pulling contest is not a Sunday dinner." These charades would continue for fifteen or twenty minutes until finally a family would agree to come over for dinner, provided they could go by their own house and bring that chocolate cake that just wouldn't wait till tomorrow to be eaten. Mind you, this was an every-Sunday ritual. It may not have been a Southern custom, but it certainly was at Salem Baptist Church in the late '30s and early '40s.

Vallie didn't just teach me which fork to use and how to dress up for church, she also cultivated my memory. In one game, she placed small items, such as a coin, a key, and a button, on the dining room table for me to observe for five seconds; then, she would remove them and I was to tell her their names. As I named each item, she would place it back on the table. When I couldn't re-

---

[5] *Roastnears* refers to corn on the cob that had been roasted in the oven. Properly, they were "roasting ears."

member a particular item, she proceeded to give me hints. She continued to increase the number so that eventually, I could name up to ten or twelve items. I also learned defensive and offensive moves in dominoes and Chinese checkers. And just for fun, all the neighborhood kids played Bingo at Vallie's house.

Vallie and Addie kept up a running game of wordplays. One in particular was "Railroad crossing, look out for cars. Can you spell *that* without any r's?" Another was the response to the question "Where does this road go?" The correct answer was "It doesn't go any place. It stays right where it is." Still another was "How do you get down from an elephant?" The correct answer: "You don't get down from an elephant, you get it from a duck." These wordplays had quite an impact on my respect for language. But I was even more affected by an experience at Mr. Rex Davis' store, located right next to Vallie's house. Mr. Davis asked me if I knew I had garments all over my back. Thinking I had bugs crawling on me, I began dancing around, trying to get them off. Of course, in doing so, I became the laughingstock of the store.

Once when I was waiting at the store to catch the bus, one of my young friends said that he told his girlfriend that her hide was so soft and pretty. She told him that he should never say *hide*, but *skin*. So, when he went to church and the congregation sang "Hide me, O my Savior, hide me," he sang "Skin me, O my Savior, skin me."

These experiences may have been the impetus for my questioning and commenting on statements made by my friends and colleagues. Once, when I was teaching high school many years later, a fellow teacher commented that I told everyone not only what to say but also how to say it. For example, a teacher said she was twice as angry at a student after he said such and such a thing. I asked her how she measured anger, by the foot or by the pound. And just the other day, Fred Bassford, one of my whirlpool friends at the gym, said he was a Pentecostal. "Oh," I said, "you practice glossolalia." Looking a little dazed, he said he wasn't sure, but if it meant he had two wives, he wasn't guilty of whatever it was I had said. I then proceeded to educate him, telling him that *glossa* was Greek for "tongue," and that *lalein* meant "to speak," actually, "to babble." He then replied that he did indeed speak in tongues, but, in his 40 years in the church, had never heard it referred to as glossolalia.

I wasn't finished with Fred, however. I asked him if he knew why *Pentecostal* was so called, inasmuch as he *was* one. After he gave me the "I don't know, and I don't care" look, I said, "Well, surely you know what *penta*, as in *pentagon*, means. You know, the Pentagon, just up the road, is a five-sided building—*pente*, five, plus *gon*, angle. And *Pentecostal* comes from *pentekoste hemera*, or the "fiftieth day" after Christ's ascension, when the Holy Spirit descended upon the Apostles." I might add that such pedantry doesn't win one a lot of friends; such ostentation can in fact lose them. Fred told me rather emphatically the next time he saw me coming into the gym, he was going to go the other way. I apologized to Fred for "educating" him. He said, "Forget it, Horace. I'll get over it." We made up, however, and we are the closest of friends. I would have hated to lose Fred as a friend, for he is one of the very finest men I know. I'm still not sure if he paid me a compliment when he said just the other day that if a person took the time to really know me, he couldn't help but like me. I asked him if I was that hard to get to know. He said, "Well, let's just say that you're different." Maybe my sister Lalar was right—I really am *different*.

As I was relating the glossolalia incident to Ric Clark, another dear friend, he said he thought Pentecostals practiced echolalia, not glossolalia. I said, "Oh, Ric, and I've been regarding you as a friend, and you don't even know the difference between them." I had to remind Ric that *echolalia* is a psychiatric term, indicating the immediate and involuntary repetition of words or phrases just spoken by others, and often a sign of autism or schizophrenia.

But now, back to Alabama—and my sister Vallie.

Vallie had an elegant home (at least, in my eyes) with a well-furnished living room, lacy curtains in every room, French doors to the dining area, and a long dining room table draped with linen. She also had a telephone and a kerosene-burning refrigerator. Electricity still hadn't made it to the country in our area.

In the guest room on the mantel was an old-fashioned clock in the shape of a bell. Though I wasn't to know the reason until many years later, many old clocks are so shaped because of Middle English *clokke*, which means "bell." It is the same word that gives us *cloak*, as in *cloak room*, because cloaks were originally shaped like bells.

Clokke also gives us the name of the German musical percussion instrument *glockenspiel*, literally, to play the bells. The glockenspiel does, in fact, resemble an old-fashioned clock, and produces bell-like tones. But what was remarkable about the bedroom clock is that it struck the hour and then chimed. So, at midnight, the clock sounded 24 times. Vallie made sure the clock was in the exact center of the mantel, saying that she liked balance and symmetry. Once, when the home demonstration ladies met at her house, the leader said the current fashion in home decorating was that of asymmetry, so Vallie moved the clock off center.

Vallie and Addie also had a scuppernong arbor, a peach orchard, a long row of cultivated blueberry bushes, two or three kumquat trees, and a garden of American Beauty roses. Although Barbour County was really too far north for growing oranges, Vallie had two small trees, each of which produced three or four satsumas a year. It isn't the fruit I remember most, but the sweet, delicate aroma of the blossoms. Addie also grew the largest strawberries, which Vallie served me with whipped cream. In the summer, we made homemade ice cream—vanilla, peach, and strawberry—in a hand-turned freezer. I practically lived at Vallie's house, absorbing the good life, as well as swaying to my heart's content on the front porch swing.

Making homemade ice cream was quite a social event in the community during the late '30s and early '40s. The church as well as families often held ice cream socials, with four or five batches of different flavors being made at a time. Of course, there was no television, and very few families had radios. In addition to ice cream socials, we also had taffy-pullings. Since practically everyone had more cane syrup than could be used during the winter, a family would hold a taffy-pulling contest and invite ten or twelve young people. A large pot of syrup would be boiled down to the consistency necessary for stretching and pulling. The mixture would then be poured into buttered platters for it to cool enough to be touched with bare hands. Then, couples pulled the mixture into fancy shapes, such as hearts and flowers. Some of the resulting taffy would be eaten, but the main purpose of the event was a social affair. Other social events were watermelon cuttings and peanut boilings.

Even though Vallie and Addy regularly made ice cream, I

longed to have an ice cream cone at the soda fountain of a drug store. One day, when I was around five years old, Addie took me with him to Ozark, the seat of Dale County, to play dominoes. He and his cronies would sit in the back of the store and play for hours at a time. Having nothing to do while they played their deuces and treys, I became bored. Addie asked the fountain attendant to give me a double strawberry ice cream cone. I didn't know I was to eat the cone, so I ate the ice cream, and took the cone back to the attendant, telling her the ice cream was all gone and gave her the cone back. She filled up the cone again and suggested I go for a walk. As beautiful as Clio was, it was nothing compared to Ozark, with its even larger houses, flowering magnolias, trees draped with Spanish moss, and Greek statues in fountains with overflowing pools stocked with enormous goldfish. There was indeed a big world out there beyond the cotton fields.

On each Mother's Day while we lived at the Phillips Place, Addie made it a point to cut the most beautiful white rose to wear in memory of his deceased mother. He would cut a red rose for me to wear, since my mother was living. It was bad enough having to wear a rose to church, and each time I wore one, I dreaded that one day I would need to wear a white one. I also thought it was sad that no one ever wore a rose to commemorate Father's Day.

Breakfasts at Vallie's were a special treat. Instead of the salt-cured mackerel, hickory-smoked ham, eggs and grits, buttermilk biscuits with homemade sausage, red-eye gravy, or syrup we usually had at home—hearty breakfasts, to say the least—I was served delicate waffles with homemade strawberry or blueberry jam, or preserves and jelly. Breakfasts were served with either orange or pineapple juice, neither of which I'd ever had before. It was also at Vallie's that I had Kellogg's Corn Flakes and Rice Krispies for the first time. Yes, there were corn flakes and rice crispies 60 years ago. As I poured milk on the Rice Krispies, I listened for them to go snap, crackle, and pop, the same as kids might do today. Vallie made Quaker oatmeal even more delicious by serving it with raisins and brown sugar, garnishing it with strawberries, blueberries, or bananas, or sprinkling it with nutmeg. And Vallie made wonderfully delicate small biscuits, topped with freshly churned butter and orange marmalade or with syrup made from sugar cane grown on the place. Though the syrup came from the same batch as that used at our house, it just tasted better at her house.

The syrup had been boiled down from cane juice by my father, who was regarded throughout our area as a champion syrup maker and hog dresser. When Daddy made syrup for other farmers, it was often my job to feed the stalks of cane into the cane mill, which was turned by a mule plodding in a circle all day. Then, as the syrup began to form on the opposite end of the ten-foot-long juice pan, I helped in trapping the scalding liquid into gallon-size tin cans. There was a definite reward for helping make syrup: drinking the cane juice. There is nothing sweeter or more delicious than cane juice right from the mill on a nippy November morning. As payment, we received every tenth gallon of syrup for ourselves.

Though Mama silently disapproved, Daddy kept a wooden barrel close by, where he saved the skimmings as the syrup formed from the boiling juice. A few days of fermenting the skimmings produced homebrew, which some people called busthead, apparently because of the condition in which it left the imbiber the next morning. This primitive form of rum would keep Daddy rosy-cheeked and happy for as long as it lasted, typically not more than a couple of weeks.

Daddy had a knack for converting just about anything into alcohol. He would tell us children to be careful to leave some peaches on the tree just in case a hungry wayfarer were to pass by. It wasn't long, however, before Daddy was redolent of peach brandy. Any luckless wayfarer would have gone away empty-handed.

Daddy's jobs were seasonal. Springs and summers would occasionally find him farming; in early fall, he rebuilt burned-out chimneys and fireplaces; in late fall, he made syrup; and in the winter, he stayed busy killing and dressing hogs for landowners. But all year long, no matter the season, he sharpened crosscut saws for loggers throughout the area. It was a truism that no one filed saws better than Nelse Danner. Mama once said she had seen Daddy file saws for so long she could do it herself if there was ever a need to do so.

A Mannerly Progression

When I was five, Vallie unwittingly introduced me to the concept of structure and organization. She taught me to set the table with china, including the salad plate and bread dish, as well as with silver, making certain the knife blade faced the plate's right side a quarter of an inch from its edge; the teaspoon was placed to the right of the knife, with the handles precisely aligned about an inch from the edge of the table. A crystal water glass was set near the end of the knife blade.

In addition to learning to set the silver, china, and crystal correctly, I was instructed to place a folded linen napkin under the fork, which was to the left of the plate. Further, if I planned to be present for the next meal, I was to fold my napkin after eating and place it *beside* the plate; if I didn't intend to eat the next meal there, I was to leave the napkin crumpled *on* the plate. Dishes were passed to the left, starting with the dish in front of one's plate. If a second helping was desired from a bowl or platter not within reach, I was to say, for example, "Please pass the cornbread," instead of reaching across the table or over someone else's plate for it. In addition, I must hold a cup by pressing the handle with my right thumb and index finger, with the other fingers reinforcing the cup—no small feat for a five-year-old. I had often noticed other people inserting their index finger in the handle of the cup, which seemed entirely logical.

I was instructed that before eating, the hands must be washed, an almost-religious ritual. In addition, all were expected to stand behind their chairs until the host or guest was seated. And if a man was to sit next to a woman, he should seat her before taking his own seat. I might add that this training came in handy just a few weeks ago when I was a guest of one of my University of Maryland students, Nancy Slomowitz, at her rather elaborate, catered graduation party. My place card was set next to hers, and as though it were second nature, I pulled her chair back to seat her. Possibly, in Maryland at least, this practice is no longer *de rigueur*, because Nancy almost fainted, but not before she said, "Oh, what a gentleman!"

When dining at Vallie's, I was to sit up straight, exchange only pleasantries, cut the meat into small pieces, take small bites, chew slowly and well, and not appear to be eating because I was ravenous, as most boys my age were. And the pickle fork was used only to spear a pickle. In addition, the butter was to be cut only from the side that had already been cut. One must never take the last piece of chicken, the last piece of fish, or the last biscuit or roll. Those were reserved for a visitor who might drop in unexpectedly. Vallie could always make room for just one more. She often had so many people for dinner on Sunday, we ate in shifts, with the adults having priority. But she made sure the children had plenty to eat, including choice pieces of chicken or fish.

Furthermore, I was to use only my right hand to eat; the left must rest on my lap, and be brought to the table only to cut the meat or to butter the roll. Resting an elbow ever so lightly on the table was a serious breach of etiquette. If I simply had to leave the table before the others were finished, I was to say, "May I please be excused from the table?" (I usually had to sit through an exposition of last Sunday's sermon or listen to a discussion of theological topics, such as "once saved, always saved," a basic tenet of Baptist theology, as well as "the priesthood of the believer" and "The Great Commission.") Finally, I was taught to show appreciation for the meal by addressing the hostess (my sister) and saying, "Vallie, I enjoyed my dinner." Only after observing these formalities was I allowed to leave the table. Without being aware of it, I was being fashioned into a Little Lord Fauntleroy. I knew of no other boy, especially my age, who could properly set a table and eat so formally.

Except for using the linen napkin, crystal, and silver properly, holding the cup just so, and reverently bowing my head for the blessing, the same manners were expected in my own home. I would never have thought of sitting down to a meal without washing my hands, cutting the butter from a side that hadn't already been cut, or leaving the table without saying to my mother, "Mama, I enjoyed my dinner," even if the meal consisted of no more than collard or turnip greens or black-eyed peas and pone bread.

Twenty years later, I was abruptly jolted out of the habit of graciously thanking the hostess for my meal. We were having brown bread and Boston baked beans at my wife's childhood home in West Hampstead, New Hampshire. My mother-in-law's blueberry and McIntosh apple pies and her strawberry shortcakes were gifts of the gods, but I had never particularly cared for this particular New England fare. I still felt duty bound to thank her for the "delicious" meal she had prepared. Out of respect for Margie and her ten brothers and sisters, I won't repeat the exact words of her scathing attack. I will only relate that she emphatically stated the beans were the worst that she had ever baked and the brown bread had

Margie, Patty & I

too much molasses and that she didn't want to hear any more of my insincerities. And, she said, I didn't have to keep turning the butter dish around in order to cut it from the side that had already been cut. Further, she said she wasn't in a wheelchair yet, and that she didn't want me seating her. So much for my Southern manners, at least in the Donovan household!

As for Southern manners, the military in later years would have no need to teach me to show respect for authority. Saying "Yes, Sir" and "No, Sir," and "Yes, Ma'am," and "No, Ma'am" was as much a part of my growing up as setting the table properly or asking to be excused from the table. I assumed that I would teach my own children to say "Yes, Sir" and "No, Sir" as well, but Margie had other ideas on raising children. A simple *yes* or *no* was all that she required. Even after all these years, I still find the unadorned *yes* or *no* a little blunt, but I'll have to admit it sounds better than *yeah* and *nah,* which I hear from a lot of young people, even when they're speaking to much-older persons.

Vallie forbade any snacking before meals, declaring that it would spoil my appetite. Later, I learned that other families actually served appetizers before a meal. And they aren't meant to spoil one's appetite, but to enhance it. After a Sunday dinner of fried chicken or catfish with all the trimmings as well as dessert at Vallie's, we would have only a light supper. What I liked best

29

was two thick slices of store-bought Dixie Maid light bread slathered with jam, huckleberry on one, and blackberry on the other, with a large glass of ice-cold milk. Life couldn't have been better—unless I'd had a cowboy outfit and a bicycle.

Daddy had withdrawn Vallie from school when she was in the fifth grade to take care of Aunt Leona, his oldest sister, who had broken her arm. But Vallie, filled with determination for a better life, joined the Clio Study Club after she became an adult, and participated in the Bay View Reading Course. She had a penchant for speaking precisely and correctly, and expected me to improve my speech as well. By the time I started school, she had extirpated "ain't" from my speech. Vallie probably didn't know the formal rules of auxiliary verbs being used with past participles, but she told me that *seen*, for example, was to be used only with *has, have,* or *had*. I would often say "I seen," and sometimes, "I seed," as Lovick's wife, with her Irish manner, was prone to say. Vallie also worked on my "third-person singulars," replacing, for example, *he don't* with *he doesn't*. There were also dicta on the pronunciation of certain words, two in particular being *chauffeur* and *chaperon*. Every word spoken must be "proper English." I can actually become somewhat depressed if I learn that I have used or pronounced a word incorrectly. Consequently, I don't use many French words!

Even neighbors got into the act of correcting my speech. Once, when I said I was teaching my dog a new trick, a horror-stricken neighbor declared, "You *teach* people, but you *train* a dog." Had she not heard the axiom "You can't teach an old dog new tricks"? I also was caught saying "That's how my parents *raised* me," whereupon I was strictly admonished that I should have said *reared*. As a teacher, I am probably more strict than most people on enunciation, diction, and pronunciation, but I dare anyone to tell me I am wrong when I say "I was raised in the South." Vallie and her well-meaning neighbors would have made excellent teachers—or Draconic military drill instructors.

Lest I have given the impression that Vallie was a homebody, baking cookies and jelly rolls, making chocolate fudge and pecan pralines, entertaining the monthly meeting of the Department of Agriculture home demonstration ladies, pruning her American Beauty roses, and correcting my speech, let me hasten to set the record straight. In the summer, she often herded the neighborhood kids into her 1936 Chevrolet and took us all to the outdoor baptismal pool at Salem Baptist Church. Even in the middle of summer, the water was ice-cold; even so, she was the first one in the pool. It was here that I learned to swim. Once every week or so, she would also take me and several of the other neighborhood kids with her to Blue Springs, about seven miles away. It's now the Blue Springs State Park. At Blue Springs, there was an extremely large, deep, cylindrical pool fed, it seems, by an underground glacier.[6] I've never known why the pool was called "blue" springs, unless it was from the color of one's body after swimming there, even for only a few minutes.

Vallie was also a high diver. At Blue Springs, there were three diving boards, and Vallie, with her hair tucked under her rubber swim cap, dove from the highest one. She executed swan dives and backward flips as well as other dives for which no names had yet been coined; she also swam a breaststroke the other swimmers tried to emulate. While Vallie was the center of attention in the big pool, I was paddling around in the shallow pool.

When I wasn't swimming with Vallie in either the baptismal pool or at Blue Springs, I was swimming with my sister Lalar and her children and their cousins and friends. On Lalar and Curtis's property was a pool that had been built near a spring on the side of a cotton field. Ideally situated among a grove of sycamores and cottonwoods, the pool was a welcome retreat from the hot sultry days of an Alabama summer.

Color Me Studious

Vallie had a prism, whose iridescence was an endless source of delight for me. Addie said the light passing through the prism was refracted into the seven colors of the rainbow. Without benefit of the mnemonic ROY G. BIV, I learned early on the colors in the spectrum from red to violet, though when I looked at the rainbow itself, the bands of color weren't nearly as distinct as the colors in the prism had been. Vallie also had a replica of the Statue of Liberty, given to her by Addie's daughter, Dorothy, an absolutely charming fashion model living in New York City. Addie's stories of the actual statue's dimensions were incredible. Could

---

[6] Lee Hunt says in *A Town Called Clio*, the pool was fed by liquid ice cubes.

there really be such a structure? For some reason, I fancied that Miss Liberty was beckoning to me, just as she had opened her arms to the poor, beckoning the huddled masses yearning to be free. I longed to see the Statue of Liberty and behold with my own eyes this magnificent structure.

Fifty years later, on a sweltering, rainy day in August, my wife and I took the ferry from Manhattan and visited Liberty Island. It so happened that at least 5,000 others must have assumed the Statue of Liberty belonged to them as well. We were indeed a huddled mass as the ferry attendant pushed and shoved to get just one more fare on board. From the Statue of Liberty, it was on to Ellis Island, where abandoned trunks belonging to the immigrants were piled high as poignant reminders of the plight of the newcomers to this free land. There are probably as many reasons for the newcomers deserting their precious belongings as there are trunks.

Though sadness like a pall shrouded Ellis Island, Margie and I had an encouraging experience as we were standing in line to catch the ferry back to Manhattan in order to board the bus that would take us back to Bolling Air Force Base in Washington. By now, I was using a cane because of my arthritic knees, and because of all the walking that day, I didn't think I could stand for another moment. We were at the end of a queue of at least 500 people waiting to board the ferry. I hobbled to the front of the line and asked the attendant if I might sit on the bench alongside the ferry while waiting for Margie to bring up the rear. Instead of merely letting me sit, he said that I could board the ferry right then. I knew I couldn't leave Margie behind, as we'd probably never see each other again in the throngs of tourists. The attendant said that Margie could come to the front of the line and board the ferry with me. I didn't know how I would be able to contact her, since my knees were on fire and exploding with pain. So, I told the first person in line to pass the word down to the pretty, blue-eyed blonde with a pink sweater tied around her waist that she could come to the front. It was quite a sight witnessing the word being relayed to Margie, who, when she received the news, came running to join me. And who says that New Yorkers, even ferry attendants, can't be gracious and kind?

In addition to the prism and the Statue of Liberty replica,

Vallie and Addie had a picture of the General Sherman Tree in the Sequoia National Park. The photo depicted fifty men with outstretched arms encircling the tree. She also had a pink conch shell, which, when held to the ear, emitted the roar of the ocean. These souvenirs and mementos sparked my imagination and my awareness of a bigger world than the cotton fields of Alabama.

Despite the dearth of reading material in our home, I learned to read fluently and to spell almost perfectly. It didn't seem to matter that *threw* and *through* were spelled differently but pronounced the same. I am confident that singing hymns in church and participating with the congregation in the responsive readings as well as reciting the Psalms with their strict parallel structure also helped me to learn new words and become familiar with the rhythm and cadence of balanced sentences. One's writing couldn't help but be improved after reading, for example, the first verse of Psalm 27, and noting the parallel structure: The Lord is my light and my salvation;/ whom shall I fear?/ The Lord is the stronghold of my life;/ of whom shall I be afraid?

Studies have been conducted in recent years that show one's writing can also be improved by reading and reciting poetry. Mr. Palmer, a teacher I was yet to meet, intuitively knew that before researchers validated it. Mr. Palmer "punished" me by requiring that I memorize and recite certain poems, the reason for which will be recounted later. Even as I teach such courses as technical, business, and managerial writing, I sometimes require that my students at University of Maryland recite William Wordsworth's "Daffodils," especially if they lack a sense of balance and proportion in their writing or speaking. Having international students read poetry is especially helpful in developing the rhythm and natural flow of the English sentence. Groups of Vietnamese students meet with me in my home on Sunday afternoons. They bring an array of colorful Vietnamese food, and we have a splendid time, eating together, checking their writing, and reading and reciting poetry. They're much more successful in learning to read and speak fluently than they are in teaching me to use chopsticks well, although I have now mastered the art of eating pho (beef noodle soup) with chopsticks and a Vietnamese soup spoon. I tell them it's not really necessary to say "Yes, Sir" and "No, Sir," since I'm not used to hearing that anymore. So, they smile, give a little bow, and say "Yes, Sir." And they still insist on leaving their shoes at the door.

Once when I was at Vallie's house, I became rather lonesome and bored. James Davis, a boy a year younger than I who lived next door to Vallie, wasn't home, and I wanted someone to play with. I was swinging alone on the front porch when I saw a man riding a horse up the road toward Clio. Without Vallie's knowledge, I ran out to ask him if it wouldn't be too much trouble, would he please tell Mrs. Horton, who lived a mile farther up the road, that Vallie wanted to see her. What I really wanted was for Patricia, her daughter about my age, to come with her so that we could play together. I was sure that Patricia would come, as she and her mother were practically inseparable. In about an hour, here comes Mrs. Horton, all gussied up in her best dress, but without Patricia. From the kitchen window, Vallie saw Mrs. Horton hurrying down the road, and not seeing Patricia with her, ran out past me to ask her what on earth was wrong. Patricia was home ill with a fever, and Mrs. Horton had to get one of the neighbors to look out for her so that she herself could come and see what the problem was with Vallie, thinking something was horribly wrong. Amazingly, I didn't get a whipping, but I did receive a not-to-be-forgotten lesson in "cry wolf."

Life with my two oldest sisters was almost idyllic—almost, because Vallie often found more things wrong with me than right. No matter when or where, she constantly corrected and upbraided me, often to my utter embarrassment, especially when in the presence of friends, neighbors, and other family members. For example, several of us boys were playing outside at her house one hot, sultry Sunday afternoon in the middle of August. All the other boys had taken off their shirts, but I still had mine on, and it was long-sleeved. Vallie told me to take off my shirt as the other boys had. When I did, she noticed I had exposed my bare torso. With utter indignation, she said, "Well! I didn't know you didn't have an undershirt on," and told me to put my shirt back on. She should have known, for I'd never even had an undershirt. In spite of her embarrassing me, she had taught me to swim and to be a perfect gentleman, and Lalar had taught me to love reading. And Lessie, bless her shamrocked Irish heart, had laid the groundwork for my ability to tell a story. Only a short time later—when food was scarce, with no way to buy it—I would pine for those bucolic, blissful, carefree days. Homemade ice cream, big Sunday dinners, waffles, strawberries and cream, Jello with whipped cream, chocolate fudge, divinity, pecan pralines, coconut cake, and pie à la mode—they all would become only pleasant, lingering memories.

I Will Not Sharpen Crayons in the Pencil Sharpener

Except for having to write a hundred times "I will not sharpen crayons in the pencil sharpener," I found the second grade one of the most enjoyable of elementary school. One reason was that I was beginning to be recognized as a serious student. David Bradley Tew and I were the champion spellers, and those students who got a certain number correct on the weekly spelling test were given a lollipop; once I got two lollipops because I correctly spelled the bonus word, February. Though David and I were best pals, my personal ambition was to best him at whatever he did. David finally beat me, however, by marrying Mary Ann Helms, the girl I thought I would spend the rest of my life with. Everyone, it seems, including Mary Ann's mother and father, thought we were quite an item in high school, especially since we both played the piano. We often walked together from school to our lessons at Mrs. Josephine Baxter's house, and then listened as the other played.

2nd Grade

The second-grade teacher, Miss Pullen, worked with Mrs. Knight, another teacher, in staging operettas. Those chosen for roles were given a pattern and material for their costume. I was assigned a part; however, because my mother couldn't sew well, I knew there was no point in taking the pattern home, so I took it to Vallie, who, with the help of her neighbor, Mrs. Esther Davis, outfitted me for the operetta. Performing on stage—singing, dancing, and speaking the lines—was absolutely delightful. I had always been something of a show-off—especially since the first day of second grade.

On that day, we had a school assembly, and the principal was awarding certificates to those who had perfect attendance the year before. Being hard of hearing, I'm not sure I even heard the principal call my name, and if I did, I didn't understand the significance of the occasion. So, when he called my name to come to be presented my certificate, I just stayed where I was. And then, Miss Pullen and everyone else started telling me to go the front of the auditorium. I didn't know what I was going for, but I made it a big event, grinning from ear to ear and skipping and dancing all the way to the front. All the students and teachers were laughing, which made me show off even more.

After we had sung and danced in the operetta, Mrs. Knight invited me to become a member of the tap dancing club. She offered the lessons for free, but said I would have to have a pair of dancing shoes with heavy taps on the toes and heels. Quite matter-of-factly, I told Daddy that evening I would need special shoes to be a tap dancer. "Boy," he responded, "I can't even buy you school shoes, much less dancing shoes!" (Once he addressed me as *Boy*, I knew there was no need persisting, because he always called me Fiddler except when he was exasperated or upset with me.) Moreover, he declared he would not allow any boy of his to become a tap dancer since that was for girls. Alas, my aspirations for dancing my way to fame were thwarted before I even started.

Clio Low School was a virtual music school. At least twice a week, the entire school met for assembly, a major portion of which was devoted to singing. Even today, I often find myself thinking the words and humming the tunes of "Auld Lang Syne," "Flow Gently, Sweet Afton," "The Spanish Cavalier," "My Bonnie Lies over the Ocean," "Annie Laurie," "Steal Away," "Swing Low, Sweet Chariot," "Tramp, Tramp, Tramp, the Boys Are Marching," "Tenting Tonight on the Old Campground," and, of course, "Dixie," as well as the Alabama state song.

The words of "Alabama, the Beautiful" further instilled in me a passionate love of my native state. The first verse is as follows:

Alabama, Alabama, we will aye be true to thee,
From thy Southern shores where groweth
By the sea thy orange tree.
To thy northern vale where floweth
Deep and blue thy Tennessee,
Alabama, Alabama, we will aye be true to thee.

We filed into the auditorium often to the stately cadence of "Largo," from Handel's *Xerxes*, played on the piano by one of our teachers. I didn't know we were marching to the music of a classical composer; when I was assigned it years later as a piano piece, I remembered the tune. At other times, the pianist played "The Triumphal March" from Verdi's *Aida*. Clio was indeed a classical little town! It certainly helped in laying the groundwork for my becoming a musician of sorts.

In the fall of 1941, the Rural Electrification Administration (REA) began installing utility poles and electrical transformers in our area. I vividly remember watching a dozen or so young men placing the poles into the ground. Each of the men had a 12-foot-long spear, called a pike; after the pole had been manually hoisted to a particular angle, the men took turns thrusting the pikes at higher points on the pole until it was finally upright.

All the landowners were getting electricity, and it seemed that each family tried to outdo the others in purchasing new appliances. Vallie bought a waffle iron as well as an electric churn. But what I remember most were the electric lights; even a 60-watt bulb produced more light than the best Aladdin kerosene lamp. Because the filaments in those early days took quite a long time to cool, the bulb faded gradually, as though it were controlled by a modern-day rheostat. Once, at Vallie's house, when I noticed the light dimming, I remarked that it was "shriveling." Naturally, I was ridiculed for saying something so silly, so inane—lights don't shrivel like dried-up oranges. As I reflect on the situation, I think my rendering was rather figurative. I was reminded to add this incident when little Angelo, my 4-year-old Colombian friend, brought me an autumn maple leaf. Bouncing with exuberance, he called the leaf a tree feather, and told me I could keep it so long as I didn't break it. Rest assured, I didn't disparage or belittle "mi amigito," or "my young friend," for his make-believe or his blissful ignorance. This little fellow speaks to his parents in Span-

ish, and then turns to
me and speaks either
Spanish or English, de-
pending on his mood at
the time or his percep-
tion of my level of understanding. Once, I asked
him to speak to me only
in Spanish; his response:
*Posiblemente usted no me
entiende*—possibly you
wouldn't understand. He
is not used to *norte-
americanos* speaking his
language.

From the age of four
until I was midway
through third grade (the
entire time we lived on my
sister and her husband's
place), we lived only about
a half mile from the
Knights. Mr. Foy Knight (no
relation to the operetta di-
rector) was a wealthy landowner, as well as a merchant, a cotton
gin owner, and a cotton buyer. When Mr. Knight felt the price of
baled cotton was at its optimum, I watched the big-muscled workers—both black and white—load long flatbed trucks with hundreds of 500-pound bales of cotton to be sold to textile mills up
north.

At the Knights' house

The Knights' palatial home, even more elaborate than Vallie's,
was furnished with gas chandeliers, Colonial-period furniture,
and a grand piano, which their teenage daughter, Alice Amika,
played with the skill of a concert pianist. Once, after she had given
a miniconcert for her family, my parents, and me, Daddy remarked that she could make that piano "talk." Sensing his admi-
ration for her talent was probably my first inspiration to become
a pianist, though it would be years before I learned to play. While
Daddy appeared to be engrossed in Alice's playing, at the time I

in my bare feet was more fascinated by the fancy little charms she wore on a gold anklet and her black, patent leather shoes.

Though the Knights lived in the opposite direction from Vallie, with whom I spent most of my time, evenings would usually find me at the Knights'. I always felt welcome there, and I made the most of it. I picked blackberries, wild plums, black walnuts, hickory nuts, pecans, chinquapins, persimmons, and wildflowers, and took them to the Knights. Of course, I knew I would be given a glass of ice-cold lemonade and cookies, and possibly ice cream as well. As Alice played the piano, I danced and sang; already regarded as a budding raconteur—probably the result of Lessie's imaginative stories—I spun tall tales the Knights all seemed to relish. It seems that I had a knack for embellishing even the most simple and prosaic event. When I told similar stories to my family, I was often derided for "just making it all up." Once, Vallie more kindly observed, however, that I had a vivid imagination.

One summer afternoon, the Knights invited Mama and me to come in for iced tea and tea cakes. Not more than five minutes later, I announced I had to go to the bathroom, and off I danced. Mama was utterly embarrassed, associating *bathroom* with the outdoor toilet at our house. Since Mama was obviously flustered by my forthrightness, Mrs. Knight said, "Oh, don't worry about Horace, the little dancer. He knows the way. He goes to the bathroom here every day. I think he likes to hear the commode flush." Later, Mama said she didn't understand what Mrs. Knight meant by a commode flushing.

A World Apart

As much as I basked in the attention I received at the Knights' house, probably what I enjoyed most was poring over the yearbooks of University of Alabama, where the Knights' only son, Herald, was then an ROTC senior. The photos of the landscaped campus and the majestic buildings staggered my imagination. The portraits of the students in business suits and evening gowns, and the pictures of campus activities suggested there was more to life than living beside a cotton field and squeezing out a meager existence. Herald told me that after he got his master's, he was going to study for his Ph.D. I had no concept as to what he was referring, but it sounded impressive. I would have thought *anything* Herald wanted to do was impressive. Little did I know that of the two of us, it was I who would eventually earn a Ph.D., and that Herald's university education would be cut short because of the Japanese attack on Pearl Harbor and his receiving a commission in the Army. Nor could I know that my own idyllic life on the Phillips Place was about to end. Herald would go on to fight the Germans, while I continued to struggle with an alcoholic father, a submissive mother, abject poverty, and from now on, an annual move.

I suppose the sound of *Ph.D.* must have left an indelible impression, because a few weeks later, one of my friends was bragging that his mother was a college graduate, the same woman who had chastised my mother for my dancing to a religious tune and had almost severed my association with Isaac. I parried, "That's nothing, my mother has a Ph.D." Though I didn't know what *Ph.D.* meant, I knew that it had to be higher than a mere bachelor's degree. It's a good thing Eddie didn't ask which university conferred my mother's made-up degree. If he had, I'm quite sure I would have replied, "Naturally, University of Alabama."

Only a few weeks after my entering third grade, my new teacher, Mrs. Mable Chandler, invited me to take a weekend trip with her and her husband to Dothan, Mrs. Chandler's hometown. Just shy of the Florida line, Dothan lay about forty miles south of Clio. It would have been my first venture outside Barbour County. I longed to make the trip with them since they were going to take me sightseeing, including a visit to a bakery. Mrs. Chandler swore one could smell the cinnamon rolls a block away. She told me that some of the stores in Dothan even had "seeing eye" doors—doors that actually opened without anyone having to push them! My parents wouldn't allow me to go, however, since I didn't have shoes to wear at the time. I would get the shoes only after the cotton was sold.

As kind, thoughtful, and caring as Mrs. Chandler was, it was in her class I met an obstacle I couldn't overcome. I experienced a feeling of outright failure. One day after we had finished a particular lesson, she told us we could use our watercolors to paint a picture of a man. Since I didn't have any watercolors, I asked one of my classmates if I could share hers. She asked why I didn't get my brother in Birmingham to buy me my own. It was quite a relief that she wouldn't let me use hers, because already I had an unreasonable fear of drawing anything, much less a man. Mrs. Chandler came to my desk and told me I could just use my pencil to draw.

I don't know why Mrs. Chandler specified an activity of "drawing a man," because it is intensely psychological, as I learned thirty years later in graduate school. I am sure she had no ulterior motives for our painting or drawing a man, but a psychologist could have had a field day analyzing the one I eventually drew. While my classmates were drawing men with smiling faces, complete with noses, eyes, and ears, I couldn't even begin. I started to cry. Mrs. Chandler told me to simply draw a stick man, and that's what I did. He had no features of any kind.

On the Phillips Place, we made 12 bales of cotton on only 12 acres, a rather high yield with the farming methods used at the time. Daddy bought me a new pair of shoes, the last pair of leather shoes I would have until after the war because of the war's demand on leather for soldiers' boots. Shoes for the next four years were made generally of reinforced cardboard. Everything looked as though our prospects were becoming brighter, however. We had whole hams and sides of bacon in the smokehouse, plenty of eggs, a milk cow, two giant hills of sweet potatoes, and canned produce that would last us through the winter. However, because of Daddy's not paying Addie his full share from the sale of the cotton, we were forced to move, which meant enrolling at a new school. I made a list of friends and teachers I especially hated to leave behind. I would miss the Knights, of course, and I dreaded leaving Vallie. At school, I regretted leaving Mrs. Chandler. Together with her husband "Doc," the vocational agriculture teacher at the high school, she would continue to play a major role in my life, even after I graduated from high school.

Also near the top of the list of people I was saddened to leave was Bennie Earl Norton, my best friend, who lived only two doors from Vallie's house. And there was Mary Ann Wallace, for she was such a kind and beautiful girl; although she came from a very wealthy family, she never ridiculed me for wearing flour-sack clothes and being barefoot. As it turned out, however, Mary Ann left Clio about the same time I did, moving with her widowed mother to Montgomery after her brothers, George, Jack, and Gerald, enlisted during the war. Until I left Alabama, I continued to call Mary Ann each time I visited my brother Ralph in Montgomery. Though I never saw her again, she continued to be such a beautiful person on the phone, even after her oldest brother, George, became governor of Alabama.

Just East of Pea River

As passionately as Mama pleaded with Daddy to move us back to Louisville, he turned a deaf ear. He didn't much like the idea of pitching his tent too close to the Dykeses, who, he thought, were just a little too pious. In fact, my grandfather Dykes' given name was William Penn, after the founder of the Quaker movement. In one of the few times I ever heard Mama assert herself, she protested that Elamville was no place to raise three growing boys—Ralph, Bennie, and me. It was common knowledge that Elamville was the wildest place in Barbour County, with Saturday night fights regularly breaking out in the beer joints. In times like this when Mama knew she didn't have a chance, she began to hum the melancholic, old gospel song, "O, they tell me of a home far beyond the skies;/ O, they tell me of a home far away;/ O, they tell me of a home where no storm clouds rise;/ O, they tell me of an unclouded day." And then, she would modulate into "There's a land that is fairer than day,/ And by faith we can see it afar,/ For the Father waits over the way/ To prepare us a dwelling place there." Mama would have to wait until she reached Heaven for that fair, unclouded day where no storm clouds would rise.

We moved from the Phillips Place only seven or eight miles to the Evans Place, a cotton and peanut farm close to Elamville, and practically bordering Pea River. The river would be a main source of food for the next several years as we moved from farm to farm, but always within walking distance of its life-sustaining waters.

As soon as we moved to the Evans Place, Daddy bought a seine that he could hardly wait to string across Solomon's Creek to catch red-horse suckers. I've never known how Daddy knew when the suckers would be running, but we were never disappointed by his efforts. When he let me go with him once, I could see how the suckers were caught by their gills in the suspended net, which had weights on the bottom and floaters on the top.

Uncle Purry had leased the Evans Place, but being a master brick mason, he never worked the farm, leaving it to his children and us boys to cultivate and to my father to supervise. Around noon on Saturday, Daddy would announce that he could hear the bullheads and channel cats inviting us to the river. We would then gather any of the big, green worms feeding on the catalpa tree in the front yard for bait.[7] When we arrived at the river, the minnow basket Daddy had made of screen wire and which he kept in an inlet would already be full of additional live bait.

After setting the poles that we would check throughout the night, and then quickly catching a few bream for supper, we would spend the night on a sandbar, eating fried fish and hush puppies, drinking coffee, and listening to my father's tales of Pea River when he was a boy. Coffee never tasted so good as that Daddy brewed with river water. The only drawback to fishing at night was crossing the river on a slippery log to check the lines. Daddy, Bennie, and Ralph, as well as my cousins, could scamper across the log with the agility of tightrope walkers. Even with the flambeaus we carried for light, I usually ended up crawling across. As we checked the lines, Daddy would announce even before we reached the line, that a particular kind of fish had been caught, from the sound it made flapping in the river. The next morning, we would usually bring in a bushel basket of several types of catfish and eels.

Daddy could also pick more huckleberries than any three people, and he seemed to know where every huckleberry bush was located within miles of every house we lived in. On a summer morning, we would set out early with our containers, each of us children vowing at least to keep up with him. Because I typically ate half the ones I picked, I might wind up with a quart in two hours; in the same time, Daddy would pick two milk pails of berries. And oh, what Mama could do with huckleberries! After she had made all the cobbler we could eat, she made the rest into jam.

Extremely intelligent, Daddy was a virtual encyclopedia. He probably didn't know what a hypotenuse was or the formula for finding the volume of a cylinder, but he knew by how many min-

---

[7] Feeding only on catalpa trees, the worms were actually called catalpa worms.

utes, a day lengthened from the winter solstice to the summer solstice and then shortened by the same increments to the winter solstice again. He could also simply look at a field and tell how many sacks of guano and cottonseed would be needed for planting. In addition, he could always tell when a juicy watermelon was at its peak of ripeness by the sound it made when he thumped it.

It was also from Daddy that I first heard the anecdote of a laborer telling his foreman that he would charge only a penny for a day's work, provided the amount was doubled on each successive day. At the end of 30 days, the laborer would be due, Daddy said, over a million dollars. Two of my "computer friends," Dr. Eric Strobel, a mathematician and physicist, and Craig Prall, a consulting computer scientist, independently calculated the exact amount as $5,368,709.12.

Elamville was a community of only twelve or fifteen homes, a Methodist church, Elamville School, two beer joints, and three grocery stores. The Central of Georgia railroad ran by the side of the village, separating most of the homes from the stores, the beer halls, and the school. So Mama didn't get her wish for us to move back to the Louisville area, where we had lived until I was four. She had grown up there, and one of her brothers, Uncle Jimmy Dykes, owned extensive acreage nearby. As opposed to our large family of ten children, Uncle Jimmy and Aunt Thelma had only one child—Merrill.

When Merrill was barely old enough to sit behind a steering wheel, Uncle Jimmy bought him a heavy-duty pickup truck, so that they would have money coming in "both ways," he said. While Uncle Jimmy was hauling a load of peanuts to Clayton to be graded and sold, Merrill would haul a load of cotton to Louisville to be ginned and baled. Merrill was the same age as Loyce, and the two got along remarkably well, despite the difference in our socioeconomic levels. War is no respecter of persons, however, and Merrill and Loyce would later fight in Germany together. Just as in our first-grade

Merrill Dykes, Germany, 1944

reader, Merrill called his parents *Mother* and *Father*, which I thought was a little stilted and high-flown, but he used the terms as casually as I said *Mama* and *Daddy*. Mama didn't think too highly of Uncle Jimmy and Aunt Thelma teaching Merrill to say "Father," however. She said the Bible taught that only our Heavenly Father was to be addressed as such. But Merrill's parents didn't think they had committed any great sin.

Visiting Uncle Jimmy and Aunt Thelma was always an intriguing experience. They were an eccentric couple who lived in a quaint Gothic house, which sat on a small promontory deep in a secluded valley. Their water was supplied not from a well, but by a hydraulic ram, a device that delivers water from a stream to a higher elevation by using the momentum of the flowing water as the energy source. In each of the bedrooms of the house were four-posters, beds that had four upright posts at each of the corners to support a canopy—insuring privacy as well as keeping out mosquitos. What was so intriguing about the beds was that each of the posts had a removable brass top, where Uncle Jimmy and Aunt Thelma compartmentalized their loose coins. In one post, there were nickels; in another, dimes; in the third, quarters; and in the fourth, silver dollars. I never did find a cache of pennies. At five years of age, I was intrigued by these caches of coins, which I accidentally discovered on my own. When no one was looking, I would very quietly take off the top of the posts just to see those bright, shiny coins. I later learned that Uncle Jimmy would wash the coins from time to time to keep them looking new. He would purposely break a dollar in order to receive change. He was a very, very odd uncle, but a rich one. On second thought, maybe he was not so odd, because I do the same thing myself, sorting and depositing my change at the end of the day. Since my bank no longer takes my loose change, I gave all of it to the church at the end of last year.

At the Evans Place, Bennie and I resumed attending Sunday School, this time at Elam Baptist Church, with Ruth Brock, a first cousin, and her five orphaned children, all of whom lived with Ruth's parents, Uncle Purry and Aunt Annie. The church itself was just one big wood-frame building, and the classes were held in the four corners of the room. This was probably the first time I was aware that I had a hearing problem. With all the background noise of the different classes talking at one time, I seldom could make out what the teacher said. It was a different situation with the singing, however. Everyone sang with gusto, and many of the older members commented about my having been blessed with such a nice, clear voice. My biggest problem with singing hymns was with the words. One hymn in par-

Evans Place
I'm on the right, in overalls.

ticular went "There is a fountain filled with blood,/ Drawn from Immanuel's veins,/ And sinners, plunged beneath that flood,/ Lose all their guilty stains." Where was the fountain? Where was the blood? Who was Immanuel? And where were the guilty stains? In fact, exactly what were "guilty stains"?

One of the things I particularly liked about living on the Evans Place was Daddy taking me with him to the grist mill to have corn ground into meal. The mill was situated across the road—which also served as the milldam—from Easterling's Pond, about two miles east of Elamville. The water from the millpond rushed through a chute onto a 20-foot water wheel that turned a shaft connected to the massive stone millstones that ground the corn. When the meal was emptied into bags, it was still warm from the heat generated by the friction of the millstones. And, oh, the delightful aroma of freshly ground cornmeal!

While the miller was grinding the corn, I bombarded him with questions of how the water wheel worked and how the corn was ground. Since my older brothers and cousins were always telling me to hurry up with my story, I felt I might be getting on the miller's nerves, so I asked if he minded my asking so many questions. Surely his response reinforces the idea that it does indeed take a village to nurture a child. He said, "You can't learn if you don't ask questions. As long as you ask the questions, I'll answer them the best I can."

On the far end of the 25-acre millpond were the most beautiful waterlilies, with the broad flat leaves and delicate white blossoms just floating on the water. I told Daddy I wanted to take one home to Mama, but he said that waterlilies were meant to be just where they were and that they wouldn't live anyplace else. I still wanted to see them up close, so Daddy borrowed a boat and rowed out to where they were. Then I saw that the waterlilies were attached to roots that extended far below the surface. Since we never went boating again, I am thankful I had the opportunity to see my father row so smoothly and gracefully, and that he took the time to satisfy my curiosity.

It was in this very millpond that a boy about my age drowned several years earlier. In fact, he was an older brother of my best friend, Bennie Earl Norton. The Norton family was picnicking at Easterling's Pond, and the boy became caught in the maelstrom, where the water became a violent whirlpool before rushing through the chute onto the waterwheel. Knowing that Daddy was a strong swimmer, I asked him why someone didn't try to save the boy. He said that although it was tragic the boy drowned, anyone who tried to save him might have been caught up in the eddy and drowned as well. But with Daddy rowing the boat, I felt safe and secure.

The Early War Years

I began attending Elamville School, which consisted of grades one through nine. Though the war had just begun, already certain critical items and foods were being rationed. There were separate ration books for gasoline, automobile

Ration Book

tires, coffee, sugar, and shoes, with each of the books having tear-out stamps. We had plenty of ration stamps but simply lacked the money to use them. The rolling store didn't run in the Elamville area; even if it had, I wouldn't have been able to buy a Baby Ruth or an all-day sucker. For a few weeks, we were on welfare—or relief, as it was then called—and again I was able to eat in the school lunchroom without paying, that is, if I was able to bring in produce from home that the lunchroom could use. Each day, a ninth grader went from room to room and wrote on the board what canned or fresh produce the lunchroom needed for the next day's menu, so that students could bring in the ingredients, a practice that health safety regulations would not allow today. The bright spot in my day was typically having half a grapefruit, a bowl of soup, and a serving of stewed prunes. To an often hungry eight-year-old, this meager fare was no less than ambrosia. Since some of my classmates didn't like either grapefruit or prunes, I usually ate theirs as well.

Once a year during my first and second grades at Clio Low School, the county health department screened the students for tooth decay. Students who didn't need dental care were given a white slip; those who did were given a pink one, which they were instructed to take home to their parents. I always received a pink slip, and as instructed, I took it home. However, I was never taken to the dentist.

3rd Grade

During the third grade at Elamville, my gums became abscessed, and several of my molars showed signs of decay. When my gums hurt, I would often press them with my finger, causing pus to ooze out. The pus was foul-smelling and foul-tasting, making it hard to focus when I was taking a spelling test, or memorizing the multiplication tables. In spite of this, I memorized, on my own, the capitals of the states and the

---

[8] The Golden Rule is a paraphrase of one of the teachings of Jesus, "As ye would that men should do unto you, do ye likewise unto them." Matthew 7:12; Luke 6:31.

states themselves in alphabetical order. Ask me at this moment, and I can recite the names of the states, but the addition of Alaska and Hawaii throws off my rhythm. Although Mrs. Botts, my new teacher, demanded perfection, she, like Mrs. Chandler, was also a caring person. Since I usually scored 100 on the spelling test, she often let me call out the words for the other students to spell.

Students' desks in those days were equipped with inkwells—or, inkstands—although I don't recall anyone ever inserting a bottle of ink into them. In addition, each student was issued a foot-long ruler, inscribed with the Golden Rule: "Do unto others as you would have them do unto you."[8] The notebooks had the multiplication tables on the back cover; for some reason, only the 9's caused me a problem. I found, however, that when the digits of the product were added, they always equaled 9, e.g., 1 x 9 = 09 (0 + 9 = 9); 2 x 9 = 18 (1 + 8 = 9); 3 x 9 = 27 (2 + 7 = 9), 4 x 9 = 36 (3 + 6 = 9), etc. I later discovered that the first digit of the product increases by 1, while the second digit decreases by 1, e.g., 09, 18, 27, 36, 45, 54, 63, 72, 81, 90. However, with the next set (9 x 11 = 99), the first digit remains the same[9], but with each succeeding set, the pattern resumes: 99, 108, 117, 126, 135, 144, etc. Though mathematics has never been one of my strong points, I am fascinated by the theory of numbers, especially those of Archimedes, Pythagoras, Pascal, Bernoulli, Newton, and Fibonacci, especially Fibonacci. On one Internet site alone, there are over 100 pages devoted to the concept of Fibonacci numbers and patterns. Basically, the last two of his numbers total the next number, e.g., 0, 1, 1, 2, 3, 5, 8, 13, ... His pattern of numbers has been observed in such diverse areas as bee hives, shell shapes, branching plants, flower petals and seeds, leaf and petal arrangements, and the geometric design of pineapples and pine cones.

Apples of Gold in a Setting of Silver

It was September 1942 when Shellye Louise Moore, my fourth-grade teacher, entered my life. Almost 60 years later as I write this memoir, the thoughts of Mrs. Moore evoke tears of both sorrow and joy. Her mellifluous voice soothed my straining ears—her

---

[9] Even though the digits (99) remain the same, look what happens when they are added (9 + 9 = 18); the digits of the sum (18) can then be added to obtain the sum of 9. Mathematics can be almost as intriguing as words!

speech was like apples of gold in a setting of silver.[10] Though I was half deaf,
I could understand almost every word
she said. I didn't know it then, but I
had suffered severe nerve damage, resulting in high-frequency hearing loss
in both ears. In 1970, I learned from
computer-generated tests administered by the Veterans Administration
Hospital in Washington, D.C., that
the hearing loss was apparently the
result of an untreated ear infection
before the age of three.

Mrs. Moore

Mrs. Moore, a graduate of University of Alabama, was the daughter of a banker and landowner in
Clio. She drove a dark blue 1939 Ford coupe. I thought Mrs. Moore
was the prettiest lady I had ever seen. She lived with her parents
while her husband and her brother, Dr. Joseph W. Moore and Dr.
T. Stroud Jackson, old buddies from their undergraduate days at
University of Alabama, were serving in the Army Medical Corps
in the South Pacific. The Second World War was now in its ninth
month, and almost everyone was wearing a pin embedded with
an imitation pearl, and inscribed "Remember Pearl Harbor."

Once, in the fourth grade, I skinned my knee quite badly. After the wound stubbornly refused to heal, Mrs. Moore brought
bandages and medication from her home and dressed it. She
changed the dressing every day for about a week until the knee
healed. In spite of my fondness for Mrs. Moore, I never had the
traditional crush on her that young boys often have on their female teachers. I suppose the reason was because to me, she was
an angel; no earthly being could have cared as much as she.

It was also during this time that my right side hurt continually; there were few days when I wasn't in constant pain. Fairly
certain I had chronic appendicitis, Mrs. Moore said that if my parents didn't take me to the doctor, she was going to take me herself to see Dr. Tillman in Clio. One Friday afternoon, after I had
been in considerable pain and had held my right side for most of
the day, Mrs. Moore drove me home after school, saying I

[10] "A word fitly spoken is like apples of gold in settings of silver." Proverbs 25:11

shouldn't be bounced around on the school bus on the bumpy, unpaved backwoods roads. My father joked I was just having growing pains. I continued having the pains intermittently, but my appendix wasn't excised until I was twenty-one years old, while stationed in the Philippines with the U.S. Air Force.

The fourth grade marked the beginning of my education in earnest. However, because of tighter food rationing for the war effort, the lunchroom program was discontinued; students had to bring their own lunches. For me, that meant a slice of fried sweet po-

*In the Philippines
Age 21*

tato, if we had any at the time. Sometimes, I brought a biscuit stuffed in my pocket. Before we moved to Elamville, I could go to Vallie's house when I was hungry; but now I could no longer visit her, for her home was on the Clio bus route. I yearned for a peanut butter and jelly sandwich like some of the other children had; often I would help another student with his homework just to get a piece of his sandwich. We were still on welfare, but what we got off the relief truck was mostly coffee, flour, and sugar— nothing that could be taken to school for lunch. We once got about a half peck of raisins, but we ate most of them in only a few days.

We produced bumper crops in cotton, corn, peanuts, and sugar cane on the Evans Place. One Saturday afternoon late in the fall, Daddy came home from Clio with a battery-powered Stewart-Warner radio he had bought after selling a bale of cotton. I cannot begin to describe my elation at our owning such a marvel. Nothing of importance ever seemed to happen on Pea River Road, where we lived, and that radio began to open up to us a previously unknown world of music, news, and comedy. Once, as I dialed the radio to the low numbers, I heard a strange but beautiful, scintillating, rhythmic sound. Though I didn't know it at the time, I was listening to Spanish from Mexico. I tried to mimic the sounds of the language, but had no idea what I was saying. It was years later, in the Air Force, when I finally learned to speak passable Spanish. Being able to speak Spanish rather fluently now is a decided asset, with the number of Hispanics living in the Northern Virginia area, where I live.

On Saturday nights in the winter, we all huddled around the fire, shelling seed peanuts for spring planting and listening to the Grand Ole Opry out of Nashville, and the Louisiana Hayride out of Shreveport; we also laughed a lot, listening to Amos 'n' Andy and Henry Aldrich, with Henry's famous line, "Coming, Mother," in response to his mother's calling "Henry, Henry Aldrich." And, of course, we devoured news of the war, now in its eleventh month. Cousins and neighborhood boys were being drafted, and already our little community had suffered its first war casualty. I can still hear the wails of Miss Armstrong, the second grade teacher at Elamville, when she learned her only brother had been killed in action.

It was on the Evans Place that my father whipped me, the only time he ever physically abused me in any way. Needam, the two-day-old son of my brother James and his wife, Ada, had died suddenly, and James came racing up on a mule to tell us of his death. It was the first time I had seen an adult cry. We had already planned on walking the two miles to James and Ada's house to see Needam that evening. I can't remember my exact question, but surely I must have asked how my little nephew had died. We were picking up pecans that had been shaken from the tree, and my father grabbed a dry limb lying on the ground and began flogging me. The result was a strange mixture of pain to my body and grief to my soul. Since I practically worshipped him, I prayed that he would tell me later he was sorry and had acted out of frustration, since I knew it was difficult for him to handle the death of a grandchild so young. There hadn't been a death in the family since Lovick and Lessie's oldest child had died about the time I was born. An excellent carver, Daddy later chiseled Needam's name and dates of birth and death on his tombstone. The subject of the whipping was never brought up; even if he hadn't seen fit to apologize, I would have liked simply to know the reason for his actions.

Though he had his faults and at times could be verbally abusive, Daddy also had a gentle side. He was generally considerate and kind, especially when he was sober. In my first and second grades, for instance, I would often find him by the fireplace warming my overalls or in the kitchen buttering a hot biscuit for my breakfast. On a bitterly cold night, he would also wrap a brick he had heated in the fireplace for me to put my feet against when I went to bed.

At the Evans Place, Mr. G. W. Phillips, a progressive farmer, lived down and across the road from us. While we plowed the fields row by row with mules, Mr. Phillips used a new Farmall tractor to plow five or six rows at a time. And from the field where I was working, I could see his son, Ladon, the same age as I, with his father, sitting in the tractor seat. In only a few days, Ladon was driving the tractor himself. And how I envied him! He had a brand-new bicycle, a Schwinn, if I remember correctly. He was not in the least bit selfish, and we had many happy hours together, riding his bicycle up and down Pea River Road. What made our times together even more enjoyable was his mother, Miss Evie, occasionally calling us in for a hefty slice of devil's food cake and a glass of cold milk.

Though not as blissful as my four years on the Phillips Place, 1942 on the Evans Place was indeed a good year—except for the war, and for Mama breaking her arm. Mama was milking the cow down by the barn. The cow was extremely gentle, but a tire I was rolling with a stick got away from me, rushing down the slope directly toward the cow. Mama was on the opposite side from where the tire hit the cow and had no time to move. Her arm was broken in three places. She continued to cook and clean with her arm in a cast, but from that moment onward, I milked the cow—when we had one—until I left home for college.

The names of states I had merely memorized began to take on meaning and relevance, as my brother Loyce left the coal and ore mines in Birmingham to work in a defense plant in Detroit, Michigan. When he came home for Christmas in 1942, Loyce said that even in Michigan's winter, with snow as high as his knees sometimes, his room was warm and cozy, with no need for even a blanket. Miracle of miracles, he said his room was heated by a steam radiator. Loyce assured us that he wouldn't be drafted since he was already supporting the war effort by helping build armored tanks at the Cadillac plant. One of my cousins, P. L. Danner, was already in artillery training at Fort Sill, Oklahoma.

1943: The Abysmal Year of My Life

If 1942 was a good year, it only served to prepare me for the most dismal and troubled period of my early boyhood. Only Mrs. Carter and Mrs. Wilkinson (two teachers I was yet to meet), Mrs. Moore, and Vallie would bring light into the abysmal darkness that year. In January 1943, when I was nine years old—soon to be ten—our family moved back to the Clio area, and I continued in the fourth grade at Clio Low School, where I had originally enrolled in first grade. I missed Mrs. Moore so much that I would have walked the eight or so miles to Elamville just to be in her class—and also to receive her attention. We were now living on the Lee Place, three or four miles north of Clio, and Elamville was four miles south of Clio.

Shortly after we moved, Loyce, who thought that working in a defense plant would exempt him from the draft, was inducted. We wouldn't see him again until two and a half years later, after the war. Mama said that if anyone had ever told her one of her sons would be fighting in a war "across the water," she wouldn't have known what to make of it. When Loyce came home from Detroit before reporting to the Army induction center at Fort McClellan, Alabama, he brought Mama a complete set of silverware, and he brought me a Mickey Mouse wristwatch.

I was the only fourth grader wearing a watch. I was also the only student who usually didn't have a pencil and who couldn't eat in the lunchroom because I didn't have the required five or ten cents. If I was able to earn a nickel or a dime, I would buy a Liberty Stamp to paste into my War Bond Book, which students were encouraged to maintain. I never did paste enough stamps in the book to buy a war bond; after the war, I could have redeemed the War Bond Book, but in all our moving, it was lost. By the end of the war, I think I had accumulated stamps that equaled almost five dollars. Mrs. Wilkinson, my teacher, must have sensed that I craved attention, for she would ask me to tell her the time throughout the day. Since I was an excellent reader, she regarded me as her assistant. While she worked with the slower students, she told me to listen to the more advanced students read.

While Loyce was home from Detroit, he bought us a new battery for the radio, which served as our only window to the outside world. Before long, even the Grand Ole Opry's appeal diminished for us as we huddled around the radio to hear the latest news of the war and Hitler's atrocities, as well as the barbaric acts committed by the Japanese in the Pacific. One of the Pittman boys in Clio had been reported missing in action in Europe, only to be later declared as killed. And James Phillips from Elamville had been taken prisoner by the Germans. The next year when I was working for the Phillipses, James' mother, Miss Della, was grief-stricken that she'd probably never again hear her only son say he loved her, as she had heard that the Germans cut out the tongues of American prisoners of war.

Ralph, then 18, had recently married and was still on the farm. His only material possessions were ten fat hogs ready for slaughtering, a couple of shoats, and three barrows. One day in March, when I came home from school, I smelled the rich aroma of roast pork and thought that today surely had been a hog-killing day. Excitedly, I anticipated a wonderful supper, complete with fresh sage-spiced sausage and crackling bread, bread made with rendered pork rinds. Innately, however, I knew this was too good to be true, for the weather was getting warm, too warm for a hog-killing.

When I ran into the house and realized that the aroma was coming from someplace else, I asked Mama what had happened. She pointed to rising smoke in a ravine near a copse of scrub pine and scraggly post oak trees and told me to go and see for myself. Beside the ravine were Ralph and my father. I overheard Daddy say, "It's a downright shame." Ralph's hogs had all been shot and burned by the county farm agent because they had contracted cholera, an extremely infectious animal disease. The next day, my father left home; no one knew where he had gone. Only my 14-year-old brother, Bennie, and I were left to help Ralph with the farming. It's difficult for a ten-year-old to harness a mule and plow a straight row, but we managed to help him get the cotton and peanuts planted. As I

Bennie, Age 14

reflect on Daddy's leaving, I think that he simply didn't know how to start over again.

About two weeks before Easter, I received a letter from Mrs. Moore, inviting me to her home in Clio for an Easter egg hunt that she was having for my old class at Elamville. Mrs. Moore's handwriting was beautiful, but it was her words—telling me that she missed me—that elated me. She added that each student should bring a decorated hard-boiled egg, and she would give a prize for the most beautifully decorated one. I walked to Clio, but I didn't have an egg to bring, much less one that was decorated. It didn't matter. Mrs. Moore hugged me and said she was really happy to see me. After we all looked for the eggs and played some games, Mrs. Jackson (Mrs. Moore's kind and gentle mother) called us in to eat sandwiches and the eggs that the students had brought to be hidden and found. While we were playing, Mrs. Jackson had deviled them and arranged them concentrically on a silver platter. She had also baked beautifully decorated cookies, which she served with fruit punch.

I was so proud of Mrs. Moore's letter inviting me to the party that I kept it in my pocket until it wore out; I must have read it at least a hundred times, and had shown and read it to as many people as would listen.

In May, while milking the cow, I stepped on a nail, which almost pierced my foot. There was no way to get to the doctor; there was no telephone to call one, nor any money to pay one. It was the first time I had missed school since the year before when my gums were abscessed; I couldn't stand on the injured foot, much less walk the mile to the bus stop. If only I had been able to contact Mrs. Moore or Vallie. I don't know why Mama or Ralph didn't tell Bennie to send Vallie word from school inasmuch as her next-door neighbor drove the school bus. Surely she would have come to take me to the doctor, even though gasoline was then acutely rationed.

Uncle Everett, one of Daddy's brothers, visited us one Sunday afternoon. Concerned at seeing my swollen foot, he said to my mother, "That boy should be taken to the doctor." Since the doctor's office was closed on Sunday, Uncle Everett said that he would come back on Monday and take me to see Dr. Tillman in Clio. I looked forward to his coming back all day Monday, even all week, but he never returned. What hurt was that Uncle Everett, so unlike his younger brother, was a dependable family man.

However, after about a week at home, I knew I had to get back to school, even though my foot was swollen to about twice its normal size. Bennie walked with me as I hobbled to the bus stop. When I got to school, Mrs. Wilkinson asked Bennie Earl Norton to walk with me to the doctor in town, about a half mile from the school. When Dr. Tillman lanced my foot, the most unsightly discolored blood spurted out. The doctor asked why I hadn't come to see him earlier, adding that it was a miracle I hadn't developed lockjaw. Within a week after I saw Dr. Tillman, my foot returned to its normal size, and I had no more problems with it.

The Kindness of Others

Since I was back in the Clio school, I could again ride the bus to visit Vallie after school. She would wash my clothes, press them, serve me waffles for breakfast the next morning, and make sure I had lunch or lunch money inasmuch as the school in Clio, unlike Elamville, had a lunchroom. At Vallie's, I was back into the ritual of bowing my head for the blessing, speaking proper English, and setting the table correctly. In addition, I now slept on a firm bed with crisp, clean sheets. I was taught to make my own bed; Vallie didn't do what a person could do for himself. I had my own bedroom at Vallie's house—at least, I called it my room. It was really the guest room.

During one particular visit, my abscessed gums were hurting again. Vallie wrote a note and told me to take it to Dr. Reynolds, in Clio. Once I was on the bus, I opened the note, which read, "Dear Dr. Reynolds, Please fix my brother Horace's teeth, and we will pay you in smoked hams or sides of bacon. Thank you, Vallie Phillips." I was quite surprised when I read it, and realized that she had taken particular notice of my discomfort. I took the note to Dr. Reynolds after school; without so much as asking a question, he immediately started filling my teeth, because he knew Vallie and Addie's word was their bond. Since I had to miss the bus to see the dentist, I walked the five miles back to the Lee Place. Thanks to Vallie, as well as the United States Air Force, my dentist—Dr. John A. Mercantini, of Reston, Virginia—says he hasn't seen better cared-for teeth in an older man. At 70, I am missing only my wisdom teeth and one molar. Checking the facts of the memoir with Vallie, she says she doesn't recall writing the note to Dr. Reynolds. But then, how many people keep an account of their good deeds or acts of kindness?

We learned that Daddy had gone to Eufaula, only about 25 miles away, to work in the cotton mill. He rarely came home; when he did, I don't recall his ever bringing groceries or money for food. Furthermore, he was almost always drunk. I could tell by his gait, as he staggered down the red-clay lane to our house, and by the way his Stetson was cocked to one side.

I must reemphasize that Daddy was neither a bad nor a mean man; he would do practically anything for anybody, except take responsibility for his own family, at least during this bleak period of my life. (I must emphasize *my life*, for Vallie says that Daddy was an excellent provider when she was young.) With scant regard for his children's education, he had often kept the older boys out of school to help a neighbor pick cotton or stack peanuts. However, he never kept me out of school, probably because he knew I would probably be more trouble than I was worth.

When Daddy was home, I hoped he would stay sober and spend some time with me. Once, when he had come from Eufaula, I got my wish; he awakened me at four in the morning to go fishing with him on Pea River. He must have known that the fish would be biting, because we brought back a long string of perch, bream, and sunfish. He would tell me to cast my line by a certain log in the river or by a cypress knee, and that I would surely catch a bream. He knew where to cast a line for a particular kind of fish, what kind of bait the fish liked, and how shallow or how deep to fish. I think he must have coined the saying now often seen on bumper stickers—*Work is for people who don't know how to fish.*

War Bonds, Victory Gardens, and Hunger

Since Loyce had practically supported us financially prior to being drafted, Mama heard that we qualified for an allotment, in which the government would match a soldier's contribution. It was in the summer of 1943 that Mama received the first check. After three or four months, we learned that the entire $25 was being deducted from Loyce's pay. So, instead of spending the money on necessities, Mama began buying a monthly War Bond for $18.75 to save for him. After the war, when Mama gave Loyce the bundle of bonds, he told her he wished that she had used the money instead. That was Loyce, always looking out for the family. Loyce was the son whom every one of us adored, and no one appeared to be jealous of his being the most popular.

Loyce
Rome 1944

When I wasn't in the fields, I made it a point to meet the rural mail carrier, to see if we had received another V-Mail from Loyce. V-Mail, which stood for "Victory Mail," was a fold-over single sheet of extremely thin paper, made especially for wartime messages. Where the stamp would ordinarily be placed on the envelope, the serviceperson simply wrote "Free." In the summer of 1943, his letters were datelined "Somewhere in North Africa." If he inadvertently disclosed any sensitive information, it would be blacked out or, sometimes, cut out by a censor. The envelope was hand-stamped "Censored by (the name and rank of the censor)," and then signed. Although I don't remember Loyce ever trying to tell us his exact location, some of my cousins used code to such an extent that their families could practically track their campaign movements. One cousin was able to relate that his outfit was in New Guinea by asking his mother if the old, speckled hen had new guinea chicks yet.

Until we received the check, there was absolutely no money to buy food. When Mama didn't know what we would eat for the next meal, she would nonchalantly say we were going to visit her cousin Augusta, who lived about a mile from us. Cousin Augusta and her husband had five teenage boys, all of whom worked as a team on the farm. Mama and Cousin Augusta would have a grand time shelling peas and husking corn for dinner. After we had eaten a good dinner, Cousin Augusta would act as though she were forcing Mama to take some of the abundance home, knowing full well that as a Dykes, Mama was too proud to beg. As I was writing this account, I called Cousin Augusta's oldest son, Marvy, to confirm the facts of our visits to their house. He remembered them quite well and then added a footnote. He said that as his mother was dying, she said in a semiconscious state, "Cousin Hettie, please take more. We have plenty."

Every week or so, Susie Mae and Ralph would walk to her family's home, about five miles from our house, and then her father would drive them back to our house with some of the basics. As ingenious as Susie Mae was, however, she had difficulty helping my mother prepare nourishing meals for Ralph, Bennie, and me. One day, after Mama and I picked butter beans from our Victory Garden, she told me to take them into Clio to see if I could trade them for some flour and sugar. Yes, we needed the flour and sugar, but we also needed the beans.

When Mama received that first government check, she and I rode into Clio with Daniel Williams, a neighboring farmer who had just bought a secondhand Buick. When Mr. Williams left us at the store, he told me to come and get him at the cotton gin when we were ready to go back home. We bought three or four bags of groceries at Baxter's Store, including a toothbrush and a tube of Ipana toothpaste, since Dr. Reynolds had said the main part of dental hygiene was up to me. Mr. Woods Baxter, the store owner, in-

With Mama
1943

formed us that to buy toothpaste, we must turn in a used tube because of the war's demand on metal. I explained to him that we didn't have a used tube because I had never bought toothpaste or owned a toothbrush before. When I went to look for Mr. Williams, someone at the gin told me that he had already left. It was raining hard, and there was no way we could get home with the groceries. My mother began to panic, for we had bought a pint of ice cream that had already begun to thaw.

Ever resourceful, I remembered that Mrs. Moore lived only a few blocks from Baxter's Store. I ran through the sheets of rain to her house and, dripping wet, hurriedly explained the situation. Without hesitation, Mrs. Moore headed for her car, the sporty little Ford coupe she drove to Elamville School. Her father was adamant that she take his Buick, saying the heavier car could handle those slick back roads better. But Mrs. Moore told her father she was quite confident in her Ford, and the two of us drove to Baxter's Store and picked up Mama and the bags of groceries. As we rode back to our house, Mrs. Moore treated my mother and me like royal guests. She would hear nothing of our offering to pay her. Mrs. Moore was the embodiment of *noblesse oblige*; not only she, but the entire Jackson clan—Alto, Sam, Shelly, Bunyan—were extremely benevolent to those less fortunate than themselves. In fact, Dr. Frank Jackson founded Jackson Memorial Hospital, one of the avant-garde medical facilities not only in Montgomery, but in the entire state of Alabama. When I asked Mr. Williams later why he had left us, he said he had "just plumb forgot."

During the time we lived at the Lee Place, Ellie Mae, my youngest sister, lived with her husband, Mixon Missildine, and their two-year-old daughter, Jacqueline, about a half mile from us. Somewhere Ellie Mae discovered a collection of Jonathan Swift's writings; of all his essays, she locked onto "A Modest Proposal." She took great delight in reading this gruesome essay to me. I shuddered to imagine that anyone could roast a child and have it for dinner—even if the succulence of the roasted two-year-old might compare with that of roast pig! Being only in the fourth grade, I didn't know the piece was a satire; if Ellie Mae knew, she didn't tell me. She also read to me Charles Lamb's (or, Elia's) essay "Dissertation upon Roast Pig." The essay told of the good that came out of a house burning—that the pig which was kept in the house was roasted, and one of the boys in the family stuck his finger into the still-hot pig, and licking his fingers, found that it was delicious. But since Swift had referred to the roasted child as similar in taste to that of roast pig, I often got the two essays confused.

In a perennial state of devotion—reading her Bible and praying aloud while kneeling on the floor—Ellie Mae regularly prayed for my troubled unsaved soul, pleading my deliverance from the raging fires of Hell, graphically describing it as seven times hotter than the fire in our fireplace on a cold winter night. Ellie Mae was an earthly saint, beautiful and loving, but in many ways a troubled soul herself.

When reading anything, Ellie Mae always held a sharpened pencil. She said it was to help focus the mind on the meaning. One of her favorite expressions was "Sharp point, sharp mind. Dull point, dull mind." Using the ever-sharpened pencil, she would write down the words she didn't know, tasking me to look up the definitions at school and bring them back to her.

This distressful year was made more bearable by Many Spot. Someone had given us a mixed-breed puppy the year before, and since she had almost as many spots as a Dalmatian, I called her Many Spot. After my father left us, I sometimes felt there was no one to turn to, and I just wanted to be alone, to try to think it all out. But Many Spot knew me better than I knew myself and followed me everywhere I went. She would sit on her haunches and peer up at me as though she were saying, "What's so terribly wrong, little fellow?" I would tell her I wanted to be alone, to just go away. But she would cock her head to one side, as if she were mimicking me, since I often tilted my head to hear a person better. If I was happy, she was happy; if I was sad, she just listened. And those sad eyes told me she understood my deepest hurt.

There was also the influence of the Pea River Presbyterian Church on Bennie's and my religious edification and educational upbringing. We had previously attended Elam Baptist Church, but now, the closest Baptist congregation was in Clio, and Mama said she didn't want us going to a town church barefoot like two orphans. So Bennie and I went to the Presbyterian church, located on the outskirts of Clio. The Presbyterians welcomed us two little barefoot Baptist boys. We both memorized the two catechisms given to us in Sunday School. For some reason, I was fascinated by the word *catechism*, literally "to sound thoroughly." At the time, I didn't know what *catechism* meant, other than I was supposed to memorize the responses to the questions, one of which, if I remember correctly, was "What is the sole purpose of man?" I believe the answer was "to glorify God with his mind, soul, and body."

I suppose it was the teachings of the catechisms, as well as Ellie Mae's graphic description of Hell, that got me, at ten years old, to begin seriously thinking of God and religion. If God created the universe—as the catechisms had taught—and if everything was good in His sight, why was evil allowed to reign? And why did Jesus have to die for my sins? What sin or sins had I committed? Though I now know of the concept of original sin, I am still not completely clear on God and the universe, Nature, sickness, and sin and evil. Maybe that's the way it was intended, that God is too awesome for us mortals to comprehend. When I look at the Milky Way and am told by astronomers that its width alone measures 20,000 light years, any further attempt to understand the Creator and the universe is unthinkable. With a light year equalling 5,880,000,000,000 miles, the width of the Milky Way alone is an unimaginable 20,000 times 6 trillion miles! Who can comprehend the expanse? *The Washington Post* reported recently that the Hubble Space Telescope has detected the faintest and most distant objects ever sighted: galaxies of stars more than 12 billion light years away.

The avowed atheist, Carl Sagan, further helps us to put the universe in perspective. He says that the number of stars we can see with the naked eye on a clear night is greater than the number of grains of sand one could hold in the hand—approximately 10,000 grains. And, he says, the number of stars we *see* is only the tiniest fraction of the number of stars that *are*. Further, the total number of stars in the universe is greater than all the grains of sand on all the beaches of the planet Earth.

With the size of the universe so truly imponderable, it's amazing that the right people sometimes come into our lives for a specific purpose. Besides Susie Mae, Ralph's wife, who often took me fishing at Shipman's Creek, the person who was extraordinary to me during this time was Estelle, Olon's wife. No matter how dire the situation, Estelle could find something to be encouraged about. An accomplished guitarist, she also possessed a beautiful alto voice. She was vibrant, beautiful, and a positive thinker. She often asked me about school. Later in life, she encouraged me to take chemistry, since, she said, chemists develop new medicines. She also told me I had the build to be a basketball player. I may have had the build, as well as the desire, but I had not a scintilla of athletic coordination.

Estelle also had a gift for interpreting the Bible. It was the one book she was allowed to read without my brother Olon complaining about her insatiable desire to learn more. As with the rest of my older brothers and sisters, Olon had gone only to the fourth or fifth grade and could barely read the newspaper, and he was extremely uneasy having a wife who was intellectually inclined. He absolutely forbade Estelle to use her time to study. It was only after he went to work that she could retrieve her Bible study materials, that is, between washing dishes and changing baby diapers. Not long before Olon died, Estelle said he apologized for trying to deny her the opportunity to learn. Even today, if I need an emotional boost, I need only to call Estelle.

But now, back to the late summer of 1943. I can't remember how well the cotton produced that year, but I do recall the peanut situation. After Ralph had plowed up the peanuts, Mama, Susie Mae, Bennie, and I shook the loose soil from them and threw the vines into windrows to partially dry. A few days later, we stacked them for the final drying. After a week or so, depending on the weather, it was time to hire a peanut picker, a machine that picks the peanuts from the vines and also bales the vines into hay, to be used for winter feed. To have the peanuts picked, one must have the money to pay the equipment owner. However, Ralph had no money and no way to borrow it. The peanuts rotted in the field. The investment in seed and fertilizer advanced by the landowner, and our months of hard work had come to naught.

Since it is from the sale of the crop that a sharecropper pays the landowner, we had not a cent with which to pay. Mrs. Lee, the landowner, drove out to our house in her 1941 Cadillac to collect her rent. In a distressed state, Mama tried to explain how Daddy had left us and how Ralph hadn't been able to obtain a picker. I will never forget the scene: Mrs. Lee tapping her left foot on the bottom step of our front porch, shaking her finger, and repeating over and over, "I must have my rent regardless." Distraught, Mama began to shake uncontrollably. It was the first time I had ever seen her cry. Possibly she cried when Daddy unceremoniously left us or when Loyce left for the war, but in front of Ralph, Bennie, and me, she was always cheerful. But now, Mama was overwhelmed, penned in, with no place to seek refuge.

Ralph was able to get a job helping another farmer and promised Mrs. Lee that he would personally take responsibility for paying her for the use of the land. Before he was able to finish paying her, however, he was inducted into the Army. Mrs. Lee allowed us to continue living in the house until we could find a place to move to.

In high school six years later, Mrs. Laird, the glee club director, took a group of us students Christmas caroling; one of the persons we serenaded was Mrs. Lee, regarded in town as a benevolent widow. As we were singing "Away in a Manger" and "Silent Night," I wanted to exclaim to her, "You are not the beautiful person everyone thinks you are. You upset my mother, making her cry." However, Mrs. Lee was gracious and kind, inviting us into her chandeliered, carpeted mansion and serving us Christmas-decorated cookies and hot chocolate. I wondered if after six years Mrs. Lee remembered me, especially after Mrs. Laird introduced us all. At 16, I now realized she had only been looking out for her business interests. But the foot-tapping and finger-shaking scene remains as graphic today as on that day in early September 1943.

A Teacher's Magic

Mrs. Mary Carter, my fifth-grade teacher at Clio Low School, once said I had the brightest, most alert eyes she had ever seen. It was during the fall of that year, however, that I remember being the hungriest that I had ever been. Since we hadn't been able to harvest the peanut crop, and since Mama was now buying a War Bond with the allotment from Loyce, we were completely without money, except for the $6.25 left after buying the bond. The lunchroom was just down the hall from our room, and I could smell the aroma of freshly baked yeast rolls. Though I usually had a biscuit for breakfast, I was so hungry by midmorning that I could hardly concentrate. There are no words to describe chronic hunger. I felt as if my mind were separated from my body. One day, when the other students were eating, Mrs. Carter asked why I never ate lunch. I replied that I had eaten such a large

5th Grade

breakfast I couldn't manage another bite.

I hardly ever played with the other boys and girls; I usually didn't have the energy. Besides that, I felt inferior to my nicely dressed classmates, who had not only lunches but also snacks. One could usually find me during recess and at noon leaning against the school building or inside in the classroom, chatting with Mrs. Carter while she ate her lunch. Once, when I was outside, an older boy tossed a half-eaten apple onto the ground; as soon as he was out of sight, I grabbed what was left of it, devouring everything but the seeds. Occasionally, a friend offered me a piece of his peanut butter and jelly sandwich. Peanut butter was a luxury we never had in our house, even though we sometimes grew peanuts. With the peanuts Ellie Mae and I gleaned from the unpicked stacks, we once tried to make peanut butter, grinding them in the coffee mill; however, the peanut butter—if it could be called that—stuck to the roofs of our mouths.

I discovered that drinking water helped assuage the gnawing of hunger. Furthermore, Mrs. Carter's enthusiasm for teaching diverted my attention. For example, she told us about the northeastern states, and why they were called New England. Mrs. Carter, like many of my other teachers, had traveled widely. We were all intrigued to hear that before the war, she had actually seen snow while visiting relatives in North Carolina during the winter. She described the hazy Great Smoky Mountains of North Carolina and Tennessee, the Blue Ridge Mountains of Virginia, and the White Mountains of New Hampshire. She showed us pictures of the white bark of birch trees and the bright oranges, reds, and purples of the autumn leaves. (South Alabama's pine-anchored lowlands and rolling hills aren't known for striking autumn colors, and I had never seen the Appalachian Mountains of North Alabama.)

I also learned the correct pronunciation of *Yosemite* and what a *geyser* was. Mrs. Carter also told us that the word *geyser* was Icelandic, literally meaning "gusher," and was the name of a certain hot spring in southwest Iceland. But it was hard to understand why the British pronounce the River Thames as *temz*. The way she taught geography made me want to visit every place we studied. In all my travels, I've yet to witness the hourly performance of Old Faithful, in Yellowstone National Park. I understand the geyser erupts on the average for about 4 minutes every 65-67 minutes, spewing a stream of boiling water more than 100 feet into the air. I later learned that Old Faithful's performance has been recorded for almost 100 years, and it has never missed an eruption.

In November or December of the fifth grade, we students noticed some white flakes drifting from the sky; we all rushed to the window to behold this wonder. None of us knew for certain what they were. Mrs. Carter explained that this was snow, the first in South Alabama in over fifty years. Most of the flakes melted before they touched the ground, but to everyone's delight, a dusting still remained the next morning.

Soon after school started in the fall of 1943, we heard that a satellite German prisoner of war tent camp was being erected in a pasture within the town limits of Clio. Nearby Fort Rucker, which had been built shortly after the bombing of Pearl Harbor, was a staging area for thousands of prisoners who were being utilized in the cotton and peanut fields of southeastern Alabama.

One afternoon on the way home from school, we students on the bus noticed a dozen or so blond young men with POW stenciled on the backs of their uniforms. The prisoners were stacking peanuts and were being guarded by unmistakably Japanese soldiers, holding rifles in the ready position. I was totally confused—we were fighting both the Germans and the Japanese, and here were armed Japanese right in our backyard. Of course, the pejorative "Dirty Japs" was already a byword, at least in our area. We were later to find that the guards were American citizens of Japanese ancestry who hadn't been allowed to serve their own United States in the Pacific war zone. The 443rd Regimental Combat Team, comprised of Hawaiians of Japanese ancestry, was fighting valiantly in Europe. However, other Japanese-Americans, especially those from California and other Western states, were utilized in more mundane jobs, such as guarding German POWs in the fields of the South. As the war wore on, and the Japanese-Americans were deployed elsewhere in the war effort, the prisoners worked in the fields unguarded.

During this time of my life, I learned what an insane asylum was. A first cousin, one of the most beautiful women I had ever known, was committed. And suddenly, Tuscaloosa stood for more than just the site of the prestigious University of Alabama; it was also the location of Bryce Hospital, where "crazy people," as some members of the community called them, were sent. I once asked Aunt Bessie when Elise was getting out of the crazy house, and forthrightly learned to be more careful with my choice of words, for Aunt Bessie, weeping and wailing, began to scream at me, declaring that her daughter was not crazy, only a little sick. I still wondered how Elise could have been committed, for she was not only beautiful, but also vibrant and charming, using similes, metaphors, and hyperboles as deftly and smoothly as a poet. Many years earlier, for example, when she was visiting our home for the Danner Family Reunion, she said she had eaten so much fresh corn that she thought she might begin to tassel. A cosmetologist, Elise owned her own beauty salon in Clio. I thought she sounded quite important when I would hear her say, "I have to be off now; I have a one o'clock appointment." I have never known for certain and have never asked why she was committed, but knowing Aunt Bessie's volatile emotions, I have a fairly good idea. Though Elise continued intermittently to be a patient at Bryce, she was eventually released, married, and led a mostly happy and productive life.

Just before Christmas of 1943, Ralph was inducted into the

Ralph
Rheims, France, 1944

Army. My father was still drifting in and out, and with Ralph gone, there was no adult male in our home. My father's oldest sister, Leona Ketchum, a widow and a landowner, told Daddy we could move to her place, and help her son Sherrod with the farming. So, in the middle of my fifth-grade year, we moved into another tin-roofed shack, this time deep in the woods, on the Ketchum Place, near Elamville. We had a rather severe winter that year, and though I had to walk over a mile to the bus stop, I had neither good shoes nor a warm jacket. But inside the house, it was warm, if only in front of the fireplace, where

Daddy kept a roaring fire. As the old saying goes, we roasted on one side and froze on the other.

When we needed stovewood or firewood, we needed only to fell a massive oak or hickory in the woods surrounding us. Daddy was so adept at felling trees that he would mark a spot and bet that the tree would fall in that exact place. I never knew him to fail. Using a two-man crosscut saw, we then sawed the trunk into appropriate-sized blocks for either the stove or the fireplace. Daddy's advice on sawing wood is still with me: *Don't push the saw.* Sawing was a pulling action, not a pushing one. I enjoyed smelling the acrid aroma of hickory and oak, as well as watching Daddy split the blocks of wood; of course, it wasn't very enjoyable stacking the wood, for he required that every piece be perfectly aligned. He said if a job was worth doing, it was worth doing right.

Not since second grade had I received anything for Christmas, but in 1944, Vallie gave me a jigsaw puzzle of a World War II aerial combat scene. There were only about 250 pieces, and I put it together and took it apart at least a dozen times, just to have something to do. Two or three years ago, I was in Alabama, visiting Ruth, when Jewell, her oldest daughter about the same age as I, recalled an incident concerning this period of my life I had completely forgotten. Jewell said that when she once asked if Santa Claus had been good to me, I replied, "Well, Mama let me use one of the chifforobe drawers as my very own." She related that I didn't appear the least disappointed or sad that I hadn't received an actual present at Christmas. If one doesn't expect anything, there's no reason to be disappointed.

At Aunt Leona's house, I was free to explore long-forgotten crannies and old trunks. In one of the trunks, I found an illustrated copy of *Gray's Atlas of the Human Body*, showing, of all things, fetuses in developmental stages; I was absolutely shocked. I also discovered a set of forceps, which I took to Aunt Leona and, in my naïveté, asked what they were and what they were used for. This was when I learned that she had been a midwife and that the forceps were used to deliver an unwilling baby into the world. This was my first lesson in sex education, and I reluctantly surmised that I too had once been a fetus as illustrated in the anatomy book. It seemed that I had not, in fact, been found under a cabbage leaf or delivered by a stork. Even though I was eleven years old, I just didn't understand how I had become a fetus in the first place. I had witnessed animals mating on the farm; however, I had yet to make the connection between animals mating and people mating. Assuming that something had occurred I wasn't yet supposed to know about—especially between my saintly, innocent mother and my kind, but rather worldly father— I wasn't bold enough to press the matter further.

My sweet, gentle, diminutive mother and straight-backed, iron-fisted, towering Aunt Leona were diametric opposites. There were certain words that I couldn't bring myself to think, much less utter, in Mama's presence; I inherently knew they were *verboten*. For example, I could not use the word *bet*, because of the its association with gambling. Not even God-fearing adults used the word *swear*, substituting instead *swanee*, as in "I swanee it's gonna rain." I heard Aunt Leona once say, "Aunt Lizzie can't help being so ugly, but I swanee she could have stayed home." Further, I would have never thought of taking the Lord's name in vain— though I was never specifically instructed not to do so, other than reading it in the Ten Commandments. Even today, when I hear someone exclaim "Oh, my G__," I feel a chill in my spine. God's name must be held in awe, reverence, and adoration, not used as a slang expresson.

My vocabulary was somewhat childish, inasmuch as I was not allowed to say certain words that were appropriate for other boys my age. For instance, a private part of the body could not be called by its correct anatomical name. Further, an uncastrated male hog couldn't be called a *boar*, nor could a bull be called a *bull*. But Aunt Leona called parts of the body as well as male farm animals by their proper names. When Mama once mentioned that my stomach hurt, Aunt Leona remarked rather bluntly, "Oh, you mean Horace has a bellyache." (Actually, Mama was right—it *was* my stomach, not my belly, that hurt.) Around Mama, I watched every word lest I offend her delicate sensibilities; but when I was with Aunt Leona, I could say any word that came naturally, even if it was *belly, boar, bull, breast*. Aunt Leona used such words matter-of-factly, as though she were discussing a thunderstorm brewing out in the Gulf. If I used any word other than the anatomically correct one, she would remark that I wasn't a little boy anymore and that I must get on with my life, regardless of what Mama might think.

One other incident concerning Aunt Leona's use of words should round out my memory of her during my early adolescence. Many years before, Uncle Rufus had extended the verandah so that there was a walkway to the well, from which we drew water with a windlass for drinking, bathing, washing clothes, and watering the animals. One summer day when I was eleven or twelve, I had drawn a washtub of water to warm in the sun so that I could take a bath, and the tub of water was on the verandah, where Aunt Leona and Mama were sitting in their rocking chairs, chatting. It was getting dark, and I wanted to wash up before I had to go to bed. Aunt Leona asked why there was a tub of water on the verandah, of all places. Telling her I had drawn it to take a bath, she wanted to know what I was waiting for. I said I didn't want her and Mama to see my "little thing." I had never seen Aunt Leona acting in the least amused, but I glimpsed a grudging smile before she said, "You don't have a 'little thing,' you have a penis, which is just as much a part of your body as your toes or your fingers. If you haven't noticed, every boy and man has one." Mama gasped as she put her hand over her eyes and turned her rocking chair so that she wasn't observing me in my natural state. I can't help but think that Mama was amused as well.

Not only must I be careful of what I said in Mama's presence, I mustn't ever let her know that I had drunk a bottled drink, which we in the country called "soda water," regardless of whether it was a Coke, Pepsi, Dr. Pepper, Royal Crown (RC), or a Nehi grape or strawberry.[11] Mama was afraid that once I upended any bottle to my lips, I would develop the thirst, as she called it, for stronger beverages. She was morbidly afraid I would grow up to be an alcoholic, like my father.

During the summer of 1944, Daddy was getting over having been drunk for a week or two, and he had the shakes awfully bad. Though I'd never said anything to him about his drinking since I was in the second grade, he knew that I hated it when he came home drunk. He was sitting on a quilt by the gardenia bush in the front yard sharpening a crosscut saw, but couldn't seem to focus his eyes. He told me to go to Scroggins Store and buy him a beer so that he could steady himself. I didn't think twice. I said,

[11] Many years later, I would learn that what we Southerners called soda water was called "tonic" in New Hampshire, my future wife's home state.

"Daddy, I've always done what you've told me to do. But I won't buy beer for you." He told me that he understood how I felt, and said he hoped I'd never take up his habit. And I haven't.

Hard Lessons

Since we were now back in the Elamville area, I again went to Elamville School. On a cold, gray, bleak December morning, I walked into the classroom expecting a new teacher. I shivered not from the cold but from frissons of delight at seeing that Mrs. Moore had been transferred to the fifth grade and would be my teacher. What more could a ten-year-old boy ask for? But however thoughtful and kind Mrs. Moore had been, she also knew how to teach a hard lesson. One morning, thinking I was her pet, I yelled out from the schoolhouse window as she was getting out of her Ford coupe and asked when her "hubby Joe" was coming home from the war. My dear, angelic teacher—the one who had dressed my knee; had driven me home from school as I clutched my side in pain; had invited me to an Easter egg hunt, and then warmly welcomed me; and had so cheerfully driven my mother

Elamville School, taken from along the tracks of the Central of Georgia Railroad

and me home with our groceries—told me sharply how I was to refer to her husband, and that some things were of no concern to me. It was one of the hardest lessons I ever had to learn. Learning from books came easily for me; it was with learning from real life I often had problems.

Mrs. Moore wasn't one to remember past wrongs; after her admonishment not to address her husband, Dr. Joseph W. Moore, as her "hubby Joe," the incident passed and was promptly forgotten. For example, not long after her scolding, a fellow student was taunting me about the clothes I was wearing—a flyless pair of coveralls made for a girl—adding that my father was a no-good drunk. Overhearing him, Mrs. Moore lectured the student and the class that regardless of what a person was wearing, it was what was in his heart and in his head that counted. (She was kind enough not to allude to the student's remark about my father.) She announced that she was expecting great things from me; and to drive her point home, she warned that prison awaited those who lacked feeling for others.

One of the best things to happen during this time was that Sherrod, Aunt Leona's unmarried son, left the farm to work in Panama City, Florida, as a welder and riveter in the federal shipbuilding yards. I was assigned to feed his livestock while he was away. When he came home every other weekend, he would bring sacks of feed, mostly sweet feed (a combination of ground corn, heads of oats, and sorghum syrup), as well as a supply of soybean meal. I consumed handfuls of the feed, both morning and evening. It was such a major part of my daily sustenance that I can still practically taste the delicious sweet feed and the nutty soybean meal. I would occasionally find a half pint of liquor in the barn that Daddy had hid.

Before Sherrod left the farm, he ordered a battery-powered electric fence from Sears, Roebuck. When it arrived, he strung a single strand of wire around a small meadow to keep several weanling calves apart from their mothers. After Sherrod got everything all set up, he told me to go to the other end of the fence and hold the wire. He said he would wave his arms when he flipped the switch, and told me to yell if I could feel the power coming through. He didn't have to tell me to yell, for the electric jolt did the whole job. I also did a few fancy steps, steps that might have made my young, black friend Isaac proud. Though Sherrod thought my dancing and yelling was hilarious, I never completely forgave him for making me the butt of his cruel joke.

During the time we lived on the Ketchum Place, I learned that in addition to Sherrod, Aunt Leona had three married sons. One, Cousin Roy, lived nearby with his wife, Cousin Inez. They were two of the dearest people I had ever known. I often worked for them during the summer. And Cousin Webster, because of his gallantry in action in World War I, had been given a plush federal job in Washington, D.C. Very polished and suave, he was now an accountant with Belk Stores, in Charlotte, North Carolina. When he came back home to South Alabama about once a year to see his aging and ailing mother, he told tales of way up north, of living in a home with carpeted floors and wearing a double-breasted suit to work each day.

And then there was Cousin Willie, who had been a guard at the federal prison in Fort Leavenworth, Kansas, but who later was transferred to one in Tallahassee, Florida. All of Cousin Willie's teenage sons were members of the high school band, and I began to ponder that if my name were Ketchum instead of Danner, I might be able to travel to faraway places, such as Washington, D.C., Kansas, North Carolina, or at least Florida, and even play the trumpet and wear a uniform in the marching band. My world was being stretched little by little as I learned that even if born into poverty, one didn't have to live that way all one's life, picking cotton and hoeing peanuts. I have often heard people say they were poor when they were growing up, but they didn't know it because everyone else was in a similar situation. We were poor, and I *knew* we were poor, mainly because others living around us were not in a similar situation.

When area farmers' corn and peanut fields, grape arbors, and fruit orchards were in season, they were never safe from invasion when I was passing by. I had no qualms about pulling an ear of field corn, swiping a cluster of grapes, or pulling up a turnip or onion and eating it. At the time, I didn't give a thought to my acts as stealing—not even as innocent peccadilloes—but as a means of survival. Sometimes when chatting with a farmer, I would ask if his grapes, peaches, apples, or pears were as tart—or as sweet—as a particular neighbor's. If he expressed any doubt, I volunteered to conduct a taste test. I couldn't afford to tell him I already knew the answer.

I knew that once a week I would get a good meal. On Sundays after church, I almost always ate at my cousin Ruth Brock's house. Though Ruth was old enough to be my mother, I was not required to address her as Cousin, as I did Aunt Leona's three oldest sons. Ruth received a monthly compensation from the State of Alabama because of her husband's work-related death and, with her five children, lived with her parents, my Uncle Purry and Aunt Annie. They owned their own home and had plenty to eat, including fabulously rich desserts, such as blackberry, huckleberry, or lemon meringue pie, and devil's food cake. Even though Daddy was often considered by some to be the black sheep of the Danner clan, I always felt welcome there. In fact, Ruth considers him her favorite uncle. When Ruth heard that I was writing my memoir, she told me rather emphatically not to say anything bad about my daddy, adding that he was a good man and that everybody loved him. I assured Ruth that I also loved him dearly. As I was thinking how I could better portray my relations with my father, Bennie called from his home in Guatemala, and I related to him what Ruth had said. Bennie summed up the difference in Ruth's and my assessments rather succinctly: "But you and I knew another side, didn't we?"

Ruth's house was also a pit stop on the way to church. Every Sunday, I always left home early enough to stop by for a peanut butter and cracker sandwich, a weekly treat. One Sunday when I was about eleven or twelve, Ruth took a snapshot of her five children and me after we had returned from church. On a recent trip to Alabama, Charles, her oldest son, gave me the picture. Not surprisingly, I was the only child in the photo not wearing shoes.

Ruth also had a piano, which I found both fascinating and bewildering, and on which I would practice several years later. From the time I first heard the piano played when I was around four at the Knights' house, I was drawn to it like a magnet. However, as hard as I tried to make some sense of the instrument, I couldn't pick out a simple tune on it.

Just before school started, I had been working in the field with twelve or so German prisoners of war on the Robinet Place; they were about the same age as Loyce and Ralph who were themselves fighting in Germany. Each of the POWs had been issued a raincoat which they kept neatly folded and strapped to their belt. One afternoon, a violent thunderstorm erupted, catching us all by surprise. It was then that I learned that only our governments were enemies: the prisoners formed a circle around me, shielding me from the pelting, cold rain with their raincoats. The differences in our languages and our governments' stances were bridged by their concern for me, an 11-year-old American boy.

Once I was working in the fields with a group of five or six POWs, hoeing peanuts, when one of them accidentally hit a rock, breaking the hoe handle. With some trepidation, he took the broken handle to the POW supervisor, who could speak some English. Expecting a tongue-lashing, together they showed it to the farm owner, Charlie Stafford. Charlie went into town and bought a whole bundle of handles, later telling the POW he could break as many hoe handles as he liked. The POW continued to write Charlie long after the war was over, often mentioning his kindness.

One day when the prisoners were working on the farm we were sharecropping, Daddy told Mama he wanted the prisoners to eat at our house, since the POW camp in Clio gave them only a couple of sandwiches for lunch. So we had ten or twelve prisoners eating with us—most of them hardly more than teenagers. Mama prepared all the Southern vittles[12]—black-eyed peas, cornbread, fried okra, and fried chicken. They had no hesitancy in eating our common fare; they were also very polite, repeating over and over *Danke schön* (thank you) and *bitte* (please). Apparently the summers in Alabama were much hotter than those in Germany, for one of their most-used words was *heiss*, as they wiped the sweat from their brow. Daddy said he was certain that *heiss* meant hot, but I thought under my breath, "What do you know? You don't have any education." Actually, Daddy was right, but at the time, I didn't know any German. The prisoners couldn't quite understand why I shouldn't be speaking their language, since they said *Danner* was as German as lederhosen.

After we had eaten, one of the prisoners noticed on the mantel a small, rather ornate, glass-enclosed clock Loyce had sent home from Germany as a souvenir. In his best English, the prisoner wanted to know how we had acquired such a handsome mas-

---

[12] *Vittles* is a dialectal spelling of *victuals*. The two words are pronounced the same (VIT l)s. The word is from Latin *victus*, food, and is further from the verb *vivere*, to live.

terpiece. We were all dumbstricken as what to say. I blurted out that one of my brothers had taken it off a German he had taken prisoner in France. Tears streaming down this young fellow's cheeks, he said he was quite certain he was that prisoner. Though Mama may not have known any German, she knew how to read a young person's heart. She took the clock from the mantel, wrapped it in a cloth and gave it to the prisoner, saying "You take it. It's yours." I was never so proud of Mama. Afterwards, Mama said she was glad to get rid of the clock; as much as she adored Loyce, she said he didn't have the right to take it off "that nice young man in the first place." Mama was never completely clear on why there even had to be wars at all—why everyone couldn't simply love his neighbor, even if the neighbor was an enemy soldier. If Mama didn't already have Quaker blood running through her veins, she would certainly have made an excellent pacifist convert. I remember her saying that those who live by the sword shall die by the sword.

Although I didn't know it at the time, the half-million prisoners of war were detained in locations throughout the United States, other than in Alabama. In Pennsylvania alone, there were more than 20 camps, which were used to house not only Germans, but also Italians, and to a lesser extent, Japanese. The exact number is not known since some of the locations were classified secret. In Pennsylvania, the prisoners finished out the war working in nearby industries. Some made hospital tents and tank coverings, some worked to maintain the camps where they were kept, and others picked fruit from area orchards. In other cases, they continued the projects the Civilian Conservation Corps had begun before the war. At the Gettysburg Civil War Battlefield, where the prisoners were first located, the youngest prisoner was 13, and the oldest was 75.

Our experiences with prisoners of war instilled in me the feeling that we shouldn't hold a grudge against a soldier who is ordered to fight for his country. Germans, Japanese, Americans—they all fought in wars not of their own making. In Pennsylvania, a warden put a suicidal German prisoner of war to work for therapy designing and building a chapel. On the bell tower of the chapel, the prisoners inscribed in Latin "for those who fought with military honor for their country."

Stern Taskmasters

Our sixth grade teacher, Mrs. Blondell Hartzog, was just out of college, and we were her first class. She had not graduated, and was given a one-year provisional certificate, I later learned. To impress her, I often volunteered some tidbit of information I had remembered from Mrs. Carter's and Mrs. Moore's classes, often calling out the answer to a question before the other students had a chance to respond; I thought I knew more than anyone else, including the teacher.

One morning when Mrs. Hartzog had to be out of the room, I appointed myself the grandmaster of sixth grade. When she returned, I was sitting at her desk calling out the spelling words. As punishment, Mr. Edwin Calhoun Palmer, the principal, had me memorize and recite before the class, the poem "Abou Ben Adhem (May his tribe increase!)." From the time I entered first grade, my teachers had always given me special attention—in some cases, deference—and it deeply hurt to be punished for doing what had come so naturally in other classes. At such times, I wanted to say, "Don't you know I'm Horace Danner? You simply can't do this to me." Nonetheless, over the next two or three months, I regularly had to memorize and recite a poem in front of the class for inappropriately speaking out in class. Even today, I remember "Let me live in a house by the side of the road/Where the race of men go by," as well as lines from Joyce Kilmer's "Trees," Sidney Lanier's "The Marshes of Glynn," and portions of William Cullen Bryant's "Thanatopsis"—literally, view of death—which was rather heavy fare for a sixth grader. I particularly liked Emily Dickinson's poem:

> *We never know how high we are*
> *'Til we are called to rise*
> *And then if we are true to plan,*
> *Our statures touch the skies.*

> *The heroism we recite*
> *Would be a daily thing*
> *Did not ourselves the cubits warp*
> *For fear to be a king.*

Mr. Palmer, from Andalusia, Alabama, typified the lean and mean image; he was a stern principal, and I quaked at the very sight of him. Even though he was deeply religious, quoting scripture as easily as he expounded the Pythagorean theorem, he had a penchant for using a particular word that caused considerable anxiety for some of the teachers as well as for me; I would have never dreamt of using the word, even after being exposed to Aunt Leona's frank language. He said he wanted to see "guts" in a young man: we needed guts to rise above poverty and guts to become educated. Mr. Palmer also had little patience with those who didn't brush their teeth. He said that every family, no matter how poor, had salt and soda in the home. He told us to use either of them separately, or to mix them. When a boy said that he didn't have a toothbrush, Mr. Palmer told him to use his finger, at least to massage the gums. (That boy was not I, for I was too afraid to speak directly to him. Besides, I now owned and used a toothbrush, although I often used soap instead of toothpaste.) Mr. Palmer lived and preached *mens sana in corpore sano,* "a sound mind in a sound body." Once, when he heard me ask the lunchroom lady if there were "seconds," as sometimes there were, he said that any extra food should go to *waste*, rather than to the *waist*, and wrote the words out on the board so that I could understand the different spellings of the homonyms, or, more specifically, homophones. Mr. Palmer could have simply looked at me to see that no extra food had gone to my waist.

His advanced age notwithstanding—with only two years before mandatory retirement—he had a great deal of energy and spontaneity; he would pop into the classrooms and announce a word for students to spell, or a math fact to recite. Whoever answered his impromptu questions correctly got to ring the bell to go home. I became rather adept at reciting poems in front of the class and ringing the bell. Mr. Palmer preached mnemonics to help us spell difficult words, one of which was *conscience*; he said to spell it as con + science. Mr. Palmer also brought to the sixth-grade class copies of *Life* and *Reader's Digest*, which I eagerly devoured. Since I wasn't assigned to a reading group, I had extra time to enjoy the magazines. In *Life*, I was able to follow my brothers' wartime movements, from North Africa to Anzio Beachhead in Italy, and finally on to France and Germany. *Life* graphically portrayed the horrors of war in both war theaters as well as Germany's stalags and Jewish concentration camps.

Earlier, I alluded to my inability to learn from real-life experiences. Just as I had asked Mrs. Moore about her "hubby" coming home from the war, one morning I asked Mrs. Hartzog how her hubby Dagwood was doing these days. Not only was she a blonde, her first name was Blondell, and some of us smart-aleck boys called her Blondie, and not always behind her back. She immediately demanded that Mr. Palmer remove me from her class, or she would resign on the spot. I suppose I had learned all the poems that Mr. Palmer knew, for he peremptorily announced that I would skip the remainder of sixth grade. He didn't talk with me about it, nor did he consult with my parents. He simply said, "Come with me, young man," and escorted me to Mrs. Lilla Tyler's seventh-grade classroom. Since school had begun in September, I had been a "big fish" sixth grader in elementary school; suddenly, I was a "little fish" seventh grader in junior high.

I became something of a local celebrity overnight; everywhere I went, someone made comments about my skipping sixth grade. Even though I hadn't been at all keen on leaving my sixth-grade friends, I became rather cocky about the whole affair, and basked in the extra attention. It was in the seventh grade, however, that most of my grades plummeted; we were learning mathematics far beyond what I was comfortable with, or probably capable of.

The more I faltered, the more Mrs. Tyler encouraged me, often sitting by my desk and helping me, especially when we were doing problems of principal, rate, and interest as well as distance, rate, and time. She told me I wouldn't be able to go back to Mrs. Hartzog's class, that I would just have to make the best of a difficult situation and study harder.

Mrs. Tyler's teenage son, Durwood, played the piano as though he had invented it. He commanded the instrument; the keys seemed to reach up to meet his fingers. I could have watched and listened to him for hours. I spent many of my waking hours "playing" the piano as Durwood played it. I executed diminished chords, augmented chords, inverted chords, full chords, arpeggios, glissandi, runs, double octaves—all before I knew these executions actually had names. As I walked to and from school, church, and the store, the air was my keyboard. I pounded out marches, dances, hymns—anything Durwood played.

Separate from Elamville School itself was a gymnasium, but we didn't have a basketball or any other athletic equipment. To play softball at recess, one of the boys would usually bring a bat and ball from home. One day, Mrs. Tyler brought in a Sears, Roebuck catalog and told us boys to pick out the basketball we would like to have. Using every opportunity to teach us, she showed us how to order from a catalog and to figure the postage. At the time, Alabama didn't have a sales tax; if it had, I am sure she would have shown us how to figure the tax as well. When the package arrived in a few days, she asked me to open it. For some reason, I felt like the ball was mine.

Although we didn't have any athletic equipment, the gymnasium was indeed used. Mrs. Tyler was an excellent pianist, and when it was too cold to go outside, she played the piano for us to dance the Virginia reel. At other times, we participated in a march as she played "Under the Double Eagle." The gym was also used in the evenings for all sorts of community activities, such as talent shows, Halloween fairs, and box suppers. The young ladies would prepare boxes of delicious food, for instance, fried chicken and coconut cake, and then decorate the boxes with brightly colored crepe paper. The boxes were then auctioned off, and the young man who bid the highest got the box—as well as a date with the young lady.

In the summer of 1944, during a protracted revival meeting at Elam Baptist Church, I could no longer resist the urgent call from the evangelist of making my profession of faith. I had been seriously thinking of making my decision public since going to the Presbyterian church near Clio two years before. It is true what Saint Augustine wrote in his *Confessions*: "Thou hast made us for thyself, and our hearts shall find no rest till they rest in

With three of my nieces

Thee." After the revival, I, along with about twenty or so others, was immersed, or baptized, in the ice-cold water of the outdoor baptismal pool, with the congregation singing "Shall we gather at the river,/ Where bright angel feet have trod,/ With its crystal tide forever/ Flowing by the throne of God?"

A lot of people thrived during the war, many of them leaving home to work in defense jobs. But for us, there was still no money for buying school supplies, not even pencils or paper. But as I was reading one of the magazines Mr. Palmer regularly brought to class, I saw an advertisement for Rosebud salve—something I haven't seen for over fifty years. The company would send a box of four containers of the salve, and upon sending in the money from the sales, one could receive ten pencils with one's name engraved on them. There were other items of merchandise one could also order, such as socks and shoe laces. For about a year, I sold several boxes of the salve and was able to receive pencils and socks, both of which were absolute luxuries.

The war was still raging in both Europe and the Pacific, and we heard on the radio of blackouts in San Francisco and Los Angeles, and New York City and Washington, D.C.; people living in these and other large coastal cities were required to extinguish lights because of a possible air raid by the enemy. I was afraid to go to sleep at night, lest our dim kerosene lamp attract both the Germans and the Japanese. Daddy assured me that they didn't even know about our little farmhouse deep in the woods. It was all I needed to feel safe and secure. And Mama said it wouldn't be long before Hitler—the Devil himself, she called him—would be only a bad dream. She said his days were numbered.

Daddy was good at putting a young boy's mind at ease in other ways as well. A sow I had been taking care of was due to farrow any day. I had been careful to keep her in the pen with fresh straw. But when I went to check on her, she was out of the pen, and I couldn't find her, no matter where I looked or how many times I called her. Daddy told me not to worry about her, that she was just following her own instincts to bear her litter in a secluded area. But that night there was a terrible thunderstorm, and I was worried that if she had farrowed already, the litter would drown. But again, Daddy said the sow would have the pigs in a safe place, and that she would protect them with her own body. And sure enough, we found her the next morning with six spotted piglets nursing away.

The War Is Over!

Just as I was finishing the seventh grade at Elamville School, Germany unconditionally surrendered. On May 8, 1945, V-E Day (Victory in Europe) was announced on the radio, and we began to have high hopes that Loyce and Ralph would soon be home. Later in the summer, we heard rumors for several days after the atomic blasts over Hiroshima and Nagasaki that the war in the Pacific would be over any day now. Each day before going to the fields, I went to a neighbor's house to check *The Montgomery Advertiser* for the latest word, since our radio no longer worked. On August 15, the headlines trumpeted:

JAPAN UNCONDITIONALLY SURRENDERS
The War Is Over!

So, in the latter part of September of 1945, just after entering the eighth grade, my two soldier brothers returned from Europe. In addition to Loyce and Ralph, all my cousins returned from the war as well, completely unscathed, physically, that is. And two brothers in the Elamville community, Jack and Eldridge Robinet, returned, Eldridge badly wounded with imbedded shrapnel. To the sheer joy of his parents, Mr. Christopher and Miss Della, as well as the entire community, James Phillips returned safely from the German POW camp—tongue intact.

James came back with his tongue intact, but with haunted memories of being force-marched during the winter along with other prisoners of war. With no shoes and with frost-bitten feet, many of the men fell along the way. James' friend, Delbert L. Wise, a blackberry farmer from Arkansas, was one of those men who kept falling. He would cry out to James to help him keep up. After several times of James helping him, the Germans starting shooting at James. Finally, James was left with no choice but to leave his friend behind, even with his calling out, "Phillips, please don't leave me. Phillips, please help me, Phillips. I wouldn't have thought you would ever have left me." James told my cousin Homer Danner in later years, "I hear Delbert Wise calling me every night of my life." James' son Laymon, born February 4, 1950, my birthday, has related to me other stories of his father's imprisonment by the Germans, some of them too heart-rending to relate. Laymon says his father never learned the fate of his friend from Arkansas.

In the early fall, when James was pulling corn for his father shortly after he returned from the war, I hid in the hedgerow of the field, trying to get a better look at him, and wondering what a former American prisoner of war looked like. During the war, I had seen hundreds of German prisoners of war, and except for their speaking German, they were just like Americans. When James reached the end of the row, he called out that he would like to meet me. I then had to confess why I had been so secretive. I told him what his mother had said about her fear of the Germans cutting out the tongues of prisoners of war. He assured me that he couldn't be speaking to me if he didn't have a tongue.

Not long after my own two brothers returned, they set about to pick up where they had left off with their lives. Ralph reenlisted and was stationed at Maxwell Field (later Maxwell Air Force Base), in Montgomery. The next year, Ralph was chosen to model the new Air Force blue uniform when the Air Force became a separate force from the Army Air Corps. Loyce immediately resumed his old job in the steel mills in Birmingham. On his first visit back to L.A. (Lower Alabama), Loyce brought me a gift I would treasure for years. It was a Parker 51 gold-tipped pen, the kind that "writes dry with wet ink," as the advertisement claimed.

I was the only student that fall who wrote every assignment in pen and ink. Mr. Palmer, who taught English, mathematics, and science, told me that mathematics problems were meant to be done with a pencil and an eraser. I had a high-priced pen, but I didn't have a pencil, much less one with an eraser. Once, however, I did have a pencil when another student told Mr. Palmer he didn't have one. I told the boy he could have mine, but in only a few minutes, Mr. Palmer gave me a problem in which I needed to use it. I told Mr. Palmer that, as usual, I didn't have a pencil. But he had seen me lend mine and told me to go to the boy and take it back. I simply couldn't do it. I can't remember the outcome.

In Mr. Palmer's math class, we learned the formulas for finding the areas of triangles, rectangles, trapezoids, and circles, as well as the volumes of cylinders. I peppered Mr. Palmer with questions. I especially wanted to know the *why* of reciprocal fractions as well as the *why* of square roots. One question Mr. Palmer wouldn't answer was why π was called *pi*, and why that particular symbol stood for the ratio of the diameter to the circumference. He said I didn't need to know that, just remember it equaled 3.14; it's true I didn't *need* to know it, but I *wanted* to know it. I wasn't to learn why until thirty or forty years later. I found that π was the first letter of Greek *perimeter*, which designated the distance around any figure, circular or sided. When the Romans conquered Greece, they adopted *perimeter* for the distance around a sided figure and kept their own *circumference* for the distance around a circle. Literally, the two words mean the same, for both *peri-* and *circum-* means "around"; *meter* of *perimeter* is the act of measuring, and *ferre*, a verb, means "to carry," or "to bear."

The summer the war was over, Daddy, Bennie, and I worked the fields of cotton and peanuts. We made fairly good crops, and before school started, Daddy had Sherrod take us to Ozark where we bought raincoats, shoes, shirts, and pants. What was unusual about this event was that I don't recall Daddy ever taking us shopping before that time or after.

The Robinet Place

Shortly before Christmas in 1945, Sherrod and Daddy had a falling out, each calling the other some uncivil, vicious, unprintable names. I heard the whole episode, as we were sitting in front of the fireplace. So, we moved again, this time to the Robinet Place, right in the middle of a cotton field. My best friend was the landlord's only son, Lomax. A year my junior, Lomax never regarded me as just another boy who lived on his father's place. In the summer, we often fished together and swam nude in Danner Creek, which flowed through the Robinet property. Apparently, the property was once owned by the Danner family when they were prosperous landowners.

Together with many of the other neighborhood teenage boys,

including the brothers Jimmy and Keith Byrd, Evans Lunsford, Ladon Phillips, and Charles Brock, Lomax and I also often dived and swam in the buff in the Elam Baptist Church baptismal pool, located in a wooded hollow about a half mile from the church. It was the same pool where I had been baptized only a few weeks before. One afternoon, all the boys except me were doing some rather fancy dives into the shallow pool. Each of them would take a running start, and then on the pool's edge, execute an airborne flip before piercing the water. Finally, I could no longer take the peer pressure; I took a running start, and when I reached the edge of the pool, I thought I flipped as had the other skinny-dippers, but hit the bottom of the concrete pool with my head. I hit the bottom so hard, I bounced back up to the surface. My head hurt for several days, and I later told Vallie that I was afraid I had damaged my brain. In a nice way, she said my head was too hard for the dive to affect my brain.

We had moved to the Robinet Place to sharecrop, but shortly afterward, Daddy took off again, leaving Bennie and me to do the farming. Mr. Robinet knew that we were both too inexperienced to hold down the farm by ourselves. Graciously, he encouraged us to stay in school; he also let us live in the little weather-beaten shack for free and paid us as well for helping him on the farm. Mr. Robinet was undoubtedly the kindest man I had ever known, and I continue to be grateful for his concern over our welfare and education.

Mr. Robinet once took Lomax and me with him to bring back a young bull that he had bought to service his cows at free range. That is, the cow would not be brought to the bull, but he would run free in the pasture to service any cow that came into heat. The bull seemed to be perfectly content where he was and had no intention of our roping him and leading him to the new pasture. After finally getting a halter on him, Mr. Robinet told me to twist his tail and Lomax to switch his rump. Still, the bull apparently wanted to stay put, whereupon Mr. Robinet exclaimed to the bull, "If you only knew the paradise you're gonna get!" The bull must have gotten the message, because he then went with us without any more problems. As we approached the Robinets' pasture, the bull apparently sensed a cow in need of his services, increasing his speed so that it was difficult for us to keep up with him. Almost before we could get him in the new pasture and his halter off, the bull was already in paradise, servicing his first cow.

I made it through the eighth grade at Elamville uneventfully, except that in the spring I suffered a bout of measles, causing me to miss two weeks of school and to lose my voice. The measles left me extremely weak, and even more emaciated. No one knew how to help me regain my voice. Mrs. Myra Robinet, Lomax's mother, brought me ice and ice cream when I had a high fever. Daddy, who was now in construction work in Bon Secour, Alabama (and who occasionally came home on weekends), thought that drinking warm lemonade would help restore it. One of my fondest memories of Daddy was his bringing home lemons and sugar; we never had lemons, and sometimes didn't have sugar. When I did regain my voice, it registered at least an octave lower than before the illness; my new, deeper voice would later become an asset.

Around May of 1946, after school was out, an ice truck started making rounds in our area twice a week. Many of the homes had iceboxes, which could hold a 60-pound block of ice. But we had no icebox and rarely had enough money to buy a large block even if we'd had one. One could buy a small chunk of ice for a nickel, enough for a day, but if I was lucky, the iceman would inadvertently chip off a piece that would normally sell for more than a nickel. But since I had asked for a nickel's worth, he would give me the whole piece, jokingly saying it was a big nickel's worth. After a while, I began asking him for a big nickel's worth. Since we had no icebox, we wrapped the ice in a quilt and put it in the fireplace. Because of the insulation of the bricks, it would keep for two to three days. Water does taste better when the ice clinks the glass.

During the spring and summer of 1946, Daddy was working on Alabama's Gulf shores in construction. Coming home one weekend, he declared he was going to move us to Foley, in Baldwin County, a stone's throw from the Gulf of Mexico. Daddy had always had a problem with asthma, many times coughing to the point he would almost lose his breath, exacerbated no doubt by smoking Pall Malls. But he said that working near the Gulf with its saltwater sea breezes, he could breathe freely. For some reason, we didn't move from the Elamville area, and I was able to continue my schooling in Barbour County in the fall.

One weekend during the summer, newlyweds Loyce and Betty visited us from Birmingham. They brought me a T-shirt which I tried on to see how it fit. Betty commented that I filled it out nicely, adding that the girls were going to go crazy over me. Not since first grade when the lunchroom lady complimented me on being cute and polite had anyone—except Estelle, Olon's wife, when she said I had the build of a basketball player—ever said anything about my looks and build, and almost immediately, I began to feel a surge of masculine power that I hadn't experienced before. As much as I tried to subdue my newly surfaced hormones, they just wouldn't lie dormant any longer. Mr. Robinet took notice of the abrupt change in me and commented that, only a month before, I never said anything about girls and that now I was preoccupied with them. I told him, "It hit me like a disease." Not realizing that the sex drive is God-given, I often brooded over my sinful thoughts. I knew of no one I could talk to about my burgeoning desires. Ellie Mae must have read my mind, however, and told me once that the human race would become extinct if there were no attraction to the opposite sex.

Since it would be at least a week before the cotton was ready to be picked, Loyce and Betty invited me to go back with them to Birmingham. It was the first time I had traveled farther from home than Troy, 24 miles from Clio. The week was full of experiences. Every day, it seems, I was invited to a cookout, where I met a lot of other kids my age. At one of the picnics, I had sauerkraut on a hot dog for the first time. I had never much quibbled about what was set in front of me to eat, but I had second thoughts about eating something so foreign—and so sour. What was wrong with a hot dog with onions and mustard? At one of the cookouts, a girl about my age said I was real cute for a boy. We continued seeing each other for the rest of the week, and then we wrote for two years. Then, I suppose she found another boy.

The week at Loyce's was a light year from anything I had known in Lower Alabama, where I was used to seeing mainly cotton and peanut fields, and the closest electric lights were in town, seven miles away. Loyce and Betty lived in a mining village called Winonah, complete with a commissary, or company store, about a half mile from the No. 7 mine entrance, where

Loyce mined for iron ore. They lived less than a quarter mile from the ore conditioning plant, which ran 24 hours a day. The lights from the plant cast an eerie, amber glow throughout the night, so that it was never dark. Back home, the only sounds at night were those of crickets and the moaning of a train in the far distance. But the rumbling of the chunks of ore being crushed at the plant meant there was never a peaceful, quiet moment. If the wind blew north during the night, the following morning, there would be a film of red ore dust covering everything outside, and often inside as well.

While at Loyce and Betty's, Betty served a type of bread that I didn't know existed, not on Earth anyway. She called it cornbread, but it wasn't like any cornbread I had ever had tasted. It was soft and spongy, not hard as a rock, like pone bread. I found that she made it by mixing cornmeal and self-rising flour, and then adding an egg. Her cornbread was tasty, but I still preferred unseasoned pone bread with collards and black-eyed peas.

And once, when Loyce had a day off, he took me to the locker room at the mine where the men covered with ore dust showered. It was amazing to see how soap and hot water could make them clean again. I also got to visit a radio station where two of Betty's aunts had a daily program of singing and playing the piano. Seeing the announcer sitting in front of a WBHM microphone set my heart on being a radio announcer. I heard he made the unbelievable sum of $150 a week. When Daddy mixed mortar, he never made more than a dollar an hour. And it was ten times what a man made working in the fields at $3 a day.

But what capped the whole week was Loyce's taking me with him to an ice cream store and buying two or three quarts of hand-dipped ice cream, packed with dry ice. There were at least a dozen flavors one could choose from other than vanilla, strawberry, and chocolate. Though Loyce and Betty's freezer was stocked with several flavors of ice cream, I looked forward each day to the Good Humor truck driving through the neighborhood. Since Loyce had given me spending money, I bought a Popsicle every day.

And at the Greyhound bus station in Birmingham for the return trip to South Alabama, it was exciting to see 20 or more buses all lined up alphabetically at an angle with their destinations on the front: Atlanta, Boston, Dallas, Jacksonville, Miami, Mobile,

Nashville, New Orleans, Richmond, St. Louis, St. Petersburg. Mine was the Jacksonville bus. It was a good thing Loyce made sure I boarded the right bus inasmuch as I didn't understand the name of a single stop the dispatcher announced over the loudspeaker. When the bus made a restroom stop in Thorsby, I wanted to call Mrs. Moore, who was now living close by in Clanton, but I didn't know how to use the pay phone, and I was too embarrassed to ask anyone.

One day after my return from Birmingham, Mr. Robinet, Lomax, Bennie, and I were picking cotton, when we stopped for water and to rest under the shade of a cottonwood tree. The others were laughing and joking, and for a change, I was silent. Mr. Robinet looked directly at me and said, "Horace, you look like you have the weight of the world on your shoulders; you're only 13 years old, but you look like an old man already." He wanted to know what could be so heavy on a young fellow's mind. He had previously commented on my newfound interest in girls, and I thought surely he was going to rib me about the country girls not being good enough for me, that I had to go all the way to Birmingham to find one to suit me. I had many pressing concerns, but none I could discuss with anyone—not even Mr. Robinet, whom I regarded at the time as a surrogate father. But I cherished the thought that he cared enough to ask what was wrong. I might have had the courage to tell him, but Bennie was right there, and the problem was with him.

Once while Daddy was home, he opened an account at Scroggins' Store, about a mile from our house, so that I could buy groceries there; he would pay the bill when he came home from his construction job every week or so. In addition to charging flour, sugar, and coffee, I also bought apples and candy bars. (At least, Daddy didn't tell me I *couldn't* buy what I wanted.) I also drank ice-cold RCs and downed moon pies, and pleaded with Mrs. Scroggins not to tell Mama that I was on my way to being a boozer. As mentioned before, Mama didn't want me drinking anything bottled. It wasn't long before Daddy put a stop to my freewheeling junkets at the country store.

When Daddy came home from the Gulf of Mexico, he occasionally brought shrimp and oysters, delicacies I hadn't even known existed. We didn't live very far from the Gulf, but it was my first taste of seafood.

During the summer of 1946, we didn't have a cow, and what milk we drank, the Robinets gave us. One night for supper, Mama, Bennie, and I had only a glass of buttermilk and some pone bread. I was so hungry that I gulped my glass of milk, and like Oliver Twist, pleaded for more. Mama said that if she gave me another glassful, she wouldn't have enough to make biscuits in the morning. I didn't care about breakfast the next morning; I wanted more right then. Delayed gratification wasn't a trait I had yet mastered. In my own defense, however, I still hadn't fully regained my strength from having had the measles earlier in the year. As Mama was about to give me a tad more, Bennie said, "Wait, Mama, he can have mine. He needs it more than I do," whereupon he reached across the table as though to give me his glass, but instead, threw his milk in my face. This incident is related not so much to vilify Bennie, but to show how hungry—as well as how self-ish—I was. In an attempt to clear my mind of some very unpleasant memories concerning Bennie and me, and which plagued my teenage years, I talked with Bennie just recently and told him how I hadn't yet resolved that particular incident. He said he has no recollection of it, but asked that I forgive him. Forgive him, yes; forget it, maybe in time. For now, the incident is riveted in my mind.

Before school started, Mr. Robinet took Lomax and me on a mule-drawn wagonload of freshly picked cotton to Clio, where it was ginned and baled. After being paid for the bale, he took me to one of the clothing stores and let me buy the clothes and shoes I needed for school. He told me it was for being such a good hand on the place. Later in the week, we returned to Clio for the circus, where I saw the lions and tigers, and also where I rode the Ferris wheel for the first time. As much as I loved Daddy, I envied Lomax for his caring and considerate father, who cared enough that I have decent clothes to wear to school.

Barbour County High School, Clio, Alabama

Without anyone else's knowledge or permission, I started the ninth grade at Barbour County High School in Clio, even though there was a perfectly good ninth grade at Elamville School. On

*9th Grade
13 years old*

the first day of school, I crouched on the floor of the bus as it was leaving Elamville School to take the senior high students to Clio. When one of the students told the driver that I was supposed to go to Elamville School, the driver threatened to throw me off the bus. However, I told him my folks would be moving back to the Clio school area any day now, and that I didn't want to start at Elamville, only to change schools in a few days. He said he could see the logic of that. I told the principal at the high school the same story. Both he and the driver probably knew I wasn't being completely honest, for sharecroppers usually don't move until the cotton and peanut crops have been sold and the debts have been settled.

For fear that the bus driver might change his mind, I boarded the train in Elamville for the four-mile trip to Clio for the next several days, getting to school just in time for first period. After I told the conductor the reason I was hitching a ride, he never charged me a fare; he said he thought the Central of Georgia could afford to give a schoolboy a short ride. On each ride, he and I had a nice chat about what was going on in my life. And he would signal the engineer to let me off at the school rather than at the depot, which was about a half mile farther down the track. I went back to riding the bus when I felt securely ensconced at the high school.

I had a good reason for finagling my way into Barbour County High: its library. Elamville School didn't have one. I wasn't disappointed; *The Three Musketeers, How Green Was My Valley, Les Misérables*, and the like now became my standard reading fare. In the library, there was also a 78-rpm record player, and I was transported by a clutch of musical offerings: Offenbach's *Tales of Hoffman* and *Gaîté Parisienne*; Brahms' *Lullaby*; Dvorak's *Humoresque*; Schubert's *Marche Militaire*; and Beethoven's "Ode to Joy," a part of his *Ninth Symphony*.

The music captured my soul. Those works and others—such as Verdi's *Anvil Chorus* and Elgar's *Pomp and Circumstance*—traditionally performed at commencements and graduations—set my heart on classical and operatic music.

In the fall of 1946, while we were still living on the Robinet Place, Bennie was quarterback for the Barbour County Yellowjackets. He was playing his third game of the season, at Luverne, Alabama. He was hurt in the game, but no one realized how seriously. He said that he heard and felt his neck crack. After several days of intense pain, it was learned that he had broken a bone in his neck. The school had no insurance, and we had no money for him to see a doctor. But Elam Baptist Church, realizing the seriousness of the situation, took up an offering for Bennie to go to University of Alabama Hospital in Birmingham. Poor guy, he had to travel all the way there—175 miles—on a Greyhound bus. He came home in a body cast that would restrict his movement for several months, until he was fitted with a metal brace that kept his head in place. The accident still causes him pain, even today, as he and his wife serve the Nazarene Church in Guatemala.

We did move that year—just as I had told the bus driver and the principal. However, the move was not back to the Clio area, but to the first of a succession of tin-roofed shacks scattered among the cotton and peanut fields in the Elamville area. In December 1946, we moved to the Middlebrooks Place, where we set up housekeeping in another run-down, tin-roofed shack beside a cotton field. Instead of living in some remote field or in the woods, we were now on a main road, and I could board the school bus in front of the house. From the Middlebrooks Place, we moved into a two-room shack on the Lunsford Place for a few months, and for my last two years of high school, we moved back to the Ketchum Place, but we now lived all to ourselves in Aunt Leona's big house, with four bedrooms, and I had a room all to myself. There was also an arbor of Concord grapes; in past years, one of the vines had been trained to twine around the verandah, making the porch a very pleasant shady place to sit on summer evenings, especially since the porch was part of a breezeway. I could simply walk to the edge of the porch and, when the grapes were in season, pick all that I wanted.

In addition to the grape vines, the Ketchum Place had two or three giant pecan trees, which bore their autumn fruit in abundance. There are very few things other than chinquapins that taste better to me than a pecan, fresh from the tree. Aunt Leona said that her husband set out the trees right after they were married, almost 50 years earlier. He had ordered the trees from Sears, Roebuck; when they arrived as nothing more than a couple of dried-up sprigs, Uncle Rufus thought of throwing them in the fire, she said. There was also a pear tree, which bore fruit as big as a man's fist; the pears were delightfully juicy and sweet. In the front yard were a gardenia bush and a camellia bush. Since the gardenia was in the yard rather than in the garden, I began to ponder why it was so named. One day at school, I looked up *gardenia*, and found that it was named after its discoverer, an American botanist, A. Garden. Since the camellia is the state flower of Alabama, I looked it up as well, finding that G. J. Kamel, a Moravian Jesuit missionary, discovered the flower in the Far East and brought it back to Europe. It would be many years before I learned that most—practically all—flowers ending in -*ia* and -*ea* are named after their founders, e.g., begonia, bougainvillea, claytonia, dahlia, forsythia, fuchsia, magnolia, poinsettia, wisteria, zinnia. The three exceptions that come to mind are *azalea* (Greek for dry), *hydrangea* (Greek for water vessel), and *petunia* (Tupi for tobacco; reason unknown).

Finding My Voice

My first year at Barbour County High got off to an inauspicious start. Early on, Miss Fountain, our English teacher, instructed the class to leave a margin on our papers, much like that of a framed picture. Before class one day, she had written our test on the board, with the questions filling it from left and right to have enough room for the comprehensive exam. Prior to having us begin the test, she asked if we had any questions. Ever the attention-seeking smart-aleck, I asked why she hadn't left a margin— and promptly found myself on the receiving end of Miss Fountain's wrath. With arms akimbo, she unleashed a scathing reprimand, warning that she would brook no further impertinent remarks from me. For the remainder of my four years at Barbour County High, I was one of Miss Fountain's model students; I was afraid to be anything less. Suffice it to say that I carefully considered every word I uttered in her class from that moment on.

Miss Fountain was in a class all by herself, using words that most of us farm boys had never heard before. Once she told us her mother was coming from Georgia to spend a fortnight. I could imagine that her mother might be coming under the cover of night, possibly in an armored vehicle. She could just as easily have said her mother was coming for two weeks, or "fourteen nights."

Miss Fountain

Later in the school year, I thought Miss Fountain was paying me a compliment when she declared I was "the most egregiously dogmatic person" she had ever known. I think she also added that I was "imperious," which, to me, only reinforced her praise. Since she said it rather pleasantly, I simply smiled and thanked her, thinking she was referring to my awesome good looks, my superior intelligence, or my scintillating personality, or possibly all three combined into one super ego. I didn't remember the word *egregious*—who would? And I had no framework upon which to make a connection for the meaning of *dogmatic*—but I later told Vallie what Miss Fountain had said about my being dogmatic, expecting her to confirm Miss Fountain's exalted opinion of me. Vallie, in fact, did confirm Miss Fountain's assessment, but said *dogmatic* meant stubborn, arrogant, opinionated; Vallie told me I didn't always have to be right, nor did I always have to have the right answer. Until that time, I wasn't aware that I usually spoke *ex cathedra* on everything, even on things I knew little or nothing about.

It was also in the ninth grade that I entered the agricultural speaking contest, more for exposure and experience than for any hope of winning. However, I won in my class. With the other winners from the higher grades, I was a contender for the title of Future Farmers of America champion speaker. I knew that the other three boys would be well-dressed; furthermore, their fathers were important pillars in the community. One was an educator; another, a landowner; a third, a banker. Only thirteen years old and somewhat of a ragtag, I found it difficult working up the courage just to be on the same stage with those older, sophisticated, well-dressed students.

I was certain that I had no chance at one of the top three prizes. However, Miss Lillian Hixon, my algebra teacher, felt that with proper coaching and a revised script, I should be able to garner first prize the next year. With her encouragement, I was able at least to give the speech. About ten minutes after we all had finished, the judges, one of whom I remember was Alto Jackson, co-owner of *Jacksons'*, the farm supply store in Clio, announced that I had won third place. Maybe Mrs. Moore had been right all along—it didn't matter what one wore; it was what was in one's heart and head that counted. In checking my diary which I kept religiously from 1946 to 1950, I recorded that my prize was $2.

It was during science class in my first year at Barbour County High that I referred to a particular black woman as a lady. I was promptly instructed by my teacher, Mrs. Ard, that *lady* was to be used only for a white woman. Not one to be easily told what to do or say, I looked up the word in the dictionary. What I found was quite interesting and may have set me on the path of being a word detective. The dictionary said that *lady* was from Old English *hlæfdige,* translated as "mistress," but literally, bread (or loaf) kneader. I also found the male counterpart to be *lord*, from *hlafweard*, literally, loaf ward (or keeper). I couldn't refrain from asking Mrs. Ard if I should call a lady's husband *lord. Husband*, literally, house-bound, seemed to be too common for a lady's consort. To Mrs. Ard's credit, however, she corrected my pronunciation of *sepulcher*, admonishing me to pronounce the *ch* as a *k*, rendering the word SEP'l ker. In those days, we pledged allegiance every morning to the American flag, read the Bible, and repeated the Lord's Prayer. *Sepulcher* was used in the account of the Resurrection.

During the ninth grade while in Doc Chandler's agriculture class, The Sears, Roebuck Foundation, in an effort to improve the strain of hogs in southeastern Alabama, offered a purebred Poland China male pig for a boy to raise, Poland Chinas being especially suitable for crossbreeding. The foundation would even furnish the balanced feed, but the boy was to take care of the pig. After it matured, the boy would then offer the boar's services to local hog growers or to any farmer who needed a sow bred. He was to charge only a minimal fee, but was to receive his pick of the litter. It would be an excellent opportunity for a young man to start his own hog-breeding and hog-raising business. Doc Chandler asked me if I was interested, and if so, the pig was mine. Though I had never pictured myself in the hog business, I was eager to give it my best effort. It just might be my ticket out of the cotton fields. Daddy, however, talked me out of it, saying that the project would be too much trouble, with our moving from year to year. Also, I don't think Mama was too pleased with my being in the breeding business. Mama got uncomfortable just hearing the word *breeding*.

In February 1947, during her first year at Barbour County High, Miss Hixon organized a weekend trip for those students interested in touring the internationally famed Bellingrath Gardens in Theodore, near Mobile. The students would sleep in a hotel and eat in a restaurant where, she said, the seafood was so fresh the fish slept in Mobile Bay the night before they were served. Everything she described about the trip tantalized me. However, I couldn't afford to go; and in my four years at the school, I was never able to participate in any other such excursions. As the chartered Riley bus pulled away from the school building for that first tour, my shame and embarrassment at being the poorest kid in school was harshly reinforced. Bennie, however, managed to go, for he borrowed the money from Bert Middlebrooks, a farmer for whom he had worked the previous summer, harrowing peanuts. After he worked off what he owed and made enough for the fare, Bennie bought a Greyhound ticket, and went to Birmingham for the summer, living with Loyce and Betty, and bagging groceries at Brown's Station

Miss Hixon

Market. When Bennie returned to South Alabama to begin his junior year in high school, he refused to live with us, staying instead with Olon and Estelle. This hurt Daddy tremendously, and finally after Daddy begged him to come home, he did so, though unwillingly. Unlike me, Bennie was not afraid of Daddy, once telling me that just because he told me to "m'kaste!" didn't mean I had to come running.

Though I missed the Bellingrath Gardens tour, Miss Hixon made up for it by regaling us with accounts of her summer vacation travels. She came from an extremely wealthy family who had extensive land holdings in, of all places, Smuteye, near Perote, just a few miles northwest of Clio, in Bullock County. Each summer she toured all over the United States. It was from her that I first heard stories about Washington, D.C., the Capitol, the White House, Arlington National Cemetery, the Tomb of the Unknown Soldier, as well as the Pentagon, which had just been completed and which would, only six years later, become my first active duty station in the Air Force.

It was in the spring of 1947 that I explored the far reaches of Barbour County, the second-largest county in the state, Baldwin County being the largest. The annual Fat Cattle Show was held in Eufaula in the northeastern part of the county. Eufaula is also one of the two county seats—right on the

Doc Chandler

Chattahoochee River separating Alabama from Georgia. It is also the river that demarcates Eastern and Central time zones. Doc Chandler took a group of us "aggie boys" to the cattle show, where we observed and participated in judging the 1000-pound steers that were being auctioned. Buyers from some of the finest restaurants in the South were there to bid on the steers. What impressed me the most was hearing the chant of the auctioneer.

Toward the end of the

school year, I was still quite frail. Dr. Jackson, Mrs. Moore's brother, had returned from the war and had set up his medical practice in our little town, although he could have accepted a position just about anywhere with a big hospital, even his uncle's in Montgomery—Jackson Memorial. I was fourteen years old, and Vallie thought it was time I should see a doctor, to get a checkup, for despite having a ravenous appetite, I couldn't seem to gain any weight. I was mortified that an adult would see me nude, or at least, partially unclothed. I should have remembered Aunt Leona's comment that every male has "one." I finally worked up the courage to see Dr. Jackson, mainly because Ruth, my favorite cousin, was working as his nurse. I shouldn't have worried, for although Dr. Jackson did check my entire body, he never appeared to regard my genital area any differently than any other part of my body. Palpating my belly, he said I was infested with hookworms and gave me medication to rid me of them. In only a few weeks, my complexion began to gain color, and I began to put on some much-needed weight.

My music career, as humble as it was, began during the summer of 1947, before I was to enter the tenth grade. Elam Baptist Church held a gospel singing school, which was held in the evening to accommodate those of us working in the fields. The teacher was hired for $25 to teach five nights. Each of us was supposed to pay $2 for the week's lessons; I hadn't planned on attending since I didn't have the money. However, my cousin Ruth said that with my singing talent, I *would* attend and she would pay my share. Since Ruth was Dr. Jackson's nurse, she now had some disposable income. And she always treated me as though I were her son, rather than her first cousin.

In the music school, I learned the treble and bass clefs, time signatures, the names of the shaped notes, and note values, as well as the patterns for directing the different time signatures; I also learned to carry the bass line in singing. Each of us took turns leading the group in gospel songs. Each of the seven notes—do, re, mi, fa, sol, la, ti—had a particular shape—squares, triangles, rectangles, ovals, pyramids, inverted pyramids.

Many years before, I had been introduced to Sacred Harp singing, which utilizes only four shapes instead of seven—*fa, sol, la,* and *mi.* The notes *fa, sol,* and *la* are repeated in sequence and then *mi* and *fa* are also repeated to obtain the full eight notes of the music scale. Musicologists can only surmise why "harp" is part of the name for this type of singing, for no harp or other instrument is used. Some think the name may have come from considering the voice a harp; others say it alludes to harps being referred to in the Bible. Whatever the background for the name, the quaint, haunting style of music dates back to Revolutionary times, and the tunes are rooted in the European tradition. There are chorales, fuging tunes, and Gregorian chants.

Once a year on the first Sunday in September, I went with Mama and Vallie to Bethlehem Baptist Church (better known as Lightered[13] Knot), near Louisville, which was the family church of the Dykeses. My mother was a Dykes, and she looked forward to these all-day singings with "dinner on the ground"; actually, the dishes were placed on outdoor tables. The singings were also a social event, where friends and relatives were able to see each other at least once a year. At the time, I didn't care for the old-fashioned style of singing; in fact, I don't recall ever hearing of another young person who tried to sing Sacred Harp. While the old folk were singing, I was outside chatting with the girls and showing off. I came to appreciate the music only after I learned of its importance in American history, first from Dr. Harry L. Eskew, Professor of Music, New Orleans Baptist Theological Seminary. In fact, Harry did his doctoral dissertation on the Sacred Harp movement in Virginia's Shenandoah Valley.

I must add that Sacred Harp in no way has died out. In an effort to find out more about the history of the movement, I searched the Internet. What I found astounded me. Sacred Harp is flourishing all over the country, from country churches to universities. Harvard University, in fact, has a website devoted entirely to Sacred Harp. Ishmael the Fiddler, otherwise known as Dr. I. J. Stefanov-Wagner, of Massachusetts Institute of Technology and Harvard University, was quite helpful in demonstrating how the four scale notes were duplicated to form an octave, or eight notes. He can be reached at either ijs@epl.meei.harvard.edu, or ijs@mit.edu. I now regularly attend Sacred Harp singings in the metropolitan Washington, D.C., area. I love its deep, rich, sonorous harmonies and haunting melodies, that is, when I am singing with the group. Just like Lee Schumacher, my singing part-

---

[13] The word is actually *lightwood,* dry, resinous pine wood that burns readily with a bright light.

ner and business associate, related, "People will travel a thousand miles to sing Sacred Harp, but they wouldn't walk across the street to hear it."

Vallie sang alto, and Mama sang treble in the Sacred Harp songs. As far as I know, Mama never owned a Sacred Harp songbook; she really didn't need one, for she had memorized practically all the most popular songs. Her clarion voice was as pure and sweet the day she died as it was in those all-day singings in the late '30s and early '40s.

Laying By for the Middlebrookses

Not long after school was out in 1947, and finishing the ninth grade, I got a job laying by Mr. Middlebrooks' corn, as well as several other odd jobs.[14] When I came in for lunch the first day, I found Mrs. Middlebrooks had prepared a good meal, including my favorite dish: potato salad, garnished with paprika-sprinkled hard-boiled eggs. I asked her if I could have a second helping; in her kindly way, she said I could have even a third or fourth helping, admonishing me only to eat what I took. She must not have known me as well as she thought, for I could certainly eat all I took and more too. Disregarding the manners Vallie had drilled into me since I was five, I cleaned out the bowl, leaving nothing for any possible latecomers.

When I went to rest on the screened-in verandah after lunch, I noticed that the Middlebrooks family had what appeared to be a complete set of the Tarzan books. Instead of a chore, plowing all morning with a recalcitrant mule became a prelude to reading those jungle adventures at lunch time. I was transported to another world, far, far beyond the cotton fields of Alabama. Mrs. Middlebrooks let me take the one I was reading home with me; I worked through each of them that summer. I also lost myself in *Treasure Island, The Adventures of Tom Sawyer,* and *Robinson Crusoe.*

Plowing in the fields was also made less arduous by daydreaming and the outlandish tales I concocted. I pictured Daddy's oldest brother, Uncle Maston, an engineer for the L&N Railroad who lived in Covington, Kentucky, making his yearly visit. I fancied his telling my father he wanted to adopt me and buy me clothes

---

[14] *Laying by* means cultivating the crop for the last time before it matures.

and pay for music and dancing lessons and enroll me—when I was old enough—at University of Cincinnati, just across the Ohio River from Covington. I imagined being the younger brother of Luther, Uncle Maston and Aunt Georgia's only son. I would have a railroad pass just like Luther and his sister, Jeannette, and I would travel all over the United States and see all the places we had studied about in Mrs. Carter's fifth grade class. I would also wear an engineer's cap and sit in the cab as Uncle Maston pulled out of Cincinnati on the rumbling ride on *The Crescent Queen* to Memphis, Tennessee, and then on to New Orleans. In New Orleans, I would get a job on a banana boat, and sail to Central America. I would then come home with pockets full of money and would buy all the fancy shoes and pretty dresses Mama could wear.

At other times I dreamed of picking oranges in Florida, grapes in California, apples in Washington State, or pineapples in Hawaii. Surely, I might be allowed to eat an orange, a sprig of grapes, a Red Delicious apple, or possibly share an occasional pineapple, but I couldn't eat the cotton I was picking. Any place other than the cotton fields of Alabama seemed to me to be paradise.

I spent a week with James and Ada over in Pike County, near Brundidge, chopping cotton and hoeing peanuts as well as feeding and watering the mules and cows, and slopping the hogs. Ada worked in the fields just like a man. She would set her two-year-old son, Franklin, on a quilt under a shade tree, checking on him each time she finished a row. Ada loved to fish and could spend an entire afternoon simply standing on the river bank, encouraged by only a nibble. I don't think she really cared whether she caught any fish; she liked relaxing and watching the kingfishers swooping into the river to catch their dinner. But she said the birds wouldn't waste their time if there weren't any fish in the river, and eventually she would catch one too, just like the kingfisher.

James said we would take Saturday afternoon off, and that I had a choice of what I would like to do: go fishing with Ada or go to the picture show in Brundidge. I had not a moment's hesitation. I could fish at home with Daddy on Pea River. I wanted to see Roy Rogers or Gene Autry conquer the Wild West. So James gave me the amount for a child's ticket, left me at the movie house, and went to park the pickup. A long line of kids was already waiting to buy a ticket, and I was afraid I would miss the beginning of my first picture show. When I gave the dime to the ticket seller, he said he was positive I had to be at least fourteen—which I was, and going on fifteen—and that I needed a quarter to get in. I didn't know what I was going to do. About that time, James—who had come up behind me and heard the interchange—plopped down a quarter and told me I could keep the dime for popcorn and a soda water. Checking my diary, I found that the name of the picture show was *Rustlers from the Badlands*.

My father didn't even pretend to farm in 1947; he worked a few odd jobs, mainly mixing mortar with Uncle Purry, who usually had a contract to lay brick for a new house. It was incumbent upon me to find work in the fields so that we could eat. With some of the money I made chopping cotton and hoeing peanuts while Daddy lay drunk or simply fished for most of the summer, I bought a secondhand banjo for $15; but even with lessons from one of my cousins, George Albert Thompson (the former owner of the banjo), I never learned to play it. My father had declared the banjo a waste of money because, he said, I didn't have an ear for playing—and I didn't. But my consuming—if short-lived— dream was to travel with a country music band, leaving the cotton and peanut fields behind forever. One weekend when Ralph was visiting from Montgomery, he picked up the banjo and played it like a pro. He said he would sell it for me in Montgomery. Just last year, I reminded him he still owed me the $15 for the banjo, not counting 50 years of compounded interest. But then, he has paid me much more than the amount of the banjo in his many acts of kindness and caring.

From the time I first started going to church, I learned that the first ten percent of what one earned was a tithe and was to be given to the church to pay the pastor, and support children's homes, Baptist colleges, and foreign missions. Through the years, I could hardly wait to start making my own money so that I could fulfill that obligation. Consequently, no matter how little or how much I earned, on Sunday I gave my tithe, even though in many cases, it was the widow's mite, sometimes only a nickel.

For a dollar, I subscribed to *The Progressive Farmer*, not that I liked farming or intended to become a farmer, but because the periodical was something to read. And for as long as I can remember, we received the *Alabama Farmers Bulletin*, which listed livestock, farm products, and farms for sale. The bulletin's inscription, "The South will come into its own when its fields are green in winter," inspired me to cultivate my fallow mind, just as farmers were encouraged to turn their fallow winter fields into green pastures and cover crops.

While reading *The Progressive Farmer*, I noticed a section on pen pals. Since stamps cost only three cents, I began to write every girl listed, and occasionally, a boy. My rationale for writing was that I wanted to find out what the cattle business was like in other states, such as Louisiana, Texas, and Arkansas. What I really wanted was to write anyone who lived far away from southeastern Alabama. Some of the girls appeared to have more on their minds than writing about cattle breeding and calf shows; in fact, one girl from St. Charles, Louisiana, wanted me to visit her so that I could see their cayenne farm, which supplied peppers to the makers of Tabasco sauce. Another girl's family grew rice in Arkansas; from her, I learned that Arkansas grows more rice than any other state in the country.

Dressing for Success ... ?

In early August, as I prepared to enter the tenth grade, my father and I got a job building a retaining wall in Louisville, seven miles north of Clio. When sober, Daddy was regarded as a first-class bricklayer, carpenter, cabinetmaker, and general handyman. This job meant a lot to me, because more than anything else, I wanted to be dressed like the other boys at Barbour County High; I wanted a plaid shirt and blue jeans and a decent pair of shoes. Daddy had promised that I could use my share to buy school clothes.

At night, I dreamed of the clothes I would wear on the first day of school; in the daytime, I pictured myself as the best-dressed boy in Barbour County High. I would stand in front of the chifforobe mirror and see myself in good clothes and new shoes, like those worn by the sons of the landowners, educators, lawyers, and bankers.

About halfway through the job, my father got so drunk he couldn't finish the wall. One day when I was out trying to find field work in order to buy groceries, he sold our only milk cow, though I didn't know it at the time. When the cow didn't show up at milking time, my friend Jimmy Middlebrooks, the landlord's youngest son, and I began searching the swamps and bogs, being especially alert for the telltale buzzards, not to mention the deposits of quicksand. We left the house about sunup and returned in midafternoon, to recount to Mama and Daddy where we had looked. As we searched, I had time to ponder the situation at home. I recalled that Mama couldn't even keep vanilla flavoring on hand, as Daddy would drink it for the small amount of alcohol it contained.

After three or four days of searching in vain, I asked my father point-blank if he had sold the cow for a bottle of Four Roses or Old Grand-Dad. With what appeared to be genuine remorse in his misty, hollow eyes, he admitted that he had in fact done exactly that. Instead of being upset that he had sold the cow and that Jimmy and I had spent three or four days searching for it, I felt truly sorry for him. I was almost overcome with emotion for the guilt I sensed in him as well as for the despair and hunger in Mama's eyes. Even though Mama never openly disparaged Daddy for his drinking, she was at the point of leaving him, she said, but she had no place to go and no one to turn to.

The lady we were building the retaining wall for didn't pay us for what we had done (at least that's what my father said). So I didn't get the school clothes I had my heart set on. I couldn't bear the thought of going back to school that fall, not being dressed like the other boys. It was then—when I was fourteen years old—that I decided to quit school and find a way to make a living for us. As noted earlier, Bennie was working as a grocery bagger and living with Loyce and Betty in Birmingham. But I was too young to leave home; besides, someone had to take care of Mama. Ultimately, I changed my mind, for, like my father, I wasn't much of a farmer, and my only hope appeared to lie in education. Other than church, school was the one place where I excelled and where I received encouragement.

Clothes for School

There were still about three weeks until school started; if I could get two or three days' work, I could earn enough money to buy school clothes. Later in the week, I heard that Roy Cecil Phillips needed extra hands shaking and stacking peanuts. I left home a little after daylight, walking the three or four miles to the field. Handy with a pitchfork, I had already been working about an hour when several other field hands began arriving. Mr. Phillips rode up on his horse and asked me what I was doing in his peanut field. I told him that I had heard he needed extra hands, and that I had been working since before sunup.

Though he'd looked and sounded angry at first, he then said in a kinder tone that if I continued working as industriously as when he rode up, he was going to pay me man's wages, $3 a day. Women and children were getting $2 a day. Despite my empty, growling stomach, I worked harder and faster. The dinner bell began to ring, and the hands retired to the closest chinaberry and cottonwood trees to eat and to rest.

One of the hands, a black boy about my age named Thomas Hardberry, had brought his lunch in a one-gallon tin syrup pail. I had eaten a leftover water biscuit—since we now didn't have a cow—and a dab of grape jelly for breakfast; however, I hadn't brought a lunch because there was nothing to bring. Not only that, occasionally I was invited to eat at the landowner's home while working in the fields, and hoped that today I would also be invited. Thomas, beside whom I had been working all morning, started eating his fried chicken wings, fried okra, and baked sweet potato. We had become good friends that morning, and I'm sure he would have shared his lunch with me. However, Mr. Phillips rode up and asked why I wasn't eating my lunch. I told him that I hadn't brought one. Declaring that no "man" was going to work for him on an empty stomach, he boosted me onto his horse, and we rode double to the farmhouse. There I enjoyed one of the best meals of my life; I ate more than I should have, as I discovered the next day.

Late in the afternoon, one of the black women began a melancholic hymn chant, ever so low and haunting. Then, the other women blended in their voices, followed by some of the men embellishing the simple plaintive melody in perfect harmony while deep-voiced men maintained a solid cadence of drum sounds. The voices of some of the women reached ear-tingling notes. Surely the Creator was pleased to hear this glorious sound—I knew I was lifted to a new height, just as when I had heard the congregation singing at Isaac's church when I was around five. A field full of blacks singing "Steal away, steal away to Jesus," "Swing low, sweet chariot, comin' for to carry me home," "Just as I Am," or "Amazing Grace," is both a treat and a blessing.

As daylight began to fade, Mr. Phillips rode up, saying he would see us all the next morning at sunup. I ran, skipped, and sang all the way home, ecstatic about having eaten a good meal and getting man's wages besides. My hands reached out to play crashing chords on an imaginary piano. Everything was a dream. The bubbling brook I had to cross to get home and the towering loblollies seemed to share my elation. The whispering cottonwoods were already lulling me into a blissful night's sleep. This had surely been my day—working like a man, eating with the landowner's family, and earning money for school clothes. Rushing into the house, I gushed out to my mother that Mr. Phillips had told me I worked like a grown man; that I'd had fried chicken for lunch, and banana pudding for dessert; that I would be paid $6 for the two days; and that I would be able to buy school clothes after all. I couldn't get the words out fast enough.

My mother was quite happy for me, but said one of our neighbors, Mrs. Della Phillips, had died that day. The funeral had been set for Sunday afternoon at Elam Baptist Church. Mama wanted to go to the services, but like me, didn't have presentable shoes to wear. Knowing that I was working especially to buy clothes for school, she had already tried to borrow a pair from a neighbor, but they were much too large for her. I told her that with the $6 I would be getting, I would walk to Clio and get her a pair on Saturday.

The next day, I arrived at the field about the same time as the others. It was going to be a great day—possibly hearing more spirituals, but definitely getting paid! Those of us who could wield a pitchfork stacked the peanut vines that had first been thrown into windrows, onto a pole with a crossbar about a foot from the ground. About midafternoon, the black hands started up their spirituals, and though we whites didn't join in, the music lifted our spirits, and we were able to finish the entire field about an hour before sundown. Mr. Phillips was so pleased with our finishing early, he said he would pay us all for a full day. In the lowering sun, there was a peculiar sadness about the scene. The once-green peanut field seemed now to be replaced by orderly stacks of hooded green-robed monks, silently brooding over the now-bare earth.

Instead of eating with the landowner today, I walked to Scroggins' Store, only about a half mile from the field, and asked Mrs. Scroggins to let me have a can of Vienna sausages, a small box of soda crackers, and a soda water. I told her that after I bought Mama's shoes the next day, I would come by and pay her. It was a good thing I ate at the store, for that evening when we lined up to be paid for the two days' work, Mr. Phillips paid me only $5.50 instead of $6. Trying to assert myself like the man he had said I was, I reminded him that he had promised to pay me man's wages. Slapping his thighs and laughing, he roared that he *had* paid me man's wages, but he had taken out 50 cents for my lunch the day before—money I had been counting on to buy Mama's shoes. I can still hear him guffaw: "The way you et, Boy, you should be paying me 'stead of me paying you." Disappointed and hurt that I wasn't getting paid the promised amount, I was also humiliated in front of the two dozen other hands.

There was no singing or playing the piano as I trudged home that evening, knowing that I would have to tell Mama that I hadn't received enough even for her shoes. The school clothes would also have to wait. Before I could finish telling her, I burst out sobbing. I had worn my bestowed badge of manhood for a mere two days. Though I had already begun to shave, I still felt like a little boy and yearned for Mama to tell me everything would work out. But Mama had more serious things on her mind than consoling a 14-year-old half-grown boy. Since she already regarded me in many ways as the man of the house, she probably didn't know what to say or do.

As it happened, I did get a new pair of pants and a shirt for school. As Jimmie Middlebooks and I searched for the milk cow, I noticed bees swarming around a partially hollow beech tree that had apparently been struck by lightning years earlier. Several days later, I offhandedly mentioned the bee tree to my parents. When Daddy asked where the tree was, I told him it was in a stand of magnolias that we often passed on the way to the river. The next morning, Daddy and I found the tree; after he smoked away the bees with a torch of rags soaked in kerosene, we found we couldn't bring all the honeycombs home in the small container we had brought. So we came back with several containers, bringing home thirty or so pounds of combs filled with clear magnolia honey—a delicacy. What we didn't keep for ourselves, Mama sealed into quart fruit jars. By selling the honey to neighbors and in Clio, I was able to make enough money to buy school clothes.

Introduction to Piano

Not long after I had settled into the tenth grade, one of our teachers, Mrs. Margaret Herring, started an experimental piano class, using a technique she had learned in New York City. One day she demonstrated the technique to those who were interested. Each of us had a scaled-down, imitation keyboard on our desks, and as she played notes on the piano, the corresponding keys lit up on a facsimile keyboard on the wall above and behind the piano. We imitated on our mock keyboards the notes Mrs. Herring played on the real one.

Then we took turns actually playing the notes and chords on the piano itself. I played my first chord—a C Major chord—that day, and it was absolutely thrilling. Though the C Major chord is the easiest for a beginner to play—with no sharps or flats, or, no black keys—it was enough for me to learn that the piano was no longer a formidable, unconquerable instrument with 88 indistinguishable keys; rather, the keys followed a successive pattern of two blacks and three blacks with white keys in between. Furthermore, I learned the keys were repetitions of octaves, or sets of eight keys; that is, the octaves followed the same pattern from the lowest notes to the highest. The piano was now an instrument that could be mastered. My dream was still to play just like Durwood Tyler.

10th Grade

Mrs. Herring said that each of us would be charged $2 a month for the instruction. Bennie and I both wanted to learn to play the piano, but neither of us had the money. Though I can't remember how we did it, together we scraped up $2.

Bennie insisted that I take lessons instead of him, because he said I had more talent. Since I yearned to play the piano, I almost jumped at his offer. As a compromise, I suggested we alternate from week to week and show each other what we had learned; however, Mrs. Herring didn't think that would be a tenable situation. Since Bennie had only one more year of school, I urged that *he* take the lessons. As it turned out, he would more than repay me for that simple gesture.

No one in the family seemed to be especially impressed about my learning to play, except Ruth, one of my cousins, and Vallie, who arranged for me to play each time I visited her church; however, Lilybelle Livingston, a neighboring lady, was almost as excited as I was. One would have thought Lilybelle was my own mother, the way she carried on about my playing the piano. But Aunt Leona told me I shouldn't even be speaking to Lilybelle, much less associating with her, because she was a prostitute. She said that Lilybelle was excited about my playing only because she was excited about my maturing young body, and that I should be careful not to be ensnared by her. I knew that Lilybelle had borne a son out of wedlock, and she was beautiful and caring; even so, I was absolutely certain she had nothing on her mind other than my being all that I could be. Though I was reluctant to tell Mama what Aunt Leona had said, I told her that I shouldn't see Lilybelle anymore. For once, Mama spoke her mind, saying I was smart enough to know whom to choose as my friends, and that Lilybelle was just as good as, or better than, overly pious, but straight-talking Aunt Leona. Mama went on to say that just because a woman had borne an illegitimate child didn't mean she was a prostitute.

Room at the Top—Hallelujah!

It was in the tenth grade that I began to do homework. There was little time to study in the evenings, however. There were chores to do—milking the new cow (both before and after school), slopping the hogs, toting firewood and stovewood from the woodpile into the house. I often had to go to bed at dark since usually there wasn't enough kerosene to burn the lamp. Without a lamp, there was no way to study.

I bided my time, trying to figure out a way to resolve the problem of no light to read and study by. One afternoon after school,

I took a pint fruit jar and visited Mrs. Eva Griffin, a black lady who lived over by Scroggins' Store. She had been my best customer when I was selling Rosebud salve. I asked Miss Eva, as I always called her, if I might borrow a pint of kerosene so that I could burn the lamp to study by, and promised that I would pay her back when I could. I wasn't afraid to ask her, because she always found time to chat with me as I walked past her house on the way to and from Scroggins' Store.

If Miss Eva thought it unusual for a white boy to be asking a black woman for such a basic necessity, she didn't say anything nor did she show it. She gladly gave me the kerosene and hugged me, saying: "Horace, honey, don't you worry about paying back any kerosene. You just stay in school, study hard, 'cause there's room at the top—hallelujah!" I can't recall how many times I went back for kerosene—or was it for those dear words of encouragement? *Stay in school, study hard, 'cause there's room at the top—hallelujah*: that has been my motto throughout life. If it hadn't been for Miss Eva, getting through high school would have been a lot more difficult. Even so, I didn't tell another person, not even my parents, where the kerosene came from.

Enticements of College

It was also in the tenth grade that I won first place in the school speaking contest. Miss Hixon, my algebra teacher, gave me the help she had promised the year before, and Miss Fountain checked my sentence structure. I had come from third place in the ninth grade to first place in the tenth grade. My prize was a 200-pound sack of guano from *Jacksons' Farm Supply*, where I was to claim my prize. However, I had no way to take the fertilizer home; furthermore, I could barely lift fifty pounds, much less two hundred. My agriculture teacher (and the sponsor of the speaking contest), Doc Chandler, took me to the store to pick up the fertilizer and then drove me home with my treasured prize. He and Mrs. Chandler hadn't been able to take me to Dothan when I was in the third grade, but he made up for it that day. Speaking was now in my blood, and I couldn't wait until the eleventh grade for the next contest, and hoped that Miss Hixon would still be there to coach me. I went on to the

Royce Abercrombie

county meet in Clayton, the principal county seat, but came in second place.

In the summer before I entered the eleventh grade, Doc Chandler took me with him to Auburn, the land-grant university of Alabama, for a state FFA (Future Farmers of America) convention. He also took a fellow student, Royce Abercrombie, who was a wealthy landowner's son. Royce and his older brother, Milton, were regarded as the best-dressed boys in school as well as the most sophisticated. They had their own car and wore expensive clothes, including leather jackets. In my mind, there was nothing Royce and Milton and their family didn't have. Normally, I would've had reservations going to any function with a wealthy schoolmate, but Royce was an exception. He was simply a great friend, and had been since I first met him in the ninth grade. Royce and Becky's home is one of the first on my itinerary when I visit South Alabama.

Before my trip to Auburn, Daddy had temporarily sobered up, got a job mixing mortar, and even bought me a pair of English Walkers, surely the most comfortable shoes that have ever been made. The shoes cost $14, a princely sum for a good pair of shoes forty years ago. When the clerk quoted the price, I was afraid Daddy would say he couldn't buy them. I was so proud of those shoes, I polished them every day whether they needed it or not. He also bought me a shirt and pair of sharkskin trousers. With my new shoes and nice, store-bought clothes, I was all ready to go to Auburn.

At the convention, Royce and I paired up to enter a calf-judging contest, and brought home two blue ribbons. We also witnessed the first instance in the United States of artificial insemination of a cow. (It was a good thing Mama was back in Elamville.) Though now commonplace in the United States, the practice was pioneered in Denmark, and had been used in Russia as well.

Sleeping in the dormitory and eating in the campus cafeteria at Auburn were enriching experiences. Royce and I also saw *Call*

Northside 777, my first movie other than Westerns, and it was all I could think or talk about for the next month. I often wonder if that one college visit was the impetus for my career as a writer and English professor. I am truly indebted to Doc Chandler for giving me that opportunity.

Speaking of FFA, I sometimes stopped by Aunt Bessie's house, which was only a quarter mile from the high school, to eat or to chat. Eager to satisfy a growing boy's appetite, she always had plenty of sandwich ingredients and could usually be counted on to have a fresh batch of chocolate chip or oatmeal-raisin cookies; not only that, she usually had a bit of gossip, and could spin quite a yarn, almost as creative as those Daddy told. When I told her that I had gone to the FFA convention in Auburn, she asked what FFA stood for. It was quite an inane question, inasmuch as everyone in the South knew what FFA stood for and that its counterpart, FHA, stood for Future Homemakers of America. All the same, I answered her question. Aunt Bessie said, "You mean you're almost a man and you still don't know what it *really* stands for?" Her eyes dancing with mischief, she then uttered the F-word. In spite of her often-risqué stories, I was aghast that my own aunt had actually said such a word, especially in front of me, an impressionable, churchgoing teenager. She was the first adult I had ever heard use it. My father used a lot of profanity, but I had never heard even him use it. Aunt Bessie wasn't finished, however. Maybe she wasn't a good speller, for she said the "H" of *homemakers* stood for a sleazy woman—one who might ensnare men, or whom some men might seek out.

Thinking that if the F-word and the H-word were all right for my aunt to utter—and since I was "almost a man"—I emboldened myself to tell Mama of Aunt Bessie's rendition of FFA and FHA, foolishly thinking that Mama might find it as amusing as had Aunt Bessie. Mama said that she gets "really mad" only about once every six months, and right now, she said she was really mad because of Aunt Bessie's polluting my innocent mind. I knew Mama wouldn't speak to Aunt Bessie about the matter, since Mama was as meek as a lamb, often appearing cowed or intimidated by the more aggressive Danners. But she did mention it to Daddy, who said, "Well, Sook, you know Bessie as well as I do." I couldn't bear to tell Mama that my mind had already been polluted from hearing my cousins and some of my schoolmates use the word, though in all honesty, I had never used the word myself.

Before I leave Aunt Bessie, I must tell how she came to my rescue later that year. All winter long when Daddy was home, he called me every morning precisely at 4 a.m. to build a fire in the fireplace and the stove. He would call, "Fiddler, Fiddler; get up; get up and build a fire!" After he was certain that I was up and had the fires going, he went back to sleep, and it was then Mama's chore to get up and bake biscuits and make coffee, while I climbed back into bed and tried to get some rest. His calling me was an outrageous thing to do to a growing teenage boy, who was only trying to get a good night's sleep, but it was useless to resist. Once when Aunt Bessie was spending the night at our house, she heard him calling out to me in the dead of night. Before I could hardly open my eyes, she marched into Mama and Daddy's room, and I overheard her tell him in no uncertain terms, "Little Brother, if you want a fire built, you get out of your warm bed and build it yourself! That boy needs his sleep." After that, I never again had to get up in the middle of the night to build a fire. Aunt Bessie may not have been an angel to Mama, but she was to me on that particularly cold winter night.

Covert Piano Lessons

In the spring of 1948, with the advent of REA (Rural Electrification Administration, now RUS, Rural Utilities Service), electricity finally made it to our area. REA had actually begun installing lines in December 1941, but the project was interrupted by the war. Now it was seven years later, three years after V-J Day, the end of the war. Although our house was deep in the woods, several miles from the main line, Sherrod Ketchum, the owner, had applied for a hook-up in 1940. Right outside our house a transformer was installed, and I couldn't wait for us to have electricity. However, Sherrod had now moved from the place and had no interest in installing electricity in a house he wasn't living in. So, the transformer sat idle for two years, when, in February

1950—only three months before my high school graduation—
Daddy said we would finally have the house wired. I made a table
lamp in shop so that I wouldn't have to study by the one glaring
light hanging from the ceiling in the middle of the room. There
was no further need to borrow kerosene from Miss Eva.

Daddy was now working almost every day with Uncle Purry.
When sober, Daddy mixed the mortar for him to lay bricks for
the construction company Henderson, Black & Green, in Troy.
Before coming home on Friday night, he stopped by the A&P in
Troy to buy groceries. A staple was Welch's Concord grape jelly,
which today is still one of my favorites. For some reason, he
wouldn't buy peanut butter, even though I hungered for it and
asked him to buy it. I kept a record of his pay stubs and found
that he was bringing home most of the money he earned, $40 a
week, less the usual deductions. And since we now had a milk
cow, we had plenty of milk and butter. From time to time, he
would buy me a shirt or a pair of pants, saying that he didn't want
his boy going to high school looking like a farmhand.

It was also during the summer of 1948 that Bennie joined the
Air Force. He gave me his clothes and shoes, all of which fit me
perfectly. After he finished basic training, he wrote that he was
going to start sending me some spending money. When I received
my first money order, I took a third of it to buy a pair of blue jeans
and a plaid shirt; with another third, I began eating in the school
cafeteria; with the rest, I started taking piano lessons.

My father didn't want me wasting money on the lessons and
declared it wasn't a boy's place to be playing the piano. Without
his knowledge, however, I asked Mrs. Red Mizell, whom I considered to be the best pianist in town, if she would teach me. Mrs.
Mizell, who with her husband, Buck, owned and operated the
Corner Drug Store, gave me short shrift, saying that she didn't
have time (she played for every funeral and wedding for miles
around) and that I was too old to begin lessons (most pianists start
when they're in grade school). She reminded me that I didn't even
have a piano to practice on, which I knew only too well.

Undaunted, I asked my English teacher, Mrs. Baxter (who
until that year had been Miss Fountain), if she would teach me
piano. She agreed to do so during her lunch period once a week,
for $5 a month. As she ate, she drilled me on the rudiments of

theory and technique. Every day during study hall and any other free activity, I found a way to get to the auditorium to practice. When I could find the time, I walked the five miles to Elam Baptist Church, where I went to service each Sunday, to practice. Many times, I would go at night, for the church had electric lights. Furthermore, I gladly did chores for neighbors and relatives in exchange for practice time on their pianos. I found it extremely difficult to visit in a home with a piano if I wasn't invited to perform. It was as though the keyboard were magnetic! (It still is.)

In only a few months, I relegated to second place the classical music, marches, scales, and études Mrs. Baxter had assigned, and started concentrating on hymns. It was one of my greatest delights to be able to play them at Sunday School and in the worship service itself. I often pleaded with my father to listen to me play. At that point, he had known nothing about my covert piano lessons; I was careful to keep the music hidden in my school books. But once I gained some experience playing in public, I yearned for Daddy to hear me, to let him see that I too could "tickle the keys," as he had once said of a boy we heard perform. Daddy didn't have a problem with other boys playing the piano, he just didn't want his own son tickling the keys. I thought my playing the piano would make him proud of me, even if I couldn't pick the banjo, strum the mandolin and guitar, or bow the fiddle (his favorite instrument). In the early years, his fiddle and bow hung by the fireplace. I'm not sure what finally happened to Daddy's beloved fiddle.

He wouldn't go to church to hear me, nor to Ruth's house, where I often practiced, even though it was nearby. But despite my father's disapproval of my interest in the piano, my teachers continued to encourage me, sometimes asking me to play for school assemblies and other activities. Daddy never heard me play the piano; neither did Mama, until a few months before her death, when I took her to Salem Baptist Church so that I could play just for her. She especially liked "There's a Land That Is Fairer Than Day," one of the songs she sang when Daddy moved us to Elamville. She would have gone to Elam Baptist Church to hear me when I was a teenager, but she didn't have presentable clothes.

My emerging skill at the piano was especially important for my self-esteem. Daddy played the fiddle, and three of my brothers (Ralph, Loyce, and Olon), one of my sisters (Ellie Mae), and a sister-in-law (Estelle, Olon's wife) played at least one stringed instrument; Estelle, in fact, was an accomplished guitarist. Before Loyce and Ralph left for the war, it wasn't uncommon for my family, as well as my cousins, to sit around the fireside or under the shade trees, depending on the season, and play guitars, fiddles, mandolins, and banjos. We would sing folk songs and Irish ballads such as "Barbara Allen" and "Wildwood Flower"; country songs, like "The Wabash Cannonball" or "The Maple on the Hill"; gospel tunes, like "Farther Along" and "Will the Circle Be Unbroken?"; as well as current numbers by Hank Williams, Roy Acuff, Ernest Tubb, and Bob Wills. However, I was never able to coax a decent sound out of a stringed instrument. I wanted to be able to play something!

Songs of the South

As noted earlier, my bout with the measles left me, a thin and emaciated 14-year-old, with a deep bass voice, much lower than the timbres of other boys my age. In the tenth grade, the girls' physical education teacher, Mrs. Mildred Laird, started a boys' quartet. She chose Chris Green, John McRae (John Mack) Hart, Robert DeLoach, and me. Mrs. Laird had made it all the way to New York City, where she was a chorus girl and had sung off-Broadway, "waaaaay-off Broadway," she would sometimes say in her lush, throaty, southern Alabama voice. She sounded like honey on gravel, no doubt from smoking two packs of unfiltered cigarettes a day. Mrs. Laird was the only woman I had ever known who smoked. Though Mrs. Laird was a product of the Deep South, her visions were of dancing and singing in exotic far-off places, images that made her voice lilt and her eyes sparkle. She was transported to another world when she accompanied us on the piano. I yearned for more of what Mrs. Laird had to offer—anything but the back-breaking drudgery of picking cotton and stacking peanuts, often on a near-empty stomach.

The songs she taught us were mostly old tunes like "Beautiful Dreamer," "Smoke Gets in Your Eyes," "Danny Boy," and "Way Down upon de Swanee River," as well as some popular songs she had arranged for us, two in particular being "I'm Looking over a Four-Leaf Clover," and "The Whiffenpoof Song." One song we did particularly well was "The Bullfrog on the Bank"; each voice part of that old college standard had a solo. When we performed it for a school assembly, it brought the house down, especially when I, a skinny kid, a year younger than the other three boys (who were all rather husky football players), hit a low A flat. It's not that I did all that well; the students just couldn't believe such a deep sound was coming from a boy who, judging by his age and size, should still have a high-pitched voice. I usually sang lead (the melody) inasmuch as it was difficult for me to carry the bass line against the other three voices. But I sang bass on the bullfrog song because I could reach the lower notes better than any of the others. In checking my memory, I called John Mack, who now lives in Florida. He said that when his wife told him the caller wanted to speak to "John Mack," he knew it had to be someone from Clio, for his name is really John McRae. Sorry, John McRae, I knew you in geometry class and the quartet as John Mack. As one of the cheerleaders, I also led the spectators at the football games in cheering for John Mack, the fullback.

Singing had now become a vital part of my life, mainly because Mrs. Laird looked past what she saw on the surface and recognized a talent that I wasn't even sure of myself. It's true I had gone to the singing school in my church and attended as many gospel singings as possible, but under Mrs. Laird, with her professional music background, I began to blossom. Playing the piano and singing have been two of the greatest joys of my life—because Mrs. Baxter and Mrs. Laird took the time to encourage and help me. And because the local churches gave me the opportunity to put my talents to use. Mrs. Laird, for example, once arranged for the quartet to sing at her church, Clio Presbyterian, for the Christmas program; among our repertoire was "We Three Kings." Robert DeLoach, who was always a bit of a comic, suggested that we retitle the song "We Four Princes."

Flashes in the Limelight

In the eleventh grade, I took geometry under Mr. Botts, who was also the principal, and the husband of my third-grade teacher at Elamville. Though I had completed two years of algebra under Miss Hixon, geometry was extremely difficult for me, and I wasn't at all certain that I could ever fathom complementary and supplementary angles, adjacent angles, or acute and obtuse angles, even though Mr. Palmer had drilled us in mathematical theorems and formulas at Elamville School. Geometry, alas, was nothing like algebra, or the math that Mr. Palmer taught, and I had resigned myself to failing the course. However, with only four in the class, Mr. Botts was able to give each of us the attention we needed, and I squeaked by—though not with an A. For Christmas, Bennie gave me a gold, 21-jewel

Mr. Botts

Bulova wristwatch for passing geometry. I made it a point for everyone to notice my beautifully crafted watch. Unlike wearing the Mickey Mouse wristwatch Loyce gave me in the fourth grade, wearing one now didn't seem incongruous with my present station in life.

In the spring of the eleventh grade, I again won the agricultural speaking contest in the school and in Barbour County. *The Clayton Record*, the county's weekly paper, ran an article headlined "Clio Boy Wins FFA County Speaking Contest." I kept the clipping in my billfold, reading it at every free opportunity. Like the letter Mrs. Moore had sent me years before, the article finally wore out.

Then it was on to the regionals in Luverne. My entire geometry class—Chris Green, John McRae Hart, and Carolyn Davis—went with me to the tournament, Carolyn chauffeuring her family's car. Though I came in second, I went home thrilled that my friends had taken the time to cheer me on that day. Mr. Botts had initially forbidden them to cut class, but finally relented

11th Grade

Mama & Daddy

and gave his blessing. I was later invited to give the same speech—*Farm Fishponds for Recreation and Profit*—at the annual Father-Son Mother-Daughter banquet, though neither of my parents was able to attend. I developed stage fright and forgot part of my speech; I swore I'd never again speak in public. But Mrs. Ard, one of my teachers and the coordinator of the banquet, consoled me and said that by tomorrow, I'd feel better and that I would go on to bigger and better things.

I was also invited to deliver a condensed version of the speech over radio station WTBF in Troy, 24 miles from Clio; the station adjoined Troy State College. The dormitories, the athletic stadium, the music building, and the spacious, magnolia-studded college campus intrigued me. It was the kind of setting where I wanted to study; Auburn, where I had visited a year earlier for the FFA convention, was much too big for me. When I returned to school the next day, Mr. Botts met me at the door and declared that I didn't have to worry about being the best in geometry, because I had a career in radio. Until I graduated, he continued to predict that my future lay in using my voice.

It was also in the eleventh grade that I was inducted into the Beta Club, an organization for high school students with a grade average of at least a B. Soon after, a request came in from the state headquarters that the school send a delegate to Birmingham for the annual spring meeting. Since Barbour County High was the newest chapter in the state, its delegate was invited to give the invocation at the banquet. The Beta Club chose me; I was delighted at the prospect of traveling all the way to Yankee City, 175 miles northwest of Clio. (Birmingham was often called "Yankee City" because it's so far north of South Alabama. Situated at the southern terminus of the Appalachians, it even snowed there occasionally.) The pastor of the Presbyterian church in Clio wrote the invocation for me. I would save on expenses by staying with

Loyce, who offered to take me back and forth to the convention center.

In my excitement about the opportunity of going to Birmingham, it hadn't occurred to me that I didn't have decent shoes to wear to the big city. The English Walkers Daddy bought me two years earlier had been half-soled again and again. I did have a blazer by then because Bennie had sent me money to buy it for the speaking tournament at Luverne, and Vallie had bought me a pair of dress trousers for the occasion. There was simply no way, however, to come up with the money for new shoes. Since Vallie had bought me the trousers, I dared not ask her to buy me shoes as well. She had never been one to dole out her money "frivolously," not even to her youngest brother. I was afraid she would say I could have the shoes I was wearing resoled—again—and polish them, and they would be good as new. In the fifty years since, I have often been tempted to ask her if she would have bought me new shoes had I so requested. I still haven't broached the subject with her.

I mustered up enough courage to approach Mr. and Mrs. Snead, the owners of a clothing store in Clio, to see if I could get a pair of shoes on credit. I was prepared to make all sorts of promises—even to the point of giving up piano lessons to be able to pay them—in exchange for presentable shoes; they didn't have to be English Walkers or anything else special. I didn't have a chance even to begin my spiel, however, for they both headed for the shoe section, fitting me with the nicest pair of dress shoes in the store. My representing Barbour County High, they said, was all the pay they needed.

I rode with the Chandlers to Birmingham, where they would be attending the annual convention of the Alabama Education Association. This was the first time I had been to Birmingham by myself, but I knew I was to walk south from the Greyhound station to 10th Street, and catch the Bessemer streetcar, getting off at Brown's Station. Standing by the streetcar stop, a scraggly, ragged old man holding a tin cup asked if I could spare him a dime. This was the first time I had seen a beggar. Feeling sorry for him, I ended up giving him all the money I had except for a dime, the streetcar fare. Even today, I haven't learned to say no to those asking for money. In fact, if a person even looks like he is hungry, I yearn to buy him a meal, and then offer to give him money for his next one.

The best and kindest brother a boy could have, Loyce gave me money to spend while I was in Birmingham. A teenage boy, he said, should always have some bills in his billfold and some change in his pocket.

The Big City: Birmingham, Alabama

Birmingham, the largest city in Alabama, was an exciting place, according to my teachers. I would see great and wonderful things, like electric street cars, tall buildings, and ornate movie theaters. But it was different for me. Though I was dressed as well as the other boys, I considered myself something of a country rustic. I found ways to be alone, avoiding group interactions as much as possible. On one occasion, a Beta Club staffer noticed me standing by myself and personally introduced me to others my age.

Even though I was 16, I had never seen an elevator; it took me some time to figure out how to get to the different floors for the small-group meetings. Nor was I certain how to use a pay telephone, but Loyce had told me to call when I was ready to be picked up each evening. Kenneth Dansby, a Beta member a year older than I, whom I had met at one of the gospel singings back home, saw me flustered and wanted to know what the problem was. After I told him I apparently didn't know how to use the phone, he dialed Loyce's number and told me the strange sound I had heard was a busy signal; he told me to wait a few minutes, and then insert the nickel, listen for the dial tone, and then dial the number again.

On the final night was the banquet, in the main ballroom of the Julia Tutwiler Hotel in downtown Birmingham. The printed program noted that the invocation would be given by Horace G. Danner, Barbour County High School—a boy not from Dothan, Troy, Montgomery, Mobile, or Birmingham, but Clio. I gave the memorized invocation, which, although my knees were shaking, went better than I had expected. Thanks to Vallie, I knew how to use the six pieces of silver next to my plate; she had drummed into me that no matter how many pieces of silver there were, one must always start from the outside. I was awed to find myself seated with the dignitaries at the head table. The appetizer—a half grapefruit with a red cherry in the middle—vividly reminded me of fourth grade, when the lunchroom at Elamville served a half grapefruit, a bowl of soup, and a serving of stewed prunes.

As a Cheerleader

New Friends, Good Sports

After I returned from Birmingham, Mrs. Baxter told me that there was more to life than studying, playing the piano, singing in quartets, and making speeches. She said I needed the experience of being with the other boys in a sports activity. Having strong legs from walking or running every place I went, I joined the cross-country track team. Since I was now eating in the cafeteria, I also had the energy to run. I began to learn something about camaraderie among athletes. We ran along the railroad tracks halfway to Elamville and back. My teammates said that with my running ability, I was going to help the team go all the way to the state finals.

Disappointed that I wasn't going out for football, however,

Cheerleading Squad

my gridiron friends urged me to become a cheerleader. The *Clionian*, the yearbook for 1949-50, shows five girls and me (the only male in the squad) doing one of our cheerleading routines. We all sported black sweaters with a yellow B for Barbour County High Yellowjackets; the girls wore pleated yellow skirts. I wore white chino pants given to me by Mrs. Tyler; the pants had originally been Durwood's. Mrs. Chandler, who was now the home economics teacher, sewed a yellow and black stripe down the outer seams.

Cheering and chanting along with my female counterparts made for one of the best times of my life. It was the first time I had been able to go to football games or any other paid school event since first grade, when I attended the dog show. Of course, as a member of the cheering squad, I didn't have to pay. At the half-time show, I particularly enjoyed getting to meet the cheerleaders (all of them girls) from the other teams. I was the envy of my football friends; they didn't let me forget that it was their idea in the first place for me to become a cheerleader. The only problem with being a cheerleader is that, after the away games, the team often stopped by Dairy Queen for a hamburger and a soda, and I rarely had any money. The players never let me go hungry, however.

Mr. Sam Price, the head football coach, told us cheerleaders we were entitled to wear the athletic jacket, and when Bennie was home from Eglin Air Force Base, Florida, he bought me the coveted jacket. I may not have been a football player, but wearing it, I fancied myself one.

When the senior rings arrived in January, Mrs. Baxter said that no one would receive them until each person had paid. Since it was difficult for a country boy without transportation to find a paying job, I knew I would be the last to pay. In fact, I was going to tell Mrs. Baxter that she might have to return mine so that the other students wouldn't be delayed in receiving theirs. But I told Vallie that the rings had come in, and without hesitation, she actually gave me the entire amount I needed. She said I could consider it my graduation present. If I wasn't the first to pay, I certainly wasn't the last, thanks to Vallie.

During the twelfth grade, I won the lead role as Ben Blayne, a young lawyer, in the senior comedy play, *Meet Uncle Sally*, further rounding out my final year at Barbour County High School. And when our class met to discuss graduation plans, they asked me to write the class song. I wrote as the refrain, "We are rowing, not drifting, to goals high and true from B.C.H.S." The 24 students of the senior class sang the song at graduation, and chose as its motto, "Rowing, Not Drifting." I can't remember if I wrote the song as a result of the motto, or if the class chose the motto as a result of my song.

12th Grade

Also, in my senior year, our business teacher, Mr. Price helped us organize a student council and prodded me to run for president. My campaign manager, Ila Mizell (no relation to the lady who had refused to teach me piano), urged the student body to "carry the banner with Danner." One day, she paraded through the halls, passing out bananas as she proclaimed, "Have a banana and vote for Dan-ah." I won by a slight margin over Bennie Earl Norton, my long-time best friend, and Robert DeLoach, one of my new best friends and a football star as well as a member of the boys' quartet. Not particularly impressed with party loyalties, Ila wrote Robert's campaign speech and directed his campaign as well. Ila had penned Robert's slogan: "Don't be a roach. Vote for DeLoach." A little irked, I asked Ila how she could find such good things to say about both of us, to which she rather smugly responded, "Because you are both nice boys, just in different ways."

The flags of the United States and the State of Alabama hadn't flown at the high school since I had enrolled there four years earlier. Since the flags reminded me upon seeing them in the first grade that I was part of something bigger—the state, the nation— I yearned to see them flying again. One of my promises in running for president of the student council was to raise the flags each morning. About a week after I was elected, we had a flag-raising ceremony in the rose garden in front of the school.

Almost fifty years after the *Clionian* was published, I looked to see what Nell Lunsford, not only the valedictorian but also the

Robert DeLoach

class prophet, had written about me and some of my classmates. She prophesied that Jimmy Byrd had become a professor at Harvard; Robert DeLoach had become a movie star (Robert *was* an Adonis whom the girls swooned over); Royce Abercrombie was president of the United States; John McRae Hart had struck it rich in the oil business; Chris Green was playing baseball with the St. Louis Cardinals; and I had become a world-renowned pianist. I haven't heard of Nell since graduating from high school, but I hope she was more of a success in life than she was as a prophet, for none of her prophecies materialized. And in the "Last Will and Testament," Ila Mizell, the class lawyer, willed my strong vocal cords and limber back which had made me an excellent cheerleader— she said—to Billy Norton (Bennie Earl's brother) and Frank Green (Chris's brother).

During the latter part of twelfth grade, I lived at Vallie's, because Mama and Daddy were now staying with Aunt Bessie in Clio. On Friday, March 10, 1950, one of Daddy's drinking pals had brought him home drunk. As my father tried to get out of the rumble seat of the car, he fell, breaking several ribs and suffering other injuries that would leave him in pain for the rest of his life. He had never believed in doctors, not even going to one when falling logs crushed three of his fingers in a sawmill accident, just two years before. But he was now in such pain that he stayed in town so that he could be close to the doctor. When Mama and Daddy weren't staying at Aunt Bessie's, they were staying at Loyce and Betty's in Birmingham, while he was being treated at University of Alabama Medical School.

Living at Vallie's house was a completely different experience, now that I was no longer a little boy as when we lived on her place. Vallie and Addie taught me to drive, and they let me take the car to church functions and to senior parties. I also made occasional trips back to the Ketchum Place to see if Aunt Leona's old house was still intact. Vallie also encouraged me to develop additional friends, even letting Robert DeLoach and me use the car to take our girlfriends for a ride.

Rowing, Not Drifting: Preparing for College

As graduation neared, I wanted more than anything else to go to college, and wrote Troy State for an application. No matter whom I asked, however, there was no money to be borrowed to cover the $10 application fee. Not be-

Graduation
May 29, 1950

ing able to borrow the money didn't keep me from telling everyone I was going to Troy State. It was clear in my mind that I was going to college—someway, somehow.

I found that I needed two letters of recommendation and promptly went to see Alto Lofton Jackson, Esquire, who with his brother, Sam, owned a farm supply and dry goods store in town. Mr. Jackson stopped what he was doing, slipped letterhead stationery into his old Royal typewriter and pecked out the nicest recommendation I could have hoped for. I wish I still had the letter, for it was one of confidence in my abilities. Buck Mizell, the owner of Corner Drug Store, and the husband of the lady who refused to teach me piano, wrote the other one.

Finally, I borrowed the fee from Vallie, who required an exacting promise that I pay her back, which I did. She let me take the car and visit the campus to make sure I hadn't left anything undone. I knew how to get to the college, but I had no idea where to find the admissions office. As a bit of serendipity, I wandered into the auditorium of Kilby Hall, to hear the most glorious and majestic sound imaginable. I will never forget the experience of hearing the 75-voice chorale and symphony orchestra rehearsing for their spring concert; I slipped in as they were singing an arrangement of "The Battle Hymn of the Republic," with Jack Knowles as the tenor soloist. Several weeks later, it would be my privilege to sing bass with the group, and to have Jack as a friend and mentor.

Just before graduation, I learned that Bennie was sending me $75 to help cover the first semester's expenses. Only the second of my own family to graduate from high school (Bennie was the first), I would be the first of any of the dozens of Danner, Ketchum, Preston, Teal, Tyler, Dykes, Olds, and Atkison cousins living in South Alabama or in nearby northern Florida and western Georgia to enter college. One of my cousins, Luther Danner, from Covington, Kentucky, was then an engineering student at University of Cincinnati; another, Adrian Ketchum, from Tallahassee, was a music major at Florida State University.

After a month, Mama and Daddy returned from Birmingham, and I moved back home from Vallie's to be with them. When he was able, he worked for Henderson, Black, and Green Construction Company. As mentioned earlier, after work each Friday, Daddy stopped by the A&P Store to buy groceries. When he was convinced that I was going to Troy State after high school, he talked to the manager of A&P about giving me a job at the store. The manager told Daddy that I could start to work there as soon as I enrolled at Troy State.

Both Mama and Daddy were able to attend my high school graduation. Since we never owned a car, Vallie picked them up and took them to the school for the ceremony. Vallie overheard one of the teachers say to Daddy, "I hear Horace is going to college," to which he responded, "That's what I hear. I just don't know how he's going to do it."

Our graduation speaker was Dr. G. Robert Boyd, Dean of Men at Troy State. In an impromptu comment in his address, Dean Boyd said he was pleased to note that the student who had written the class song would soon become a student at Troy State. However, being hard of hearing, I didn't understand him; it wasn't until the audience and senior class began applauding and asking me to stand that Robert DeLoach, who was sitting next to me, gave me the gist of Dean Boyd's remarks. The dean also announced that under a work scholarship, I would become an aide in his office, starting with the summer session, right after high school graduation. His announcement of my working in his office was news to me, and I was so elated, I kept thinking about what he said for the rest of the program.

The word *college* itself was a foreign word in the family. Not a single family member, except Vallie, Estelle, and Ellie Mae, seemed to appreciate the importance I attached to continuing my education. Estelle thought I should study chemistry; Vallie thought I would make a good pharmacist. But I told them all, I wanted to teach English composition and literature. Possibly Ellie Mae was still fascinated by "A Modest Proposal," and "A Dissertation upon Roast Pig," for she wanted to know what was terribly wrong with a Danner teaching literature. From that moment on, no one tried to stop me from going to college, although no one else as I recall encouraged me.

Just before enrolling at Troy State, I went to Troy to check into the stock clerk job that the manager of A&P had promised Daddy I could have. Since I didn't have transportation, not even a bicycle, the manager said that he felt the distance from the college to the store would be too far for me to walk. I thereupon went to see Dean Boyd, telling him the only job I would have was the one in his office. He said that with my clear speaking voice, he would arrange for me to be the college radio announcer, a job I held for the entire time I was at Troy State.

Memories of Troy State

Dean Boyd was a trusted friend and mentor throughout my two years at Troy State. He once remarked that students usually made the Dean's List because of good grades; with a wry chuckle, he added that to the best of his memory, I was the only student on his "list" for poor grades. I excelled in music and English, but I

Dean Boyd

was close to failing in algebra and biology. The dean asked Bobby Anderson, from Hatchechubbee, Alabama, a senior majoring in mathematics, to tutor me. A World War II veteran studying under the GI Bill, Bobby was one of my roommates. With his help, I squeaked by in both courses.

On June 25, 1950, only four weeks after enrolling at Troy State, Communist-controlled North Korea invaded South Korea, and we were at war again. I recall that very few students seemed to know where Korea was even located, much less what our interests in the region were. It wasn't long, however, before many of the older students began withdrawing to enter the conflict. By winter, we would have hardly enough athletes to field the basketball team.

Registration each quarter was a traumatic time for me. It seemed that all the students could write a check for their full tuition and books, or had a work scholarship that cancelled out most of their tuition. The World War II veterans didn't need a checkbook; their statement was stamped, "Paid in full by the Veterans Administration." I never had a checkbook while I was in school, because I never had enough money to put in the bank. Word circulated that I didn't have money to buy textbooks. Some of my veteran friends—Fred Searcy, from Dothan, is the one whose name I remember—let me use their books from a previous quarter, and some friends my own age often let me study from a particular one of theirs when they weren't using it.

As I was writing the memoir, I called Fred and thanked him for his helping me get an education by lending me his books. In the course of our conversation, I told him that I had written several books and was a professor of writing at University of Maryland. He was absolutely aghast, remembering, of course, that I had withdrawn from Troy State after only two years, and with less than a sterling academic record. He said, "I thought you had to have a Master's degree to teach at a university." I told him I had not only a master's but also a Ph.D. He said he never realized I was all that smart. I should have told Fred that there are many intelligent people who don't hold a Ph.D., and that it takes more than intelligence to earn one. More than anything, it takes perseverance, as later accounts reveal.

About six months after I had matriculated at Troy State, I was on my way to class one morning with my friends Wade Hall, Sam Young, and Buddy Windham, when I spotted a man mixing mortar for a new dormitory being built. It looked like my father; when he was able, I knew he sometimes worked for a construction company in Troy, but I just couldn't picture him on the stately manicured grounds of Troy State. As I neared the work site, I was certain that the worker was my father—there just aren't

In Front of Pace Hall, my dorm

that many Lincolnesque men wearing a Stetson at construction sites. I didn't want him to see me, and I surely didn't want to talk to him, especially in the presence of my sophisticated pals. I was afraid that he had been drinking, and I was always embarrassed to be associated with him in public, even when he was sober. But he saw me, and I told my friends not to wait for me.

Leaving his mortar box, Daddy strode in my direction, like he was really happy to see me. Sporting that big friendly smile, he asked how my classes were coming along and how my finances were; he also asked how I was doing in piano. I managed to tell him I had no money at all. Never one to easily show my emotions, I just couldn't help myself—as soon as I left him, I burst out bawling, I suppose for the interest he now showed in me. At least, I was happy my friends had gone on to class and didn't see me lose control of myself. I hadn't cried since I was fourteen, when I had to tell Mama that Roy Cecil Phillips had taken out fifty cents for my eating at his house, and that I hadn't even made enough to buy her shoes.

When I returned to the dorm after class, Mrs. Montgomery, our "house mother," gave me an envelope, telling me that my father had left it for me. In it were a half dollar and some smaller coins, amounting to less than a dollar. Again, I was embarrassed that Mrs. Montgomery now knew who my father was and that she knew the small amount of money he had left me. I was certain she knew how much I received, for the money was in an official Troy State envelope, the same kind Mrs. Montgomery left us notes in. As I reflect on the incident, Daddy left me probably all the money he had or all that he could borrow.

When I returned to my room to get ready to go to work at the drugstore, one of my roommates, Joe Tom Dyess, asked if I would help him with his abnormal psychology assignment. Though I was in a hurry and not in the best of moods, I said I would help him if I could. He proceeded to ask me about a dozen questions, smiling at each of my responses. After finishing the questions, he said

Dr. Ervin

that I had passed the test—that I was definitely abnormal. He would have to ask me all those questions on a bad day!

At Troy State, I also resumed taking piano, now under Dr. Violett Ervin, a former professor at Juilliard Conservatory of Music in New York City, and a true virtuoso. She was the first Jewish person I had ever met. She had come to Troy all the way from New York because her husband had accepted a professorship and later became head of the psychology department. Dr. Ervin helped train my left hand to play full octaves and my right hand to play full chords, and worked with me on my arpeggios and glissandi. It was from Dr. Ervin that I learned to play "The Star-Spangled Banner" with the pomp and grandeur it deserves. On Saturday afternoons when I had a three-hour break from my job at Byrd-Watters Drugs, I would walk to her house to practice on her grand piano and electric organ. Dr. Ervin was a bit of an eccentric, as evidenced by what she wrote in my college yearbook, *The Palladium, '51*: "To Chum Horace! From one Pilgrim to another. . . Be punctilious with alacrity on the wings of a dove. Amen. Violett Gross Ervin." Exactly what she meant I'm still not sure, for I had always been quite careful of details—at least, in piano—and willingly eager—again, in piano. She was right about my being a pilgrim however, for I had already set out on a voyage of discovery.

Mrs. Stephenson, the choral director's wife, who was also a piano teacher and had heard me play in a recital, wrote, "Best wishes and good luck. Keep up the good work in piano—you've made an excellent start."

Earlier I alluded to my being a part of the Troy State Chorale. It was the hour that I looked forward to each day. When the chorale and orchestra presented Gilbert and Sullivan's *H.M.S. Pin-*

Troy State Freshman

afore, Mr. Stephenson instructed that only the male soloists were to wear bow ties. I wasn't a soloist, but I was the only non-soloist who showed up wearing a bow tie. Frankly, I hadn't remembered him giving such instructions. Maybe that was one of the things he was referring to when he inscribed his note in the yearbook: "Dear Horace, It was good to hear the progress you have made in piano. Why not apply the same effort to everything you do?"

Mr. Botts had been correct all along; not only was I able to meet part of my college expenses by working in the dean's office, I also announced for the college radio station. And at the drugstore, I tended the fountain, a popular college and high school spot in the 1950s. I still found time to practice the piano and played every opportunity I could, for daily student devotionals on campus and for Wednesday and Sunday evening services at First Baptist Church in Troy.

In addition to not being able to pay my tuition in full each semester, my first semester at Troy State was traumatic for still another reason—I was required to take physical education. In high school, I had never felt confident enough to catch a ball, throw a ball, hit a ball, kick a ball, or sink a ball in a basket. I was quite willing to resign myself to running track and playing the piano, not playing ball. But deep inside, I wanted to be good in all sports. We were playing softball at Troy State. I had been able to absent-mindedly miss catching a ball that came my way in the outfield, but there was no way I could get out of my turn to bat. I shouldn't have worried. Coach Fuller Brooks noticed me holding the bat as though I was going to swat a fly, instead of slamming the ball out of the ballpark as many of my teammates had. He came over to where I was standing at home plate and said, "You hold the bat this way." Then he instructed the pitcher to hold up while he placed his right arm along mine to demonstrate the intended carry-through. Then he told me to keep my eye on the ball and to simply connect the bat with the ball. One of my greatest thrills was hitting the ball over second base and making it all the way to first.

About the only other thrill of physical education at Troy State—but certainly one that could have insspired me to become a professional athlete, that is, if I could count on this amenity—occurred after we were off the playing field. As we boys were hustling out of the shower, a gym attendant handed each of us a nice thick towel that had just come out of the dryer. The hot towel alone was enough to keep me coming back.

Academic Influences: Inklings of a Career

Shortly after becoming a student at Troy State, I joined the newspaper staff and had my first article published. In it, I reported on the demographics of the student population, noting that the majority of the students hailed from southeastern Alabama, with a few coming from as far away as Bayou la Batre, near Mobile, and a few from as far north as Birmingham; we also had a goodly number from northern Florida and southwestern Georgia. The rest were from Puerto Rico and New York. There was no need to indicate that none of the students were black. If Isaac, my black friend when we were five years old, had still been living in Alabama, he wouldn't have been able to join me at Troy State, because that was at least ten years before integration of higher education in Alabama. With newspaper writing in my blood, I would write a newspaper column, "A Way with Words," many years later.

One of my most colorful professors was Dr. F. Bashinsky Rainwater, who, with his stately bearing, was the embodiment of an eminent academician. Literature came alive in his class. Short stories, poetry, Greek dramas, Shakespeare's sonnets and plays, even essays were read and studied with relish. His trenchant interpretation of Faulkner's "A Rose for Emily" still permeates my college teaching of literature. And his poignant rendering of Sophocles' *Antigone* inspired my willingness to give my life for a worthy cause. Because of his artificial leg, he used a cane and was often late to class; in a puerile attempt to be in charge, I volunteered to call the roll for him so that he could begin lectures immediately upon entering the classroom. Though I am no longer proud of it, I also imitated his limp, grandly hobbling into the classroom amid applause and

Dr. Rainwater

cheers from cretins like myself, but eliciting jeers and sneers from the more mature members of the class.

Still another professor at Troy State who greatly influenced my future career was Miss Thelma Goodwin, who was not only my speech teacher but also my boss, and a most stringent one. She supervised the "College Hour," one of the radio programs I announced for. Just like Vallie, Miss Goodwin had no qualms about correcting my diction at any time or any place. She also had me listen to the tapes after the programs and coached me in toning down the southeastern Alabama bright *i* in *night, right,* and *sight.* She helped me produce a darker, less strident, tone, pronouncing the sound as the diphthong *ah-ee.* I sometimes think she also coined the phrase "How now, brown cow?"

A stern taskmaster, Miss Goodwin warned that if I planned to continue as the college radio announcer, I *would* indeed eradicate *idn't* from my speech, both on and off the air. When she was finished with me, I wanted to shout to the world, "There is no such word as *idn't.* And don't you ever forget it!" No excuse for a failing or a shortcoming would she accept. Once when I wanted to hitchhike home to try to

Miss Goodwin

persuade Vallie to lend me money to buy a book, Miss Goodwin advised me to grow up, that I had the Faculty Forum radio program to announce for on Sunday. She didn't give me a chance to tell her I had planned on hitchhiking back on Saturday afternoon. She was undoubtedly the firmest with me of all the teachers, professors, or any other adults in my life (including Vallie and my first sergeant in military police school at Camp Gordon, Georgia). Only Miss Fountain could have been considered for that dubious distinction when, in the ninth grade, I asked why she hadn't left a margin on the blackboard. However, Miss Goodwin did instill in me self-confidence in my voice and my abilities as a speaker.

Another of my duties was to tape the lectures of the visiting speakers for convocations, graduations, and other important events. By listening to them, I picked up additional pointers in public speaking. In replaying the tapes for editing, I was able to hear the speakers again. This responsibility also gave me opportunities to meet and talk with those dignitaries and to see my name printed on the program. The cotton fields were vanishing into the distant past, one day to become only bittersweet memories.

Although I worked four or five nights a week at Byrd-Watters Drugs, Mr. Byrd gave me a week off so that I could join an evangelistic team formed by the Baptist Student Union at the college. The team consisted of a youth evangelist, a pianist, and me, the soloist and song leader. We had been invited by the Parkview Baptist Church in Eufaula, about 40 miles from Troy. Each night we had dinner at a church member's home before the service started, and everything went well until the last night. After we had been served and had already begun to eat, the hostess said she had prepared for us her favorite meal: rabbit casserole. Until she announced that, I had no problem, thinking the dish was possibly chicken, for it did have a chickenlike flavor. For some reason, I had never beem able to coax myself to eat rabbits, squirrels, possums, coons, and birds, or any kind of wild meat, though I had gone trapping for coon with Daddy. Although I began to feel queasy, I managed to finish everything else on my plate, and even nibbled at the rabbit dish. I then excused myself to go the bathroom where I vomited my entire dinner.

The church gave us a very nice honorarium, and although the evangelist usually receives the most, he wouldn't hear of his getting the lion's share. So, the honorarium was divided equally, and I had the most money I had ever had at one time while at Troy State, a total of $35. Half-jokingly, I told the group I should receive even more inasmuch as I had to sing the last night on an empty stomach. Utterly devoid of sympathy, they said it was my problem that I had a weak constitution for rabbit.

Turning Point: Finding the Words

To my other professors at Troy State can be attributed many positive influences, but the pivot upon which my ultimate career turned was a remark by my American history professor, Dr. H. Eugene Sterkx. A Creole from New Orleans, his vocabulary was rich; his voice, powerful; his enunciation, invariably precise. By his voice and demeanor, he commanded attention from the class. Once, for instance, when a student was clipping her nails, ever so discreetly, he declaimed,

Dr. Sterkx

"The one thing I hate worse than smelling bacon frying first thing in the morning is a young lady clipping her nails behind her history text."

In my blundering attempts to emulate his preciseness of speech, I had been trying to express myself in the class discussion but stumbled for the right words. Later, at the drugstore where I worked, and where the professor often dropped by for an ice cream soda—which I made with two scoops of ice cream instead of one, that is, when Mr. Byrd, the owner, wasn't looking—he told me in his usual candor that although I appeared to be a fairly intelligent young man, I had the vocabulary of a backwoods twelve-year-old.

He said that I must have words to convey my thoughts, to express my ideas. His statement was most ironic, for I had always been interested in words, how they originated, where they came from. For example, I once asked Daddy why a skunk was often called a *polecat*. A man of little schooling himself, he responded promptly: You wouldn't want to touch one of them fellers with a 10-foot pole. That answer seemed logical and satisfied my curiosity; years later I learned that the *pole* of *polecat* was an Anglo-Saxon respelling of French *poule*, chicken, the same base as *pullet*, and a cognate of Spanish *pollo*, as in *arroz con pollo*, rice with chicken. My father was well aware that polecats often raided the chicken coop, but I am sure he never knew that polecats were literally *chicken cats*. On another occasion, I asked Daddy how mushrooms got their name. Again, his answer was simple and direct: They look a little mushy. In fact, the word is an English transliteration of French *moisseron*, which translates as "moss." I also asked Daddy what *turnip* had to do with the verb "to turn." That question was the easiest of all for Daddy; he said it was because turnips turn up at the table too often.

Although Daddy didn't quite understand the background of *mushroom*, he did teach me my first French word, though neither of us was aware that it was French. After our fishing expeditions at Pea River, he would say something like, "We caught bookoo fish." Naturally, I assumed the word was spelled *boo-koo*; I knew that it meant "plenty of," or "a lot." Many years later, I discovered that the correct spelling was *beaucoup*, and that the correct pronunciation was *boh KOO*. Just a few years ago I told Vallie (who had taken such pains to see that I correctly pronounced words when I was five or six years old) that we had been mispronouncing the word all along; as might be expected, she retorted, "It's not incorrect—it's the *Alabama* pronunciation." Just recently, one of my students, who is from Indiana, pronounced it *bookoo* as well.

I learned another French word, *chaud*, but I assumed it was a dialectal past tense of *chew*, as in "He *chawed* his tobacco." Consequently, I was careful never to use the word outside of South Alabama, and then only in my own social group. Since I left Alabama, I have not heard the word used by anyone, anywhere. Meaning "hot," the word is perfectly acceptable, that is, if one is speaking French. It is difficult to explain how the word is used, but I'll "wager" Robert Hanssen was "chaud" when he was arrested for spying by the same agency he had served for 35 years.

Professor Sterkx's assessment of my wordhoard, Anglo-Saxon for *vocabulary*, stunned me because even in high school I had faithfully read Frank Colby's syndicated word column, "Take My Word for It," which ran in *The Montgomery Advertiser*. Reading the column one day, I noticed on the same page a large square of smaller, numbered squares alongside clues under the headings "Across" and "Down." It took me a while to decipher what it was all about, but finally getting the idea, I began doing the crossword puzzle each day. At first, I could come up with only about a fourth of the words; anxiously, I would await getting the neighbor's paper the next day, after his family had finished it, to look up the answers. Since I didn't own a dictionary, I kept a list of the most frequently recurring clues and definitions.

Then, one day at school, I found a dictionary with its covers torn off, about to be discarded. I told Mr. Botts, the principal, I would give it a good home. It became only the second book in our house. Next to the Bible, this dilapidated old high school edition of a dictionary became my most treasured possession. Fascinated by the backgrounds of words, I actually read the dictionary. Reading the etymology of a word, I noticed that the word was often cross-referenced to another. The dictionary also helped me complete the crossword more quickly. With my morning cup of coffee, I still do the crossword puzzles in *The Washington Post* and *The Potomac News* before beginning my daily writing, teaching, and speaking activities.

At any rate, the professor's remark about my "backwoods" vocabulary jolted me. By that time I honestly thought that indeed I had arrived, that my natural interest in words, my crossword experience, my love of the dictionary, my making speeches, and my reading the word column had qualified me for a level above "backwoods."

Searching for Roots

I didn't know it then, but Dr. Sterkx had set me on a path toward a writing and teaching career. I began listing unfamiliar words from my texts and the lectures. Before long I had a rather extensive list of words. One day I told the pastor of First Baptist Church in Troy that

I was "amassing an academic vocabulary," and that I had learned about 25 new words. Dr. Claude T. Ammerman, not only an excellent college-town pastor and former seminary professor, but also a noted scholar of Greek, Hebrew, and Latin, suggested that I commit to memory Latin and Greek *roots* of words rather than *words* themselves. He said that at least 60 percent of English is from Latin and about 15 percent from Greek. He said that by knowing a single root, one could open up a whole family of English words. I was intrigued by this novel idea. I had heard of both Latin and Greek, but I didn't know exactly how either of them had influenced the English language. Many times when I was a young boy, Dr. A. Y. Napier, pastor of Elam Baptist Church—and a retired missionary to China—elucidated the meaning of a particular Bible passage by explaining what it meant in Greek.

Dr. Ammerman got me started by telling me that *hypo-* was Greek for "under," and that one can place this prefix before roots to obtain such words as *hypochondriac, hypocrite, hypodermic, hypotenuse, hypothermia*, and *hypothesis*. That sounded fine, but I didn't see how the concept of "under" fit with *hypotenuse*, which I had long known was the longest side of a right triangle. He explained that if the triangle is turned so that the hypotenuse is lying on a plane, the *pleura hypotenusa* would indeed be the "side subtended," or "side stretched under," the right angle. I later discovered that the majority of mathematical terms derive from Greek with a smaller number being from Latin.

Dr. Ammerman's advice was all I needed, and for the next 25 years I continued to add to my reservoir of word roots, all by sheer memorization. Increasing my vocabulary added depth to my reading and variety to my writing. Over time, I also added to my repertoire the backgrounds of hundreds of interesting words—for example, *hysteria, ink, mile, muscle, mushroom, school, siesta, ventriloquist, vermicelli*. The origins of these words, as well as about 500 others, are given in the "Wordextras" section of *Discover It! A Better Vocabulary, the Better Way*, which I co-authored with Dr. Roger Noël, Chairperson of the Department of Modern Foreign Languages at Georgia College and State University in Milledgeville, Georgia. With show cards illustrating these and other words, I have given talks to talented and gifted students throughout Fairfax County, Virginia; Prince William County, Virginia; Prince

Georges County, Maryland; and Montgomery County, Maryland. I also hold workshops for teachers at all levels on presenting Latin and Greek within the context of their own disciplines.

On the last day of summer session in 1951, as I was walking past the finance office in Bibb Graves Hall, Mr. Edward Caruthers, the business manager, waved me inside. He had always been friendly to me, when every quarter, I had to obtain his approval to register without having the full tuition. Quite fatherly, he related that he knew I was having financial problems, which Dean Boyd had told him were affecting my grades. As I went to leave, he rose and put his arm on my shoulder, assuring me he would help get financial aid for me in the fall so that I wouldn't have to work three jobs and would have more time to study. As I thanked him for his concern, my lower lip started trembling. I hurriedly left his office and couldn't wait to get out of earshot, for I started sobbing. I had never before had a man talk with me so caringly. I never saw Mr. Caruthers again to thank him for his taking the time to talk to me so warmly. When I returned to Troy State in later years for a visit, I learned that he had died.

Into the Wild Blue Yonder: The United States Air Force

The day after Mr. Caruthers talked with me, I used all the money I had to ride the Greyhound to Birmingham to see Loyce and Betty. I wanted to talk over my predicament of mediocre grades and low finances. Loyce was the one person with whom I could share my soul. I just didn't see how I could continue my studies and work three jobs. Mr. Caruthers had promised to help me, but I'd had promises before, promises that never seemed to materialize. While at Loyce's house, I saw television for the first time, and as providence would have it, I watched a program on the U. S. Air Force. At the end of the program, there was an announcement that the Air Force needed motivated young men. Without a moment's hesitation, I decided to enlist. Since I was now 18 and didn't need my parents' approval, I didn't even return to South Alabama to see Mama and Daddy.

Somewhat saddened that I wouldn't be continuing my college education, Loyce said that the military would give me at least a fighting chance at life. When he knew that I had made up my mind to enlist, Loyce, who had served in the military during the war, advised me about some of the problems I might encounter in the military. What he told me came quite close to Polonius' advice to Laertes in Shakespeare's *Hamlet*: "Unto thine own self be true, and it shall follow as night the day, thou canst not be false to any man." In the same serious vein, he told me that if I didn't want to be made fun of by the Northern boys, I must eradicate "y'all" from my speech. Never mind that they would say things like "youse guys," just don't ever utter "y'all," or I would become a laughingstock in the barracks. I took his advice to heart and to this day, have not uttered "y'all," except in recounting his advice. He added that I must be especially careful around "polacks, dagoes, and krauts, especially them that's from New York."

Before I boarded the streetcar for the recruiting station, Loyce, with a twinkle in his eye, said that the polacks, dagoes, and krauts were the salt of the earth and would turn out to be some of my best friends, especially them that's from New York. As though it were prophecy fulfillment, four of my best friends in the Air Force were James Chiodo (pronounced CHI doh), Anthony Bachigalupo, Mario Santamaria, and Leonard Bonfanti, all "dagoes" from New York. And there was the "kraut," Gerald Hertzfeldt, but he was from Hooper, Nebraska; the "polack," Edward Barkowski, hailed from Boston.

Reporting to the recruiting station, I didn't have an opportunity to say a final goodbye to Loyce and Betty. That night I tossed and turned in a seedy hotel room in Birmingham, and the next day was on a flight to San Antonio, Texas. It was the first time I had ever seen an airplane up close, much less flown in one. August 30, 1951, was the beginning of an Air Force career that would span 36 years of active and reserve duty, ending with my retirement as a Chief Master Sergeant with the Air Force Intelligence Service.

Even before I took the oath of enlistment, I was determined that I wouldn't so much as even hint that I could type or play the piano. I wanted to be a real soldier, though I had fired a weapon only once in my entire life, when, at sixteen years old, I almost blew Jimmy Middlebrooks' foot off with a double-barrel 12-gauge shotgun. Jimmy was showing me how to shoot squirrel nests out of tall oaks. He demonstrated how to aim at the nest and how to squeeze the trigger. I did as he said, but nothing happened. And then I pointed the shotgun to the ground, about a foot from where Jimmy was standing, and asked, "Like this?" It was a good thing the end of the barrel was almost touching the ground; even then, the blast made a foot-deep hole in the marshy, sandy ground.

I *was* a good soldier except on the firing range. Bill Miller, a lanky cowboy-type from Big Spring, Texas, was my firing partner. An absolute deadeye, he emptied his magazine, including the ten familiarization rounds, right through the middle of the bull's eye, making just one ragged hole. It was then my turn. For the first five of my familiarization rounds, I hadn't even hit the frame surrounding the target, much less one of the rings around the bull's eye. Each time I fired, the spotter sent up "Maggie's drawers," a red flag indicating failure to hit the target. Bill said he wanted to check to see what could possibly be wrong with my weapon. Checking the M-1 closely, he waited until the range sergeant wasn't looking our way, and then sprayed my remaining rounds onto the target, being especially careful, he later told me, not to hit the bull's eye. I walked away from the firing range a sharpshooter, not as an expert, but high enough to keep me from having to clean weapons for the rest of basic training. I asked Bill how it was that all the Texas boys were so friendly, telling him that they were big enough to push us little guys around. His reply still brings a chuckle: "Well, pardner, it's either be friendly or be dead. If in Texas a man ain't friendly, we just shoot 'im." Years later, when asked if there were any embarrassing incidents in my life not covered in the security questionnaire, I confessed the rifle range incident to a security clearance official at the Pentagon. When he asked how old I was at the time, I told him I had just turned eighteen. He told me to forget it.

I made high scores on the battery of aptitude tests administered in basic training except on the ones testing for critical skills the Air Force needed. Just about all my unit had received orders to attend rather exciting technical schools, such as aircraft mechanics, aircraft communications and warning, and radio and telegraph. Two or three weeks passed after graduation, and still there were no orders for me. I was one of only six or seven airmen in casual status. I had come to the conclusion that I was a misfit as far as the Air Force was concerned and that I would soon be discharged for scoring low in the technical areas.

My brother Bennie was then serving as a Portuguese linguist for the Air Force in Brazil, and I began to think that being a linguist would be a good job for me. Continuing to read my Bible each night and even kneeling by my bunk to pray—which no one ever made fun of—I asked permission to see the Protestant chaplain. I abdicated my high-flown principles of wanting to be a regular soldier and told him I could type 50 words a minute and play the piano as well and I thought I could become a pretty good chaplain's assistant. He mustn't have thought it highly unusual I could type, because he said, "Well, now, let me hear you play a hymn, Private Danner." He escorted me into the sanctuary, handed me an armed forces hymnal and told me to take my pick. I told him I didn't need a hymnal to play "What a Friend We Have in Jesus," or "Amazing Grace." I played both hymns in a manner that I believe would have made my idol Durwood Tyler proud. The chaplain told me that I could begin as his assistant the following week and that he would send me to chaplain's assistant school as soon as there was an opening.

The Army's Military Police School, Camp Gordon, Georgia

The very next morning, the Squadron CQ (Charge of Quarters) of my basic training outfit at Lackland Air Force Base awakened me at 4 a.m. and told me to pack my duffel bag, that I was catching a flight from San Antonio in three hours. Two thoughts were running through my mind: I was being booted out of the service, or I was being sent to chaplain's assistant school already. I chose to dwell on the more positive alternative. I thought, "My, that chaplain surely worked fast; he found an opening for me already." I had made up my mind that I wouldn't at all mind typing and playing the piano for four years. All agog, I asked the corporal where I was being sent. He responded, "Looks like you're heading to the Army's Provost Marshal General School at Camp Gordon, Georgia." At the time, I had no idea what *provost marshal* even meant, so the CQ said I would be training to be a military policeman. I was quite certain that the CQ didn't know the full score, and I showered and shaved, quite certain I was really on my way to chaplain's assistant school. Or, possibly, the chaplain with whom I had talked didn't think I needed any training and was sending me as a chaplain's assistant to Camp Gordon.

The small, chartered plane made an emergency landing in Birmingham, the same airport I had flown out of just a few weeks before. The emergency turned out to be a lucky break for Bill Cunningham, with whom I had enlisted, and who was my best friend in basic training. Bill was from Birmingham, and he called his mom and dad, who came to the airport to see him, and I called Loyce and Betty. I teased Bill that he must have had an "in" with the pilot. The airline treated all of us to milkshakes and hamburgers while we waited for the plane to be checked before continuing its flight to Augusta, Georgia. The olive drab personnel carrier waiting to pick us up at the Augusta airport confirmed my worst fear—we were indeed on our way to Camp Gordon. If it had been blue, I would have known I was at Chanute Air Force Base, Illinois, for chaplain's assistant school.

On the first day of military police training—November 2, 1951—after a 5-mile appetite run, the drill sergeant mustered us for the orders of the day. Before he began barking the orders, he called out, "Private Danner, on the double, front and center." I couldn't believe that anyone at Camp Gordon even knew my name, and here I was singled out from almost 500 trainees. I rushed up to the sergeant, who commanded I report to the orderly room on the double. Not thinking that I had done anything terribly wrong already—I hadn't even had breakfast yet—I cherished the thought that the Air Force had realized its mistake of sending me to the Army's military police school when I was supposed to be at Chanute Air Force Base, Illinois.

When I arrived at the orderly room, the first sergeant told me to go to the mess hall and have breakfast and then report back—that the adjutant wanted to see me and right now, he was having breakfast himself. Army chow never tasted so delicious, and besides that, by noon at the latest, I would be on a plane to Chanute with a full apology from the Secretary of the Air Force, as well as the Secretary of the Army, for inconveniencing me. I reported as ordered, and the adjutant quite abruptly informed me that the Air Force had overbooked the school. I was being removed from the class and assigned to the Army's casual company where I would be cleaning bachelor officers' quarters, washing pots and pans, and cleaning weapons.

I was the only Air Force person in the casual company; the others were a wild sort of boisterous, foul-mouthed soldiers being processed for discharge for a number of unsavory deeds. They played cards and told dirty jokes until three or four in the morning. Practically all I owned was stolen, and I had never been so discouraged. If I couldn't be a chaplain's assistant, at least I had rather be with my Air Force outfit. At other times, I yearned to be back at Troy State, even if I had to work three jobs, arrange with Mr. Caruthers to let me pay my tuition by the week, and borrow books from friends. But I went to chapel services as often as I could, read a good portion of the 150 Psalms, and prayed for deliverance from my harrowing nightmare.[16] I didn't even care if the soldier misfits laughed at me—I sank to my knees every night beside my cot and prayed for help. After a month of doing every menial chore the Army had, I was ordered to report to the next military police class.

I hated everything about military police school— performing calisthenics, sit-ups, and pushups every morning with a rifle and bayonet before the moon had even said good night; marching, running, throwing hand grenades; firing every pistol, rifle, shotgun, bazooka, and machine gun in the Army's arsenal; crawling on our bellies under barbed wire while being fired on with live ammunition; being thrown to the ground in unarmed defense training; attending classes on riot control; learning to direct traffic; and watching films on installation security. Not only all that, we celebrated Thanksgiving in the field, with the cold rain soaking our turkey and dressing, and making the cranberry sauce and mashed potatoes run together.

Our week in the field camping among the Georgia pines wouldn't have been so traumatic if I had been told that *bivouac* was originally from French *biwacht*, or literally, "to watch by." To me, *bivouac* simply meant standing guard at night, sharing a tent with another guy and cuddling up to a cold rifle, using my helmet for a basin while shaving in cold water, eating C rations, and praying to get back to garrison for a hot shower and a hot meal. I could have also appreciated reveille more had I known that the word originally meant "to wake up."

---

[16] Psalm 70, by King David, echoed my plight: Make haste, O God, to deliver me! Make haste to help me, O God. (Verse 1)

A few days after our week in the field, the school gave us an afternoon off. While most of the trainees were either playing cards or softball, I thought I could best use my free afternoon by seeing the provost marshal. Already halfway through the school, I told him I was sure the Air Force was probably showing me as AWOL (absent without leave)—that I was really supposed to be in chaplain's assistant school. I also told him I didn't think I ought to have to endure the rest of military police school to be a chaplain's assistant. I was quick to remind him that I could best serve my country by typing and playing the piano. He was also quick to remind me that I was Air Force and he was Army, and there was nothing he could do for me. He did suggest that I might ask the chaplain to let me play the piano to my heart's content if I ever had another free afternoon.

My bunkmate, Paul Merritt, of Ravena-Coeymans, New York, didn't much like the school either, but we toughed it out, even coming to appreciate the growth in our muscles and the increased stamina. When I went home for Christmas, my family couldn't believe how much weight I had gained and how nice I looked in my Air Force blues. To them, the one stripe on my sleeve made me a hero. I, however, knew I was anything but a hero; I wanted to be a chaplain's assistant.

There was one pleasant day at the school. We were out in the field, and at the break, one of the trainees known for impersonating the training sergeant started on his routine. We all thought the sergeant was in the tent talking with the operations officer. But they had both slipped out of the tent and had come up behind us just as the impersonator was at his zenith. We were howling with laughter that the sergeant could be imitated down to the last nuance. Just like the sergeant, he was barking orders and telling us we were a despicably sorry lot, and how even our own mothers would disown us if they knew just how inept we all were. We looked up to see the operations officer and the sergeant laughing so hard that they had lost all sense of military decorum. Later, when it was time to return to garrison, the sergeant told the truck drivers who had come to pick us up to leave without us, telling us to get back to the barracks as best we could. Chow would be late that night, and the cooks and the kp's (kitchen police) were not at all happy over our shenanigans, causing them to have to work late.

The Nation's Capital: Washington, D.C.

Constitution Avenue
Washington, DC
1952

On January 10, 1952, about a week before graduation, the first sergeant called ten of us who had excelled in the school to the orderly room and told us we were being given a special assignment, that we were headed to the nation's capital—Bolling Air Force Base, D.C.—where we would work as town patrol with the Army, Navy, and Marine Corps. During the long bus ride from Augusta, Georgia, to Washington, I began to become quite excited about seeing the city of my dreams for the first time. I would see all the places Miss Hixon had told us about when I was in high school. Departing the Greyhound bus station in Washington on New York Avenue, I was weighted down with an overstuffed duffel bag, an overnight bag, and a radio. A street photographer said he would like to take my picture for only two dollars. Giving me a receipt, he said I would be receiving the picture in a couple of days. This was my introduction to the world of scam.

I asked the cabdriver to swing by the Capitol before heading to Bolling, sprawled along the Potomac, across the river from Washington National Airport (now Reagan National Airport), which is on the Virginia side. The ride was even more exciting than I had expected, seeing the towering obelisk of the Washington Monument and the colonnaded Lincoln Memorial as the cabdriver drove down Constitution Avenue. At that time, the west end of the Mall along Constitution Avenue—where the Vietnam Memorial is now—was inundated with temporary office buildings that had been erected during World War II. And within a mile from the gloried monuments and the Capitol, I witnessed the first slum I had ever seen. Southeast Washington was, and still is, a disgrace to the Nation's capital city. I was crushed that its streets were not paved with gold. Not only that, I was anything but dazzled by Bolling; it was a far cry from anything I had expected. With its open-bay World War II barracks, the base was purely and simply another Camp Gordon—an Army post—simply transported from Augusta, Georgia, to the banks of the Potomac, and in sight of the Capitol. On my weekly trips to Bolling nowadays, as I teach classes for University of Maryland held on base, I am pleased to see that the base bears little resemblance to its 1950's look. The enlisted men are now well housed in high-rise, air-conditioned dormitories. And where the runway used to be in 1952 is now one long parade ground and soccer fields.

When I was interviewed for town patrol at Washington Navy Yard, the Marine sergeant in charge said I was too scrawny to be breaking up bar fights between the tars (sailors) and the leathernecks (marines), or the ground pounders (soldiers) and the flyboys (airmen). After he told me that, I was greatly relieved that I wasn't accepted; I thought all I would have to do was strut up and down Constitution and Pennsylvania avenues, looking all sharp wearing my spit-shined boots with a .45 Colt automatic strapped to my side.

And then, I was relegated to waiting around in the barracks at Bolling with nothing to do but make my bunk, read, eat, sleep, and go to the movies. It was the epitome of a saying I would hear many times in the military—hurry up and wait. What a life—and a boring one at that!

But I did make a new friend—Frederick (Freddy) Faust—of Chalmette, Louisiana, just outside New Orleans, and right on the Mississippi. We had been in training at Camp Gordon, but we hadn't met until we were at Bolling. On January 22, 1952, after about two weeks at Bolling, Arthur

Freddy Faust at 55 Years Old

Atley, Freddy, and I were called into the first sergeant's office and told we were being assigned across the Potomac to the 1120th Special Activities Wing, South Post, Fort Myer, Virginia, where we would support the Pentagon. Fort Myer would be my home for the next eighteen months; it was the longest time I would live in one place since I was seven years old. At first, Freddy and I shared Room G115, Alabama Hall; each of Alabama Hall's 12 wings—designated A though L—had 30 two-man rooms. Built to accommodate the young women from across the country who took the places of soldiers in combat during World War II, Alabama Hall was distinct in that it had no urinals. In addition to a bank of shower stalls in each bay, each of the latrines had a bathtub, but I never knew an airman luxuriating in one.

South Post, which had been built during World War II, was just across the street from the Arlington National Cemetery; because of the many casualties in Korea, "Taps" could be heard at military funerals all day. Now, all fifty or so buildings on South Post have been razed, and the area has reverted to its original, intended use as a burial site. On my last visit to Fort Myer, I couldn't tell where Alabama Hall or any of the other buildings once stood.

I might add at this point that I have been asked over the years why I didn't become a commissioned officer, with all the education and degrees I've accumulated. It's certainly not because I didn't yearn to be an officer or because of my lack of trying. Shortly after finishing military police school and being assigned to Fort Myer, I boned up on mathematics, my weakest academic area, and took the Air Force Officer Qualifying Test, with the idea of becoming a pilot or, at least, a navigator. After scoring rather highly on the test, I was sent to Samson Air Force Base in upstate New York to be administered several coordination tests, including a psychomotor test, which required holding a stylus on a white dot on a revolving disk, something like an old phonograph record. Not the most coordinated 19-year-old in the Air Force, I failed the test miserably.

Those of us who failed the psychomotor test were told that once we reached the age of 20, we could apply to Officer Candidate School, to become a non-flying officer, provided we were still single. But by the time I was 20, I was already engaged to be married, which automatically disqualified me from attending Officer

Candidate School.

It snowed shortly after my arrival at Fort Myer in January 1952. I was so excited that I ran out into the snowstorm with only my shorts and undershirt on. It was the first snow I had seen since the dusting we received when I was in the fifth grade at Clio Low School.

During Mardi Gras in New Orleans, I thought my roommate, Freddy, would go AWOL, just to be back home during the festive occasion. I just couldn't believe that anyone could become so despondent, since I had never before even heard of Mardi Gras. Freddy tried to describe the gala event with its parades and floats, but for a country boy like myself who was barely out of the cotton fields and had never even seen television but once, I simply couldn't fathom it. For Freddy, however, it was like spending Christmas away from home for the first time. Freddy would remain a very special friend, even after almost 50 years.

Since my old buddies at Fort Myer won't ever let me live it down, I must relate an incident that led to some embarrassing, life-threatening consequences. We had been taught in military police school that unless our lives were threatened, we were to call out "Halt!" three times before firing our weapon. Not more than three months after being assigned to Fort Myer, Staff Sergeant Musiel and I were dispatched to Alabama Hall, where it was reported that two civilians from the District were winning all the airmen's money by using loaded dice in a crap game. As soon as the sergeant and I approached the huddle of crapshooters, one of the civilians yelled out "Police!" and scraped up all the money and jammed it in his pocket. The two men then bolted for the entrance, which was about 50 feet from where the game was being played. I struck out down the corridor after them, and as soon as I emerged from the building, I yelled out "Halt!" three times, cocked my .45 Colt automatic, and fired two rounds in quick succession. The man with the pocketful of money fell face down in a puddle from the pouring rain; I thought I had killed him, and apparently he thought so too, as he lay in the puddle motionless. But as soon as I reached him and rolled him over with my boots, he jumped up running and could very well have earned a medal in the Olympics. We never saw him or his accomplice again. But the point of the story is that in later training sessions, the sergeant would say "And you don't try to break up a crap game, like Danner did!" I was relieved of duty until an investigation was completed, and then I was called in to see the wing commander. He said the only thing I did wrong was that I wasted the government's ammo by not taking better aim. I put on my second stripe not long after that.

It was also at Fort Myer that I developed two other close friends, John Bawsel, from Richmond, Virginia, and David Clark, from Olean, New York. Bawsel, Clark, and I would later ship out to the Philippines where we often patrolled together and pulled guard duty at the 13th Air Force Military Prison. For a short time, Clark and I were also roommates in the Philippines. On the same orders, Freddy was transferred to Greenland. I wouldn't see him again until I entered the seminary in New Orleans six years later. By that time, he and his wife, Rhoda, had four children, on their way to having eight in all.

Not long after arriving at Fort Myer, I asked one of my Hispanic friends, José Innamorato, from Laredo, Texas, if he would teach me a few Spanish words, such as "Thank you," "You're welcome," and "Please." The next day he gave me the book *Learn Spanish in 20 Easy Lessons—the Cortina Method*. I don't know why José had the book in the first place since he spoke fluent Spanish. In the book was a card advertising a set of twenty 78-rpm records as a companion to the book. When the records arrived, I spent virtually all my off-duty time listening to them, mechanically repeating the *palabras y frases*—words and sentences—in the book. In a short time, I was able to parrot such phrases as *pan y mantequilla* (bread and butter), *taza de café* (cup of coffee), *café con leche* (coffee with milk), *vasa de agua* (glass of water), *cerveza* (beer), *vino* (wine), and *pasemos el comedor* (let us go into the dining room). Note that all the phrases have to do with food and drink.

Other than carrying on elementary conversations with my Hispanic friends in the service, I had little opportunity to practice this sparkling language. However, twenty years later, I passed the foreign language mastery test in Spanish for the Ph.D. at both George Washington University and American University, both in Washington, D.C. Over the years I had maintained a modicum of reading ability in Spanish, and was able to qualify on the written tests with only minimal preparation, especially since I was allowed to use a Spanish-English dictionary during the examinations. I am quite certain that my knowledge of Latin and Greek roots also helped in my ability to do as well as I did. Though it is not common knowledge, Spanish traces its background to Greek as well as Latin. For example, *gymnasium* is Greek for "a place to exercise in the nude." In Spanish, the word is spelled *gimnasio*, and is pronounced hem NAH si oh.

One of my roles at Fort Myer was a cross between a concierge and a maître d' at the Green Room, the beer garden that personnel from all the armed services in the area frequented nightly to drink and to dance. Possibly one reason I was assigned this post more often than any of the other squad members was that I didn't drink and I couldn't dance. It was my job to make certain that everyone was in proper dress before entering and that no fights erupted between members of the different services. One night, the Army's Singing Sergeants staged a program at the Green Room, and I was the escort of Eddie Fisher, who at the time was a member of the group. He autographed a dollar bill for me, and I kept it until I arrived in Kwajalein on my way to the Philippines.

It was at Fort Myer that I had my first regular paying job as a musician. At only the second Protestant Chapel choir rehearsal, the director asked me to direct in her absence the following Sunday. I wasn't too worried about being able to handle the situation, because as a teenager I had learned the directing patterns in the gospel singing school. Not only that, Army Master Sergeant Elsie Davis, from St. Louis, Missouri, was the organist. If I had any questions, Sergeant Davis was the quintessential musician. I might add that Sgt. Davis continued to keep in touch with Margie (my wife-to-be) and me until she died, thirty years later. The choir director never returned, so the chaplain asked me to continue, with a stipend of an unbelievable $25 a month, a handsome boost to my monthly salary of $85. Here I was, a one-striper Airman Third Class (the new designation of Private First Class), fresh out of the cotton fields of Alabama, and directing the South Post Protestant Chapel Choir, composed of members from all the armed services in the area, including the Marine Corps at Henderson Hall, just around the corner from South Post, Fort Myer.

In the choir was a soprano from New Hampshire, an Army

PFC *Donovan*

sergeant serving as stenographer and receptionist for Mr. Archibald Alexander, Under Secretary of the Army at the Pentagon. This pretty, svelte, and charming young sergeant asked me what my name was. I told her it was *Danner*. Sergeant Donovan (Margie, I later learned) responded that *Danner* sounded like a last name and then asked what the boys in the barracks called me, to which I replied, "Private Danner." She remarked rather smugly that she would call me "Danny," but with her New England accent, it sounded more like *Denny* or *Dainey*. She has continued to call me Danny for almost 50 years. If she says, "Horace Danner, now let's get something straight," I know I'm in trouble, big trouble, for something like playing the piano instead of doing my share of the housework.

After Margie and I talked that night, I couldn't wait to get back to the barracks and tell my buddies that I was going to the movies with the prettiest sergeant in the Army. In later years, I would often say I *married* the prettiest sergeant in the Army, always raising a few eyebrows. She helped me raise three children, and she is still one of the prettiest women in Prince William County, Virginia.

Graduating from the Army's stenography school at Fort Benjamin Harrison in Indiana, Margie had been assigned to the Pentagon as a reward for being the top student in a class of mostly males. She was to report to Major Donald Geer, a former professor at the United States Military Institute, and had memorized the military procedure: snap to attention, salute smartly, and say "Private Donovan reporting for duty as ordered, Sir." She knocked on the major's door, expecting a brusque, "Come in." But to her surprise, the major flung the door open, motioned to a chair, and said, "Have a seat, young lady." Flustered by the informality, Margie said she was nonplused as to what to say or do. The major wanted to know what she would like to be called, to which

Margie said, "Private Donovan, Sir." Major Geer then said, "No, no. What do you *want* to be called? I mean, what does everybody else call you?" Margie replied, "The girls in the barracks call me Maggie. But, back home in New Hampshire, my family called me Sis."

The girl who was called Sis "back home in New Hampshire" had never talked on a telephone, except in a secretarial class at her high school, Pinkerton Academy, in Derry Village, New Hampshire. But now, Margie had an office to herself, with a telephone banked with an array of push buttons. Margie said she wasn't awed by the telephone; she knew she had a job to do, and simply did it. In her position, she received dignitaries from around the world. She probably saw more dignitaries in a month than most of us would see in a lifetime. She made PFC the week after she arrived, and before she could get used to having one stripe, the Army made her a corporal, and then a sergeant. Margie has often said I was attracted to her because of her rank—and, I might add, her uncanny way of managing money. On payday, after buying a few toilet articles, she sent most of her monthly salary to her mother, who Margie knew could surely use it, with eight younger siblings still at home. But Margie always kept back a little money for herself. In later years, when money was scarce, Margie was fond of saying, "When I was single, my pockets did jingle."

About a year ago, I was in physical therapy for a dislocated shoulder at Fort Belvoir hospital with another gentleman. In the course of our conversation, I related to him something of my military and academic background, and he told me his. He said that he had taught at West Point, and then was assigned to the Pentagon. Finally, we told each other our names. When he said "Donald Geer," I asked him if he had ever had a stenographer from New Hampshire by the name of Sergeant Donovan, to which he replied that he remembered Maggie quite well, recalling that she was one of the most pleasant and efficient military personnel he had ever known. I then asked if he had been an aide to General McNamara, and if his office number was across the corridor from 3E609—Margie's room number. Finally, I told him that we had already met while I was visiting Margie in her office at the Pentagon. He was quite surprised that I was her husband, that Margie and I had three grown children and six grandchildren, and that she had completed not only her bachelor's degree but her master's as well.

The Protestant chaplain at South Post Chapel was Major Harry C. Rickard, a Methodist from the Shenandoah Valley of Virginia. He already knew Margie, since she had been stationed at Fort Myer for six months before I arrived and had attended chapel services every Sunday. The chaplain heard me play for evening worship on only my first Sunday at Fort Myer, and immediately after the service, invited me to accompany him for a 12-month tour in Eniwetok, an atoll in the Marshall Islands, and the site of the atomic and hydrogen bomb tests between 1948 and 1954. Finally, I would become a chaplain's assistant. But, as had been the case with me and the Army Provost Marshal at Camp Gordon, Georgia, Chaplain Rickard was Army and I was Air Force, and even after pulling a few strings at the Pentagon, he found that regulations prohibited an Air Force enlisted member accompanying an Army officer. Though he wasn't aware of it, his wife, Reba, knew of the spark between Margie and me, and suggested that he not pursue the matter further. I have often wondered what turn my life might have taken had I not met and married this blue-eyed, Irish beauty.

Ours, I am convinced, was a most unusual courtship. Our main pastime was attending the movies at the South Post Theater. Though I had no major financial obligations, I was completely broke by the middle of the month, even with the extra pay I received from directing the choir. I would ask Margie if she wanted to see a particular movie, and if so, I could accompany her if she could pay my way. At the time, admission in military theaters cost a quarter. Once, one of my friends wanted me to pay his way to a movie, but I told him I was going with Margie. I suggested that if he came along, Margie would probably pay his fare as well, which she reluctantly did, saying later that I had left her with little choice. The armed forces ran movies before they were released to the public, and we saw Humphrey Bogart and Katharine Hepburn in *The African Queen*, and I do believe we saw all the Dean Martin and Jerry Lewis comedies.

Margie was also quite an aficionada of hot chocolate sundaes, and we kept Marriott's Hot Shoppes, just across US Route 1 from the Pentagon, in business—with Margie's money, of course. Though Interstate 395 with its ten lanes of congested traffic now separates the Pentagon from the old location of the Hot Shoppes, at that time Shirley Highway (US1) had only two lanes, and we were able to cross the highway on foot with little problem. But what was probably most unusual in our courtship was our long strolls on Sunday afternoons in Arlington National Cemetery. We observed the hourly changing of the guard at the Tomb of the Unknown Soldier, visited the Lee Mansion, and read the names of those who had been killed when the *USS Maine* was sunk by an undersea mine in Havana's harbor in 1898.

Before going for a stroll in the cemetery, Margie almost always ate the noon meal with me at the Air Force dining hall. Our serving line offered a wide choice of entrees, at least six vegetables, and a variety of breads, salads, and desserts. Even at that time, almost 50 years ago, the dining hall was on a par with any civilian cafeteria in the area. At the Army mess hall—notice *mess* instead of *dining*—she went through a chow line and took what she was served, even if it was liver with onions. The Army didn't allow choices—in fact, in the rather Spartan menu, there were no choices.

Since the Mall was just across the Potomac from Fort Myer, Margie and I either walked across Memorial Bridge or caught the military shuttle to visit the Lincoln Memorial, the Jefferson Memorial, the Smithsonian Institution, and the Washington Monument, even climbing the stairs of the 555-foot obelisk. While I was content to stay in my room and listen to my Spanish records, Margie wanted to get out and see things. She said we wouldn't always be stationed in the Nation's Capital. One of the most beautiful color snapshots I now have is one of Margie standing underneath a blossoming Japanese magnolia on the Tidal Basin, off Independence Avenue.

For Christmas in 1952, Margie gave me a silver identification bracelet. What was so remarkable is that it was the first wrapped Christmas gift I had ever received, and I was like a little child opening his first present from Santa Claus. Though my wedding band was lost, I still have the bracelet.

During the time I was stationed at Fort Myer, there were many important landmarks in history. On February 6, 1952, for example, only a week after I arrived, King George VI of England died, and the flags around Arlington National Cemetery as well as the streets of Washington were lowered to half-mast. And in January 1953, General Eisenhower was installed as the thirty-fourth president of the United States. It so happened that on Inauguration Day I was scheduled to work from 2400 to 0800 hours. I had thought that I would catch a couple of hours of sleep and then join the other onlookers on Constitution Avenue and possibly get a glimpse of my new Commander-in-Chief. But as I was ending my shift, the operations sergeant informed me that I was detailed to extra duty from 1000 hours to 1400 hours. So, on this historic event, I guarded an empty parking lot on Fort Myer. The last major event was the death of Joseph Stalin on March 5, 1953, in Moscow. Again, the flags around the cemetery and throughout Washington were lowered to half-mast.

A year after Margie and I met, we were married in the South Post Chapel, where I still directed the choir and where we had first met. Since we were both under the age of 21, both the Army and the Air Force required a notarized statement from our parents giving us permission to get married. My commander urged me not to make the mistake of marrying too young. I told him I was in love and that nothing could stop me. Since neither of our sets of

parents was able to attend the wedding, Major General McNamara, for whom Margie worked at the Pentagon, acted in her father's stead. We set the date for the first Sunday after Chaplain Rickard returned from Eniwetok. By that time, I had put on another stripe, and Margie was now a Staff Sergeant. Shortly after we married, I put on my third stripe; even so, she still outranked me. (She has always outranked—and outflanked—me.)

I will never forget our wedding day, Sunday,

Margie & I on our Wedding Day

April 12, 1953. The cherry trees and the Japanese magnolias were in full blossom, and Saturday had been a perfect day in Washington. But today, there were lowering clouds, making it the most dismal imaginable. Just before the wedding, the clouds gave way to a shower and then a downpour. Mass had just been celebrated, and the Catholic chaplain said to me, "Son, this is your last chance; you can run and still be a free man." But in spite of the pouring rain and the advice of the chaplain, Margie and I had a beautiful wedding. Don Gamache, a Catholic from Lowell, Massachusetts, was my best man. My ushers were all from my military police unit: David Clark, a Catholic, from Olean, New York; and my roommate at the time, Samuel Goodman, a Jew, from White Plains, New York. Margie's attendants were all WAC (Women's Army Corps) corporals and sergeants.[17]

Since we didn't own a car, Don Gamache took us after the reception to our apartment, the rent for which was one dollar more than my salary of $94 a month, and the apartment wasn't even air-conditioned. But the apartment did have its redeeming values. Just outside our second-floor bedroom window was a cherry tree in full bloom the day we got married. In two or three months, it was a sight to behold with luscious, red cherries hanging in clusters. That was when I knew life would be good with Margie. We climbed up the tree and picked at least a peck of cherries. She baked a cherry pie in the twinkling of an eye. With the Betty Crocker cookbook that we had received as a wedding present, she also baked a spice cake with a butter-caramel frosting.

From time to time, I drive by 1609 North Queen Street in Arlington, just to see if the place has been torn down yet. But we were close enough to North Post, Fort Myer, that we could walk to the commissary and the movies. It was in May 1953 that Margie and I saw Alan Ladd in *Shane* at the North Post theater before the movie was released to the public. Margie could also catch a shuttle from North Post to the Pentagon. And I walked to my duty station at South Post.

The amazing thing about the Air Force was that no one ever asked if I had ever eked out a living as a sharecropper's son, lived in a shack deep in the woods or in the middle of a cotton field, gone to school barefoot and hungry, moved from farm to farm, or borrowed kerosene to burn the lamp. Once an airman is issued

---

[17] WAC, and its counterparts, the Air Force WAF, and the Navy WAVE, are no longer used.

a uniform, all outward socioeconomic differences disappear. For all anyone knew, I could very well have been a banker's son from Seattle, a doctor's son from Boston, or a lawyer's son from Philadelphia. What a person makes of oneself is the only thing that counts in the military. An airman was encouraged to go to school and make the most of every opportunity. It was all the encouragement I needed, and I enrolled in psychology and sociology correspondence courses in USAFI (United States Armed Forces Institute).

Leaving the Nation's Capital

Only two months after Margie sewed on my three stripes of Airman First Class (or, buck sergeant), and three months after we were married, I received orders to report to the Military Port of Manila, on the island of Luzon. Though I lacked the fourth stripe of Staff Sergeant necessary for Margie to accompany me at government expense, she was bound and determined to be with me in the Philippines. Early on, I learned no one tells Margie what she can or can't do. She would pay her own way and, if necessary, board a freighter to Manila. Consequently, she sought and received an early release, and was discharged on her birthday, July 3, 1953.

Margie and I went by train to Boston to visit her family in New Hampshire. While there, Jim, one of her brothers (and who was later killed in a motorcycle accident in Waco, Texas, while stationed there with the Air Force), helped us tour New England, climbing Mount Washington, the windiest site in the United States. We also saw the Old Man of the Mountain, the Flume at Franconia Notch, Lake Winnipesauke, and Portsmouth Naval Yard (not for a moment having the faintest idea that our first two children would be born there). We stuck our toes in the Atlantic Ocean at Hampton Beach, near Portsmouth, the water so cold, even in the middle of summer, only the hardiest of souls can stay in more than a minute. On the rocky coast of Maine, we savored a bowl of New England clam chowder on a cold, blustery, windy day. When I need to calm my mind, I only have to remember that summer day in Maine.

After our stay in New Hampshire, we ventured to South Alabama to visit my family. Between Atlanta and Montgomery, the conductor went from coach to coach taking orders for breakfast, which would be brought on board at the next stop. Margie wasn't feeling all that well and decided to order scrambled eggs, something rather bland, she thought. What she didn't expect was that the eggs were apparently fried in bacon fat, with a nice dollop of grits on the side, a welcome sight for me, but anathema to her. While we were in Alabama, Margie became quite ill every morning. I had assumed her queasiness was from eating Southern food, such as grits, black-eyed peas and pone bread, foreign fare for a New Englander. After a few days, Mama called me aside and whispered that she was sure Margie was "expecting." My first thought was to respond—especially to Mama—"My, how in the world did *that* happen?" The weather so unbearably hot after our chilly two weeks in New England, we left Alabama sooner than we had planned and headed to Los Angeles to visit my brother Bennie and his wife, Alberta.

On the train ride from Montgomery to Los Angeles, somewhere across the barren plains of Texas, the conductor went from coach to coach, announcing that the Korean War had ended. We stayed together in Newhall, a suburb of Los Angeles, for about a week with Bennie and Alberta. Even as we were on the way to Newhall from the train station, I began to have my doubts that Margie and Bennie would get along, especially when Bennie pointed out to us the San Bernadino Mountains. Being used to the truly majestic White Mountains of New Hampshire, Margie retorted in true New England humor, "Yeah, you can see right over them." They gave us the grand tour of Los Angeles and the San Joaquin Valley. I took a picture of Margie picking an orange, the first time that either of us had seen oranges while still on the tree. They had invited Margie to stay with them until she could obtain passage to Manila. Before she could do so, however, interpersonal problems developed between Margie and Bennie. Although four months pregnant, she returned to New Hampshire to live with her parents while I was overseas. Not feeling secure or safe at Bennie and Alberta's home, she stayed with a female friend she had cultivated until she left California.

After our time together in Newhall, Margie stayed with me for a week in the guest quarters at Park Air Force Base, near San

Francisco, until a few days before I sailed. She would have stayed longer, but she had to return to Los Angeles for an appointment with a gynecologist. I sailed on the *USNS Barrett* from San Francisco on August 20, 1953, with the military bands playing all the service songs, such as the Navy's "Anchors Aweigh," and the Air Force's "Off We Go into the Wild Blue Yonder." There was a lot of hugging, kissing, and crying, as the soldiers, airmen, sailors, and marines pulled away from the embraces of their wives and sweethearts.

Although Margie wasn't there for me to kiss and embrace, I cried unabashedly along with the others. As the ship was about to sail, the mood changed palpably, as the bands shifted to playing the service hymns, beginning with the Air Force's "Lord, guard and guide the men who fly/ Through the great spaces of the sky;/ Be with them traversing the air/ In darkening storms or sunshine fair." As the troop ship maneuvered under the Golden Gate Bridge, we could still make out the lingering strains of the last hymn—the Navy's "Eternal Father, strong to save,/ Whose arm doth bound the restless wave,/ Who bidd'st the mighty ocean deep/ Its own appointed limits keep,/ O hear us when we cry to thee/ For those in peril on the sea." A week later, we docked in Honolulu, where the ship was greeted by a musical gala of the military bands playing and the islanders strumming ukuleles and performing the hula. I had never felt so proud to be serving my country.

We docked for 24 hours and were given shore leave. My Fort Myer friends, John Bawsel and David Clark, and I ventured downtown, where we had a steak dinner at Ciros Restaurant. Although I had no more money than the others, I paid for everybody's meal, as Bawsel, who lives in nearby Richmond, Virginia, reminded me recently. It was on Hotel Street that I witnessed slums even worse than in Southeast Washington, D.C. The streets of Washington hadn't been paved with gold, and the streets of Honolulu weren't strewn with orchid petals. I might add that Honolulu has homeless, wandering men and women as well as soup kitchens, just as in Washington, D.C., and other large cities. As soon as we debarked, little Polynesian children came rushing up, begging for money. This wasn't how it was supposed to be! During my Air Force career, I would return to Honolulu on numerous occasions. And only once did I ever visit Waikiki. When I was sent to Hawaii, I always went on assignment, not on vacation. Anyway, to me, Waikiki looks better in the tourist brochures than it does in real life.

A few days after leaving Honolulu, we crossed the International Date Line. As we crossed the 180° meridian on Friday, September 4, 1953, we entered the Domain of the Golden Dragon. The ship's captain called us all on deck, where we had a simple ceremony. The crew then passed out individualized certificates that indicated that, in the flash of a second, we had indeed gone from Friday to Saturday and were now in the Eastern Hemisphere. I still have the elaborate certificate, embossed with mermaids.

Clark Air Force Base and University of the Philippines

We continued steaming toward Guam over the vast expanse of the Pacific. At Guam, we docked for 36 hours, and I looked up a cousin, Charles Brock—Ruth Brock's eldest son—who was stationed with the Navy about ten miles north of the port. I didn't know the way, but I hitchhiked and kept asking for directions with each ride. After spending a few hours with Charles, he checked out a jeep and drove me back to Agana, where I boarded the ship again. From Guam, it was on to Kwajalein Atoll, where we were required to surrender American currency and coins for military script, in an effort to thwart blackmarketing once we arrived in Manila. Consequently, I had to give up the dollar bill autographed by Eddie Fisher back at Fort Myer, Virginia. And then it was on to our destination, Manila, arriving September 13, 1953, just in time for the monsoon season. It rained continually from September to April, and often continuously for 24 hours a day.

Margie and I promised to write each other every day and append "P.S., I love you," the name of a popular song at the time. During my 17 months in the Philippines, I missed writing several letters, especially when I was in the field, and often forgot to add the postscript. Margie, however, never failed to write every day and always wrote the agreed-upon note. Though I still can't believe I actually did it, I made suggestions on her sentence structure and circled any misspelled words and returned the letters for correction. I operated in a "revise and resubmit" mode. We now laugh about my pedantic crudeness, but it wasn't funny to her at the time, being separated by 12,000 miles and getting her grammar critiqued and her spelling checked. I should add there was once a lull in her writing, and it is because of something I am ashamed to admit. I nonchalantly wrote and told her that I had smoked a cigarette and that my unit had toured the San Miguel Brewery in Manila where I had drunk beer. She immediately responded that the letter she was writing would be the last until she heard from me that I had given up my sinful, dirty habits. Of course, I wrote back and told her that I had learned from my debauchery and was now clean again. Even in the meantime, she continued to write. She always dated her letters on the back so that I would know which one to open first inasmuch as I usually received seven letters at a time, the mail coming by surface rather than air in those days.

Just outside the main gate of the sprawling, 125-mile perimeter of Clark Air Force Base was Mount Arayat[18] and to the west was 9,000-foot Mount Pinatubo, which erupted a few years ago, covering the base with ash and eventually causing it to cease military operations. Mount Arayat is distinct in that it was concaved, like a giant bowl had been pushed down into the top. Attaching a religious significance to almost everything, the Filipinos declared that the mountain was where Noah's Ark landed. The mountain was also a bastion for the Huks,[19] a group of communist-led rebels who were extremely active the entire time I was stationed there. In fact, the primary mission of our security unit was to safeguard the perimeter of the base as well as key communications facilities from infiltration by the Huks. In conjunction with the PCs (Philippine Constabulary Police), we patrolled the perimeter with M-20s, or armored personnel carriers, armed with quad50s. It was on one of these patrols that I witnessed a Huk being severed at his midriff by the machine-gun fire of a PC. It is not a sight I wish to see again. I also don't want to ever see again the living remains of a man who had accidentally stepped on a land mine that had been left from World War II.

Adjoining Clark was a village of Negritos, literally "little blacks." The Negritos migrated to the Philippines many centu-

[18] The name of Noah's landing is Ararat. The name of the mountain in the Philippines is spelled as I remembered hearing it. I called the Embassy of the Philippines in Washington, where the spelling was confirmed.

ries ago; they are true pyg-
mies, with an adult height
of under five feet, about
that of a 13-year-old
American boy. Their small
size, black skin, and kinky
hair make them look en-
tirely different from other
Filipinos. Foraging for
food, they roamed the
mountains and valleys surrounding the base. I spent
many Sunday afternoons
in their village, clowning
around with the children
and the children's mon-

With the Negritos

keys. The young men tried with little success to teach me to shoot
with the bow and arrow. In some of our field exercises, the Air
Force hired the men of the village to be the "enemy." It came as
no surprise to either them or us that we were always captured.
They also helped us to become more adept at camouflage.

While stationed in the Philippines, I continued my studies at
University of the Philippines, studying anthropology and Philippine folklore. Though I took the initiative to attend the university, the Air Force was most supportive. On the nights I had class
but was standing lone guard on Lily Hill or FM Hill or securing
the main gate with as many as seven others, the shift sergeant
would send a replacement for me as well as a jeep for me to drive
to class, which was held on base.

After a few months of juggling classes and a shift schedule, I
succumbed to letting the provost marshal's office know I could
type. Until I returned to the States, I was chief clerk in the Office of the Provost Marshal, where I reviewed, corrected, and
helped type the incident reports completed by the security police-
men. Since I had my hands full correcting the grammar, spelling,
and sentence structure in the reports, I no longer had the insatiable urge to correct Margie's letters.

An incident I am reluctant to relate happened in the Philippines, but it's necessary to round out my memoir. I was implicated

[19] *Huk* is short for Tagalog *Hukbong Magapapalayong Bayan*, or People's Liberation Army.

in an alleged offense, for which I felt that I was completely inno-cent—innocent, at least, in my own mind. The Air Force had other ideas. Two airmen and I, a sergeant, were charged with vio-lating Article 135 of the Uniformed Code of Military Justice (UCMJ), "disobeying a written order." The other two freely ad-mitted their involvement and were duly charged. But, while work-ing at the Pentagon, I had bought my own copy of the UCMJ and spent many hours reading its articles of offenses as well as its pro-visions. Based upon my knowledge of the UCMJ, I adamantly re-fused to sign the charges, declaring that we were being charged *ex post facto*; in other words, the so-called offense occurred before the particular regulation we were charged with was promulgated in order to prevent future incidents of this type. The military's trial lawyer said, however, that even in the absence of a regula-tion, we all should have known better. Although I wasn't person-ally involved, I was charged because I was the ranking person present when the incident occurred.

The incident involved the 5th Air Force commanding general's plane. The general had flown in from Tokyo to meet with the commander of the 13th Air Force, headquartered at Clark. On the midnight shift, an airman third class (one-striper) was posted at his plane to insure no unauthorized access. An air-man second class (two-striper) and I (a three-striper) were mak-ing the rounds of the guard posts, making sure that all the guards were alert and bringing them hot coffee. While chatting with the guard, my partner said he had never seen inside a general's plane. Although none of us were on the access list, he told the guard he wanted to look inside. When he tried to close the door to the plane, it wouldn't close. Consequently, he placed the ramp ladder against the door to secure it, and we went on our merry way as though all was well. About two hours after our shift ended, the guard was called in, who then implicated my patrol partner and me. We found out later that the cost for repairing the door amounted to less than $25, but it upset the general to the point that he demanded that all of us be held accountable.

Prior to being indicted, I had never been so much as even "chewed out," as the military expression goes. At the time, Margie was expecting our first child, halfway across the world, in New Hampshire. Margie had regarded me as Prince Perfect—since when she met me, I didn't smoke or drink, and I played the piano for chapel besides—I didn't think that she could handle my committing even an innocent peccadillo, much less an offense for which I could have been confined. If convicted, I stood a good chance of receiving what was commonly called six, six, and a kick, meaning six months of confinement, six months of two-thirds forfeiture of pay, and a BCD, or a Bad Conduct Discharge, also known as the Big Chicken Dinner. I had always read my Bible daily, prayed every night—on my knees—and sang in the choir (or directed it). Now, with the impending court-martial, like my sister Ellie Mae (when in 1943, she warned me of the wrath to come in the raging fires of Hell), I stayed in a constant state of devotion and prayer. I prayed that the Lord would take me home while I was still a free man. I had no appetite, and had to force myself to eat. My weight dropped from 150 pounds to a mere 110. I made a promise to God that night: if He delivered me from this ordeal, I would never fail to give Him credit.

Two nights before the slated court-martial, I was scheduled to pull duty as assistant desk sergeant, monitoring by radio a crew of over a hundred security personnel, both military police and Filipino guards. As I was lacing up my boots in my room in order to begin the midnight shift, a piercing pain jabbed me in the abdomen. In spite of the pain, I finished dressing, and reported for duty. About two o'clock in the morning, the pain became so intense I couldn't concentrate or give a coherent response on the radio. The desk sergeant, S/Sgt Anthony J. Bachigalupo, from New York City, said, "Danner, go back in the armory and lay down for a while." Jokingly, he continued, "I know you're just trying to get out of work anyway." The pain subsided after about an hour, and I returned to my job as the radio dispatcher. I finished the shift, and that day being the first of the month, March 1, 1954, I stood in line to get paid.

I didn't go to sick call at the prescribed hour of 0700, as I wasn't in a great deal of pain at the time. But about noon, the pain shot through me like a rifle. Almost doubled over, I trudged through jungle overgrowth to the hospital, about a mile from the barracks. Perspiring profusely, I finally arrived and reported to the sick call desk; the medic told me I would have to wait till after the dependents had been seen, which would be about two hours. All I could do was lie down in the adjoining hallway, moaning and groaning, and writhing in pain. Hardly before I could get straightened out on the floor, a doctor noticed me and immediately asked the medic on duty rather abruptly, "What's this man doing lying on the floor, of all places?" The medic replied rather cursorily, "Oh, he missed regular sick call. Claims he's got a bellyache. We're gonna make him wait till dependents' sick call's over, just to see if it's for real."

Dr. McFall, as I later learned was his name, ordered the medics to help me into the examining room on the double. He then pressed down on my belly and said, "Prepare this man for immediate surgery." I had acute appendicitis. After being prepped and sedated, I was wheeled into the operating room around 6 p.m., and Dr. McFall said, "Sergeant Danner, I'm going to make a little . . . ." The next thing I knew it was the next day.

When the mail clerk brought me my usual seven letters from Margie, I asked rather groggily, "How's my court-martial going?" As if he were passing the time of day, he remarked, "Court-martial? What court-martial?" Not in the mood to be kidding around, I said, "My court-martial! The one everybody's been talking about!" Rather nonchalantly, he replied, "Oh, yeah, now I remember. The old man said to tell you to take it easy; they dropped the charges on you."

I later found that the special court-martial was reduced to a summary, which carries a maximum penalty of only thirty days' confinement instead of the maximum of six months with a special. Both airmen were fined a mere $25.00—to pay for the damage caused—and the incident was expunged from their records. Before I left the hospital, they were already back in the States; in fact, their rotation was delayed because of the court-martial. Since the charges were dropped on me, I was glad I didn't have to face them again. I might have had to go back to the hospital for more than just appendicitis.

Two or three days after the operation, Dr. McFall told me that if I'd had to wait for two hours to be seen, I would probably have died of a ruptured appendix. Until I left the Philippines, I asked for Dr. McFall when I had to go to sick call, and I never let him forget how thankful I was for his concern—and for the successful operation!

Shortly after I was discharged from the hospital and was

recuperating in the barracks, I received a telegram that I was the father of a baby girl, named Patricia Ann, born at the Portsmouth Naval Hospital, Portsmouth, New Hampshire, on March 9, 1954. When I went to the orderly room to thank the commander for sending me the news about the charges being dropped, I told him I was a proud new father. He immediately gave me two weeks' recuperation leave and sent me in a staff car to Camp John Hay (a military rest and recuperation base) in Baguio, the summer capital of the Philippines, as well as the site of the Philippine Military Academy. Like Mrs. Moore in the fourth grade when she said she was certain I had appendicitis and drove me home from school, the commander said that in my condition, I didn't need to be bounced about on a rickety Filipino jitney.

At Baguio, high in the majestic mountains of north-central Luzon, I was able to rest and relax in the cool, refreshing air and stroll among the towering pine trees. I also got to drink real milk. (At Clark, the milk had been reconstituted.) Also while at Baguio, I enjoyed a one-day excursion to the South China Sea and rode waves 10 to 15 feet high. On the way back to Clark, I stopped by Dagupan City to view the Lingayen Gulf of the South China Sea where, only nine years before, General MacArthur had landed to liberate the island of Luzon, and where on the beach, a monument is erected to him and his liberation forces. Many of the coconut palms lining the beach were nothing more than shreds, from the mortars fired during the war. Knowing that I was innocent and with the court-martial behind me, as well as being a new father, I had begun to live again.

Only a few weeks after my recuperation leave, our military police unit returned to Dagupan City on a training expedition, as it was called officially. It turned out to be more like a beach party, and at age 21, I tasted beer for the second time. Not only did I taste it, I drank a whole can; unlike the smooth taste of San Miguel brew, I hated the taste of Budweiser, and wondered why anyone could drink anything so bitter.

Memories of Dagupan City and the Lingayen Gulf are quite pleasant, however. We brought tons of food, including fresh fruit and blocks of ice. As soon as we arrived on the beach, dozens of the most beautiful little boys and girls came rushing up to us, ask-

John Bawsel, from Richmond, Virginia

Filipino Children on the Beach

ing for a centavo. We gave them more than a few centavos; we gave them oranges and apples—and ice water. I was pouring the ice water and had planned on giving each child a cup of the water. But as soon as I gave a cupful to the first of the children, they took a sip and passed it on to one of their friends, not acceptable hygiene, but beautiful camaraderie. I have dozens of pictures of the children, and each time I look at them, I see the beauty of a child with so little sharing all that he had. And any one of the boys would gladly shin a palm tree there on the beach and bring a coconut down to us.

Unlike one of my friends who joined the camera club so that he could tour the island (even though he didn't have a camera), I had never relished seeing the sights of the Philippines on my own. Because of the Huk insurrection, travel throughout the island was severely restricted, and we were advised not to travel alone. I was content to stay in the barracks and study on my three days off, after working for nine days straight. But I made a new friend, Gerald Hertzfeldt, who insisted I get out of the barracks and visit

[20] Jai alai, Basque for "merry festival," is a game similar to handball. The ball, called a *pelota*, is harder than a golf ball and travels 150 miles an hour.

Manila, 60 miles south of Clark. To save money, we stayed at the military port. One of the highlights of our trips to Manila was attending a jai alai game.[20] We also enjoyed a juicy steak in one of the fine restaurants overlooking Manila Bay. The sun setting in the Pacific was a glorious sight, marred only by the half-sunken hulks of American and Japanese warships rusting in the harbor, from World War II. I have been told that today, the hulks have been salvaged and that the bay is now even a more beautiful sight to behold.

One of the ways I coped with being away from Margie for 18 months was to check out a book from the base library every two weeks. It seems that the due date for the book always came around too quickly, before I had time to finish it. So, I would check it out again. I continued checking out books to make the time go by faster.

On January 31, 1955, seventeen months after arriving in the Philippines, I was awakened before reporting to duty and told I had only a day to put my affairs in order before returning to the States. The first thing on the agenda was to visit the base office of University of the Philippines, since I was due to graduate the following month in Quezon City, just before my scheduled departure. Since I had already completed the requirements, I graduated *in absentia,* and my degree was mailed to me at my home in Alabama.

I had arrived in the Philippines on a troop ship, but I left the islands by Flying Tiger, a contract airline serving the military. We departed Clark on February 1, 1955, and then landed on Kwajalein,[21] an extremely narrow atoll—covering only six square miles—that seemed to appear out of nowhere in the vast Pacific, to convert our military script back to U.S. money. It was a grand feeling to hold such a simple thing as a thin dime between my fingers again. It was American, and it felt good. On February 2, Lt. Howard Short, the pilot of Flight 352-1, issued us all a Certificate of Membership in the Ancient and Royal Order of International Dateliners. Instead of skipping a day as we had when we crossed the International Dateline heading toward the Philippines, we now had two Wednesdays. After spending a day and night in Hawaii, and still dressed in a tropical uniform, I landed at Travis Air Force Base, California, on February 4, my birthday. I was 22, and the father of a baby girl I hadn't yet seen. Even

---

[21] It was at Kwajalein 17 months before that I had to surrender the dollar bill Eddie Fisher autographed.

though wearing a short-sleeved shirt on this blustery, cold, but sunny day, I was thankful to be back in the States and on my way to see Margie and Patty.[22]

Since I had no time to write Margie I was coming home, and since her family didn't have a phone, she had no way of knowing when I would be arriving at Logan Airport, in Boston. So, I placed a long-distance collect call from California to Francis Gates, the neighbor who lived across the road from Margie. Meeting me at the airport the next day, Margie had Patty with her, and we planned to stay in a hotel in Boston overnight. Margie had shown my picture to Patty every day, calling me "Daddy." When Patty saw me, that sweet, little, darling girl who had never even so much as cried, began to yell and scream. Not wanting to disturb the other hotel guests, we checked out of the hotel in a hurry and left on a rickety train from Boston to Lawrence, Massachusetts, just south of the New Hampshire state line. It was there that Margie's brother Harvey (pronounced HIGH vi by Margie) picked us up in the 1954 two-toned Chevrolet that Margie had bought in anticipation of my coming home. Snow-blanketed New England was a welcome change from the hot, monsoon season of the Philippines. While I was in the Philippines, Margie had knitted matching wool, reindeer-design sweaters for the three of us.

Back Home in the States

My new assignment was Barksdale Air Force Base, Louisiana, near Shreveport, where I was an aide to the Provost Marshal of 2nd Air Force, Strategic Air Command. The day I reported in, the first sergeant asked the new group of ten or so men how many of us were married. I raised my hand. Then, he asked how many of those married could type. I was the only one who raised a hand. And that's how I got the job as aide to the Second Air Force Provost Marshal. Though I hadn't been promoted while in the Philippines, I made staff sergeant only a month after being assigned to Barksdale. My main job was as liaison between the Office of Special Investigations (OSI) and the Command. Toward the end of my four-year tour in August 1955, I wanted to return to college, as I was eligible to study under the GI Bill. I wasn't certain

---

[22] In 1955, Hawaii was a territory, not a state.

what I wanted to study, however, and with Margie expecting our second child, I knew it was no time for indecision.

So I reenlisted for another four years, and asked to be transferred to Grenier Air Force Base, Manchester, New Hampshire, to be close to Margie's home. On March 22, 1956, our first son, Jerry, was born at Portsmouth Naval Hospital, the same hospital where Patty had been born two years earlier. Margie had wanted to name him Horace Gerald Danner, Jr., but I made

Margie, Patty, Jerry & I

a scene in the hospital, exclaiming that I didn't want any son of mine tagged with either Horace or Junior. The vital statistics lady from York County, Maine, said, "Well, you could call him "The Second." And that's what we tagged him with. Although the Portsmouth Naval Base is in New Hampshire, the maternity section of the hospital juts into the boundary of Kittery, Maine; consequently the birth was registered in Maine. It would be seven years before our next son was born, and Margie agreed that Stephen Alan Danner had a nice sound to it. I had always liked *Alan* after seeing Alan Ladd in *Shane*.

Not long after we arrived at Grenier, Margie's childhood friend, Jennie Lumly, a Catholic, planned to be married and asked that I sing Schubert's *Ave Maria* at her wedding at Saint Thomas Aquinas Catholic Church, in Derry. When I purchased the music, I found there were four sets of words: English, German, French, and Latin. I assumed I would sing it in English, since it was the only language I knew. But Dorothy Weatherbee, a good Catholic and the organist who played for the Protestant chapel service and accompanied the choir I directed—and who also played for the Catholic service—said I must sing it in Latin, or the wedding wouldn't be valid. She said I couldn't help it for being a Baptist. So she set out to teach me the Latin version. It was good that she coached me on the Latin version since I have been asked to sing the song at a number of Catholic funerals and weddings in the years since.

Though I had been trained as a military policeman, I didn't have the heart of one. At Bolling Air Force Base, in Washington, I had been turned down as a member of the town patrol because I was so small. At both Clark and Barksdale, I had mainly worked in the provost marshal's office. Consequently, throughout my seven years in the Air Force, I had never been fully tested, or "baptized of fire" until just before midnight in late January 1957. My shift was just getting off duty. A father had come on base from nearby Manchester to meet his son, a young lieutenant, who was flying a jet in from Maxwell Air Force Base, Alabama. They had just left the main gate, headed down the steep hill toward the city, when we at the guard office heard an awful crashing sound. Though my shift was just ending, three of us were detailed to investigate.

First on the scene, I discovered bodies lying all over the road, and I immediately began a triage to determine who could possibly be saved. The father's car had crashed head-on into another. The father was killed as well as several others in the other car. I rode in the ambulance with the lieutenant to the hospital, and was the one who had to tell him his father didn't make it. Four hours after our shift ended, we were released from duty, and I had 12 miles to go before reaching our apartment in Derry Village. I finally arrived, splattered with blood, and began to tell Margie what had happened. The thoughts of the lieutenant losing his father coupled with my being safe in Margie's arms with our two children sleeping peacefully were hard to take. In about a week, the City of Manchester as well as the New Hampshire State Police wrote letters to the military commander, commending us for our taking charge of the accident scene, and doing it so professionally. I continued my contact with Lieutenant Lovering (or, Lovinger), visiting him in the hospital until he was well enough to return to uniform. My military friends said I could have been a chaplain as well as a policeman.

Only two or three months after the accident, we moved from our Derry Village apartment to base housing at Grenier. And every Saturday night we visited Margie's parents in East Hampstead, having the usual Boston baked beans and brown bread. On this particular night, we were on our way back to our apartment at Grenier the day after a snowstorm, and the roads were banked five or six feet with plowed and drifted snow. As we crested the hill at Grenier, where the fatal accident had happened, I must have hit an ice spot. I lost control of the car, skidding into a snowbank. All the way down the hill, we careened from one snowbank to the other. Luckily, everyone else apparently was at home where they belonged on this New England winter night because there was not another car on the hill. That night we said a special prayer of thanks for our safe arrival. Our four guardian angels were working overtime that night.

One of my duties at Grenier was sergeant of the honor guard, which participated in funerals for Air Force personnel in the state of New Hamsphire and in northcentral Massachusetts. I was in charge of the firing party and was the one who presented the folded American flag to the next of kin. After a funeral in Massachusetts, the Veterans of Foreign Wars (VFW) held a drinking party at their lodge, to which we were practically ordered to attend. I told the driver that he would have to wait until we got back to Grenier for him to drink his beer. The VFW members didn't have any problem with the driver not drinking, but they insisted that I take a drink. I told them politely that I didn't drink alcohol, that I would have a soft drink. That didn't satisfy the old salts; they wanted the sergeant in charge of the military detail to drink to their deceased comrade. After I told them three times I didn't drink, one of the veterans wanted to know what kind of sergeant I was anyway. That was all it took for Staff Sergeant Robert McKenna, the lead sergeant of the firing party. Sergeant McKenna squared off with the veteran and told him in no uncertain terms, "Sergeant Danner is our squad leader, and he's a sergeant because he stands up for what he believes." The veteran backed off, and Sergeant McKenna earned his stripes that day for coming to my defense.

To supplement my staff sergeant's salary at Grenier, I directed the base chapel choir, set pins by hand at the bowling alley, worked in the Base Exchange, and worked part-time in a direct mailing company in Manchester, where we labeled, bundled, and mailed advertising circulars. It was a grueling routine; when I finally got to bed, I felt I had been drubbed.

Though I played the piano for Sunday School and directed the Protestant Chapel Choir, I still felt that my musical talents could be better utilized. So, after being a military policeman for seven years, I told Margie that I had "heard the call" to enter the ministry. Margie enthusiastically supported my decision, even though her father insisted on knowing how I planned to support a wife and two young children. I remember his rather stern advice, "You don't give up security for insecurity." In my usual cocksure manner, I told him I had already checked with personnel and learned I was eligible to receive the GI Bill and that we would all be just fine. So, on August 30, 1958, I reverted to reserve status after seven years and *one day* of active duty.

Margie and I left Grenier Air Force Base, after my directing the choir for the last time, and as soon as chapel services were over on the first Sunday of September 1958. Chaplain Chester L. Smith requested that the congregation sing a valedictory hymn, the comforting words of which we would need only too soon: "Be not dismayed whate'er betide,/ God will take care of you./ Beneath His wings of love abide,/ God will take care of you."

Be Not Dismayed Whate'er Betide

We drove our '56 Chevrolet with two preschool children—Patty and Jerry—first to Alabama, and then on to Louisiana, where I would enroll in New Orleans Baptist Theological Seminary, to study church music and religious education. We had an apartment on campus, 4543B Seminary Place. After two months without receiving a check, I visited the Veterans Administration (VA) office on St. Charles Street in New Orleans, with the grand hopes that I would be issued a check on the spot for two months. Alas, after the counselor had gone over my records, I learned that I had missed the GI Bill by one day. The Grenier Air Force Base personnel office in New Hampshire had led me to believe that I had three years after my discharge to enroll in a program of study, but the VA said I had to begin school within three years of my *first* discharge. In appealing the VA's decision, I learned the Air Force would have discharged me early enough to begin a program within three years if I had so requested. If only I had listened to my father-in-law when he asked how I was going to support my family!

I trudged back to our apartment and told Margie the outcome of my visit to the VA office. I told her we would have to leave the seminary, and I would reenlist in the Air Force. The Air Force allowed reenlistment at one's last rank for 90 days, and that period would soon be over. She would hear none of it, saying that if the Lord had called me into the ministry, He would surely provide a way. And provide He did. "No matter what may be the test,/ Lean, weary one, upon His breast."

The very next week, the Reverend Seab Hayes, a pastor from Patterson, Louisiana, in St. Mary's Parish—Cajun bayou country, 105 miles due west of New Orleans—visited the seminary, looking for someone to direct the church's music activities. We served First Baptist Church of Patterson for three years. Most of the church members were offshore oil workers and their families from East Texas, and those Texans had generous hearts. The church members would often invite us for the weekend, and when they did, it was Texas-style outdoor barbecue, with grilled Gulf shrimp on the side.

We would leave our apartment on the seminary campus three hours before Sunday School started, with Patty and Jerry still in their pajamas. We then crossed the Huey P. Long Bridge over the Mississippi, and drove on US10 along the bayous to Patterson, passing through such French-sounding towns as Houma, Paradis, Des Allemands, and Thibodaux. Another town, Raceland, was just as Cajun, even with its English name. At Raceland, Domino has giant sugar refineries, and we once toured one of them. It was quite educational to see how blackened sugar cane entered the refinery at one end and came out as granulated sugar on the other. I say "blackened," inasmuch as the cane would be cut and left lying in the fields for the husks to dry. Then the farmers set fire to the husks, in order to cut down on the labor of stripping cane, as we small cane farmers used to do in Alabama. I was educated in another way too. For years, I had thought that brown sugar was that which hadn't been fully refined, but found that a syrup is poured over the granulated, white sugar to give it its brown color and soft texture.

On the 105-mile trip to church, we sometimes played a game of how many brown pelicans and snowy egrets we would see along the bayous, bordered by cypresses draped with Spanish moss. Occasionally, we would also see local fishermen paddling pirogues on the bayous. About ten miles before arriving at Patterson, as we crossed Atchafalaya River at Morgan City—the shrimp capital of the world—Margie began dressing the children in their Sunday clothes. In Morgan City, Santa comes by shrimp boat. In the median of the main thoroughfare sits a shrimp boat that's decorated with lights and poinsettias at Christmas. Morgan City is home to the annual blessing of the shrimp fleet on Labor Day weekend. With the advent of the offshore oil industry, the event is now termed Louisiana Shrimp & Petroleum Festival.

On those Sundays when Margie and the children couldn't go with me, I caught the Greyhound bus from Canal Street; the bus left New Orleans at 6:30 am, getting me into Patterson a whole two hours before Sunday School began, giving me time to freshen up and get a cup of coffee at the pastor's house. The problem with using the bus was that I had to wait until midnight for the return bus from Houston to New Orleans. Getting up to go to Air Force Reserves the next morning was well-nigh impossible. Many times, I would tell Margie that I just couldn't make it to Reserves, that I had to get some sleep; I knew, however, that young children have to eat, and there was also rent to pay. Tuition, however, was free, thanks to the support of the Southern Baptist Convention.

It doesn't sound like much now, but the $25 check we received at the end of the evening service would buy our groceries for the coming week. The next day, we would go grocery shopping, buying five pounds of hamburger and two boxes of breaded shrimp at Schweggman's Supermarket on Chef Menteur Highway, or, translated from French, "Head Liar Highway." With her New England ingenuity, and with good-grade hamburger costing only 25 cents a pound, Margie provided delicious and nourishing meals for our family of four. She invented a lot of ways to serve ground beef.

If my missing out on the GI Bill wasn't enough, the Army discovered upon auditing Margie's financial record while she was stationed at the Pentagon that she had been overpaid $22 for separate rations. The Army demanded full payment by return mail. If we'd had that amount, we would've felt we were millionaires. So I wrote, explaining our financial situation. The Army allowed us to pay two dollars a month until the debt was repaid.

In spite of our lack of money, Margie found a way to make each of the children's birthdays special. The children were always given a small present, and Margie baked a cake. As they became older, she baked the cakes in special designs to celebrate their activities and achievements. Jerry's request was for a cherry pie instead of cake, and in later years, when Stephen came along, his request was for Boston cream pie, which Margie could make in the twinkling of an eye.

Classes met at the seminary from Tuesday through Friday to accommodate ministerial students having pastorates as far away as Mississippi and northern Louisiana; the Air Force Reserves allowed me to put in my time in the Air Force Office of Special Investigations (OSI) in New Orleans on Monday mornings.

Most of the seminary students were supported by their home churches or their parents, or by their wives, many of whom taught in Jefferson Parish Public Schools—Louisiana being the only state in the country to call counties *parishes*. But Margie and I had no home church to support us, since I had served only military chapels. And we had absolutely no financial support from our families. But we did receive a Air Force check each month for the days I served with the OSI. While we didn't receive any financial support from our own families, Vallie did keep Patty supplied with the most beautiful dresses she had made herself. Vallie guessed Patty's size, and the dresses always fit perfectly.

When I first enrolled at the seminary, I obtained a secretarial job for a professor of New Testament, Dr. Frank Stagg. I didn't know shorthand, and many times, I couldn't read my hieroglyphics and had to ask him to repeat what he had already dictated. I am sure, at times, he was exasperated with me, but he exemplified the patience of Job. When I found that I had missed out on the GI Bill, I asked Dr. Stagg if Margie could take over my job while I looked for better-paying work outside the seminary. When he learned that Margie had graduated from the Army's stenography school and had served as a stenographer for the Under Secretary of the Army at the Pentagon, he was elated. With our children in the seminary's laboratory preschool, Margie also enrolled as a special student in theology, ecclesiology, education, and music. I say "special," because only those with college degrees were classified as regular students. Margie's grades often excelled those of the ministerial students. More important than the grades, however, was the confidence she gained.

Around Thanksgiving, I was able to land a job at Sears, only two or three blocks from the seminary, selling boys' clothing. But the prospects of our first Christmas in New Orleans seemed bleak. Even with the $25 weekly check from the church, it was almost impossible to make enough to live on. One day, only a couple of weeks before Christmas, Patty, then four years old, was with me at Sears, when we passed the bicycle display. I was hoping she wouldn't notice them, since she had already mentioned that the other children on campus had bicycles. But notice them she did! After she looked at two or three of them, she showed me the one she liked the best, but then said rather nonchalantly, "But if I don't get one, I'll know that Santa just had to share." She got the bicycle, but it took Margie reading the instructions, and Donald Coppedge, a fellow seminarian and our upstairs neighbor, and me until 3 o'clock in the morning assembling it.

Since I had come to the seminary from the military instead of directly from college, I hadn't needed a book satchel. But at the seminary, all the students carried their books and music in satchels. I carried mine in my arms. Shortly before Christmas, we were sitting at the dinner table when Patty, who was always in charge, told Jerry, "We are not supposed to let Daddy know he's getting something for Christmas to put his books and music in." Hearing her innocent remark was my Christmas present; I could very well have done without the satchel.

After the Christmas rush, I was offered a 30-hour-a-week job as cashier, which I held for the entire time we were at the seminary. So, I had three jobs: the church, the Air Force Reserves, and Sears. Amazingly, I was never ill for the entire time we were at the seminary; however, Margie came close to dying of viral meningitis at the Veterans Administration Hospital in New Orleans. At the same time, both children had the measles. "All you may need He will provide,/ God will take care of you./ Nothing you ask will be denied,/ God will take care of you."

Margie and I had absolutely no one on whom we could call for help, except Vallie, who at that time had never traveled outside the state of Alabama. But she caught a Greyhound from

Dothan, and came to cook and take care of Patty and Jerry while I worked at Sears, served the church, and visited Margie in the hospital. The crisis over, we drove Vallie back to Alabama and continued northward on to Margie's home. In the middle of August, we left the sweltering, humid New Orleans climate for a restful and even chilly two weeks in New Hampshire. Before we left Louisiana, one of the church members at Patterson slipped me two $20 bills to use in case we needed some extra cash. He didn't explicitly say he was giving the money to me, but he didn't say anything about my repaying him. We were on the way back to New Orleans from New Hampshire, when somewhere in Kentucky, I told Margie I had $40 in my billfold and that we could stop and treat ourselves and the kids to a hot meal in a restaurant—there were no McDonald's in 1960. Her response reveals the kind of person she was and continues to be. She said we had food in the car, and that I would return the money as soon as we arrived in Patterson. I am confident Charles Newkirk never thought he would see his $40 again.

I might add that we could have never survived without Margie's attention to money. If we needed something, my first inclination was to buy it and pay for it later, like Patty's bicycle. But Margie had three principles for buying just about anything: First, the article had to be truly needed; second, save up the money to pay for it in cash; and last, buy it only after it had been marked down at least three times. With her managing the money, we never had a past-due bill, and our credit has always been such that we could get any type of loan we needed, even today.

Though I had never really liked to fish—even as a boy—I had always wanted to take my children fishing, just like my father had taken me to catch our dinner on Pea River. So, early one Saturday morning, 3-year-old Jerry and I went fishing on a bayou close to Chalmette, only a quarter mile from the Mississippi, with big ships easing up the river to New Orleans. I didn't know we needed a license or that there was a size limit. Jerry and I had caught several small fish when a game warden drove up. All excited, Jerry held up our catch and exclaimed, "Mister, look at all the little fish we caught." It was at that moment the size-limit sign loomed in front of me, larger than life. I truly hadn't noticed the sign before, but after the stone-faced warden pointed it out to me, I wondered how I could have possibly missed it.

All the time that Jerry was showing off the little fish, pointing proudly to each one, I was telling the warden I was a student at the seminary, that we drove round trip 210 miles to Patterson every Sunday, that I worked 30 hours a week at Sears, and that this was the first chance I had to take my son fishing. Officer Pierre Robert (pronounced roh BAIR) said he simply didn't have the heart to drag a seminary student and his little boy into court for catching a few little fish. He said he had a son of his own, and he didn't want to upset my son by having him throw the fish back in the bayou. Further, he told me to take the money I would have paid as a fine and stop by a roadside market and buy that boy a really big fish to take home to his mother. And who says this world is not a decent place to live?

Recounting life in New Orleans wouldn't be complete without describing our experience at Mardi Gras. I don't need to tell anyone what a day of revelry Mardi Gras is. I had no really compelling desire to attend the festivities, but remembering Freddy Faust's fascination with the holiday, we bundled up the children and took the streetcar down through the French Quarter to Canal Street—just to say we had witnessed it. Jerry, only two years old the first year we attended, needed to go to the bathroom, so I asked someone who looked important where I could find one. The man peered at me, let out a whoop, and exclaimed, "Man, the street's your bathroom on Mardi Gras."

One woman, in an advanced state of pregnancy, sported a sign over her belly, which read "George did it." And on her back was a placard that read "I'm looking for George." I declared that I would not subject myself or my family to this travesty of religion again. But, caught up in the activities, we were back on Canal Street for the next two years, trying to catch some trinkets and a few pieces of hard candy, and practically getting trampled and mauled in the process. One drunken man tried to step on my hand as we both tried to pick up a trinket that had been thrown from a float.

It seems that everyone but me knew I had a hearing problem. After I had been in music theory class at the seminary for only a few days, the professor remarked that he couldn't understand my problem of not being able to match particular tones and to identify certain inverted chords he played on the piano. The professor suggested I see an audiologist. The doctor tested my hearing, and was astounded that even he could discern the sounds that only I was supposed to be able to hear in the earphones. He took a complete medical history and could only surmise that the mishap while firing quad50s in the Philippines was the cause of my hearing impairment. He started me on a prescription of Vitamin B_1, which I thought was helping me.

In spite of hearing difficulties, I continued to sing solos, sing in the seminary chorale, and play the piano. To set the scene of the next incident, I must relate that New Orleans Baptist Theological Seminary is often considered to be the most conservative and the most evangelical of all the seven Southern Baptist seminaries. Our chorale sang the Christmas portion of Handel's *Messiah,* with our own small ensemble augmented by members of the New Orleans Symphony Orchestra. One of the cellists, a beautiful, devout-looking, conservative-appearing woman seemed to be putting her deepest devotion into her playing. After the concert, I simply couldn't resist telling her how her Christian faith was certainly exemplified in her rendition. She let out a laugh that jarred the seminary chapel, exclaiming, "Man, this is only a gig for me. I play where I get paid to play. Last night, I was jiving on Bourbon Street." And with that, she encased her cello, leaving me with a dumbfounded expression.

Growing up, the only church music to which I had been accustomed was hymns and Southern gospel music. So, being introduced to the great oratorios, such as Handel's *Messiah*, with its recitatives, arias, and choruses, was a completely new experience. While at the seminary, the 100-voice chorale also sang Bach's oratorio *The Passion According to St. Matthew* as well as Mendelssohn's *Elijah.* For my recital, I sang as my required recitative and aria "It is Enough" from *Elijah.*

My senior recital was quite an experience. I had to memorize six or seven religious art songs, from Bach to gospel and rock. Unbeknownst to me, Bennie, who was still living in California, had made arrangements with the seminary audiovisual department to have the recital taped. Margie, our children, most of my co-workers from Sears credit department, and some members of my church attended, although they had to drive over 100 miles from

Patterson to New Orleans. The tape Bennie had made was circulated for several months afterward, as he sent it to all my family members to hear. Most of them had never before heard songs from Bach, Handel, Mendelssohn, and Franck.

Toward the end of our seminary days, I needed to use a music dictionary. I could have used one in the library had I only had the time, but I went to class in the morning, grabbed a quick lunch, and then went to Sears, working until the store closed. Margie and I had both hoped that we could finish seminary without having to buy another book. However, when Margie was convinced I really did need the dictionary, she was able to save on our food budget in order for me to purchase it. Even today, as I use *Harvard's Dictionary of Music*, I am especially thankful for Margie's being able to stretch the food budget for us to buy it.

It was July 1961. As Margie and I were practicing the lineup for the graduation processional, the registrar rushed up to me, telling me there was no need for me to continue, since I was shy a fourth of a credit necessary in order to graduate. I had already accepted a position with the Orange Baptist Church in Orange, Virginia, and Margie and I had planned on leaving the seminary the very next day, right after the ceremony. It so happened that Dr. Claude Rhea, Dean of the Department of Church Music, was assisting with the lineup, and overheard the registrar. He attested to my practicing overtime, preparing for my recital and using the studios to the fullest. Dr. Rhea signed off on the fraction of a point, and we both graduated the next morning without further incident. We then loaded our U-Haul trailer and set out for Orange, but not until Margie had once more vacuumed, recleaned the bathroom, and given the entire apartment a white glove inspection. In her usual manner, she said we would leave the place better than we found it.

Our First Full-time Church: Orange, Virginia

At Orange Baptist Church, I directed the educational activities and directed six choirs, including an all-boys choir. This church spoiled me. Working with Althea Pace as the choir accompanist and church organist, I assumed that all large churches must be blessed with someone so talented and easy to work with. Not only did she play for the adult choir, she also accompanied two of the children's choirs. Once, in an activity for 6-year-olds, my plan called for walking music; I asked Althea if we could then have some skipping music, then running music, and on and on. She modulated from one to the next without missing a beat and without a piece of music in front of her. Of all the accompanists I've worked with, Althea was the only one who used a free organ accompaniment on the last verse of a hymn. Quite uplifting to congregational singing, such an embellishment follows the traditional melody of a hymn, but the harmony utilizes varied chord patterns not found in the hymnal. Althea's organ meditations for the prelude, offertory, and postlude were based on the liturgical year and were mainly Bach chorales, two in particular being "Sheep May Safely Graze," and "I Call to Thee, Lord Jesus Christ." Without a doubt, she was the *ne plus ultra* of church music, at least in the churches I served.

Since I had worked for Sears for three years in New Orleans, the company gave me an employee discount certificate to be used when we arrived on the church field. We bought an Early American sofa and a chair for the living room, and a maple dining room suite. However, when Margie figured out that we couldn't afford the payments on my salary, we returned the dining room suite; we then ate on a card table until one of the church members happened to visit one day. The church member said she had a small dining room table we could use.

Only four miles from Orange is Montpelier Estate, the home of James Madison, fourth president of the United States; it was at Montpelier that I was invited to give a musical program of Early American hymns for the music and arts society. The Sacred Harp songs that Mama sang when I was a boy were the centerpiece of the program. While at Orange, I was also invited to perform my Bach-to-rock repertoire for various music clubs.

In early December 1961, on a Friday evening, my family in Alabama called to say that my father would probably not live through the night. They called the next evening to tell me that he had died, and that his funeral had been set for the next afternoon, a Sunday. We didn't have enough money to fly down, and it would have taken twenty hours to drive, since it was before there were interstate highways. The pastor announced Daddy's death to the congregation, and as soon as the service was over, the deacons assembled rather quickly and gave me more than enough money for the plane ticket. Then, one of the deacons drove me to Washington National Airport to catch a plane to Alabama. I missed the funeral, but since my family knew I was on the way, they waited until the next day for the burial. As far as I know, Daddy had never been inside a church, but he had a church funeral, and was buried in the Salem Baptist Church cemetery. Salem was the first church where I attended Sunday School with Vallie.

Since the church paid only $100 a week, barely enough for us to exist as a family of four, we had no money for entertainment. Not only that, the IRS disallowed a claim of my ministry exemption; ministers are not required to report the amount of money that the church designates as rent. Even though my title was Minister of Music and Education, and though I had completed professional training for the position, the IRS disallowed the claim because I wasn't formally ordained. I was, therefore, required to pay over $100 in income tax for the year before. A rather wealthy church member, Mr. Otis Jones, advanced me the money to pay off the debt, and I worked in his flour and grist mill every Saturday morning for the next several months to repay him. My fingers became blistered and calloused from shoveling corn and wheat, and I came in from the mill exhausted and covered from head to foot with flour dust.

After soaking in a bath to relieve my aching muscles—muscles that hadn't been used during the week directing choirs and playing the piano and the autoharp—Margie and I took the kids to every Civil War battlefield in the area: Fredericksburg, Chancellorsville, the Wilderness. We also ventured to Appomattox, Manassas (or, Bull Run), Sharpsburg (or, Antietam), and Gettysburg. We soaked up more Civil War history during our time in Orange than I had ever learned in a history class. Even today, Jerry says that our Saturday afternoon trips were probably his inspiration to excel in school. And on a trip to Charlottesville, about 30 miles from Orange, Jerry, not even in first grade yet, saw University of Virginia, and told us that was where he was going to college. And he did. If I'd had a dream that a linguistics book I would write 30 years later would be adopted as a textbook there,

I would've surely thought I was hallucinating.

My work at the mill ended when I missed the final stop on the one-man elevator and was dumped headfirst onto a concrete slab just inches from the roiling Rapidan River, the rapids of which turned the giant water wheel that in years past had powered the mill. Cornelia Craun, the church secretary, who always thought I was a little funny anyway, dubbed me Horsecollar Horace, after I had been fitted with a neck brace at Martha Washington Hospital in Charlottesville. Cornelia, one of our best friends even after almost 40 years, doesn't seem to recall any of the important things I did in music and education at the church; she seems to remember only the horse collar. She had two children, Phyllis and Dougie, who were the same ages as Patty and Jerry, and we had a lot of good times together.

The first Christmas at Orange didn't appear very promising. Earning barely a living wage, supplemented slightly by Margie's earnings as a typesetter for *The Orange Review*, I wondered how we could possibly brighten our children's prospects for Christmas. Around the middle of December, the pastor called me in to say that an anonymous church member had given us $100 for Christmas. In 1961, a hundred dollars made a lot of difference in our lives. Over the years, I have wheedled Cornelia to tell me who was so generous. Being the stubborn professional she is, even to this day, she has refused to tell me.

Due to the excellent music training over the years, the church had practically grown its own talented choir. There didn't seem to be an anthem that the choir or the accompanist couldn't sight read. Once, I told Cornelia, who sang in the choir, that she had misread an A flat. We still get a chuckle out of her remark: "I don't know an A flat from G minus." Cornelia was probably the only choir member who couldn't read a note of music. But she made great ham biscuits and fried apples, neither of which Margie and I had tasted before coming to Orange.

There was no ready reserve outfit in the immediate vicinity of Orange, so I joined a group of officers who met weekly in a study group in Fredericksburg. I was able to earn points toward retirement, but I didn't get paid. And we could surely have used any additional income, with what the church was paying me. But Margie made her own clothes, as well as Patty's. There seemed

At the Bradbury Piano

to be nothing that Margie couldn't do.

While visiting Vivien Roberts, one of the tenors in the adult choir, I naturally took notice of his and his wife's piano, which I surmised from the design and wood grain to be over 200 years old. I learned that the piano had been in their family for several generations, and that it was the piano on which William Bradbury, almost a hundred years ago, had composed the tune to "Just As I Am," and "Jesus Loves Me." Since neither of the Roberts still played the instrument, I persuaded them to donate it to the School of Church Music at New Orleans Baptist Theological Seminary. The donation was carried in *The Charlottesville Progress,* and Dr. Rhea, the Dean of the School of Church Music, suggested to the editor of *The Church Musician,* Southern Baptists' music monthly magazine, that I write an article concerning its history, the owners, and their donation. So, my first article, "The Bradbury Piano," was published in July 1963.

It was at Orange that Margie developed an extremely high fever. My first thought was that she had contracted meningitis again, as in New Orleans, when she prayed that she could live long enough to see the two children grown. The doctors told us she needed to be admitted to a hospital immediately. Since the church didn't provide any type of hospital coverage, I wasn't able to take her to University of Virginia Hospital or the Martha Washington Hospital in nearby Charlottesville. Since Margie was a veteran, I was able to get her admitted to the VA Hospital in Richmond. While Cornelia kept our two children, I drove Margie from Orange to Richmond—60 miles—with her almost at the point of death in the back seat of the car. Since her head hurt so bad, she couldn't even bear the pain of combing her hair, and she looked like she might not make it to Richmond. With her hair disheveled as she writhed in pain, she was an awful sight to behold. While I was visiting Margie in the hospital, John Bawsel and his wife, Lois, often had me over for dinner. They embodied the Spanish expression *mi casa es su casa*, my home is your home.

While Margie was in the hospital, a piano salesman with whom I had negotiated for a new instrument at the church, told me he would like to put a brand-new Baldwin Acrosonic in our home for a month, just to see how we liked it. He said I was under no obligation to buy it. The salesman knew what he was doing—he knew that once I played the piano, I couldn't live without it. After ten days in the hospital, the doctors were unable to determine the cause for her condition. Nevertheless, her fever and headache subsided and her condition stabilized, and I was advised to bring her home to rest. On the way back to Orange, I casually mentioned that a salesman had left a beautiful piano in our living room for her to play as she recuperated. After she got completely well, I told her, the salesman said he would have it picked up.

Margie isn't one to be easily duped; she knew my ruse—that I had maneuvered obtaining the piano for myself. (We didn't actually need it; we didn't have the money for it; the piano wasn't on sale; and it certainly hadn't been marked down three times.) But Margie let me keep the piano, and I gave lessons to neighborhood kids to pay for it—at $26 a month for three years. Margie may have played the piano four or five times in the 35 years since we bought it. But with all the gusto Dr. Erwin at Troy State had instilled in me, I awakened the kids each morning throughout their school years by banging out "The Star-Spangled Banner." Will they ever forgive me?

As soon as we arrived on our church field at Orange, I enrolled in a classical record club and had already received a number of LPs, but didn't have a stereo. When church members invited us occasionally for dinner, I sometimes asked if they had a stereo player so that I could listen to one of my records, but mainly one by the Mormon Tabernacle Choir. I made it a point to obtain a hymnal of the Latter Day Saints, simply to get the music and words to "Abide with me, 'tis eventide," surely one of the most peaceful pieces of music ever written. As far as I have been able to determine, the song is in no other hymnal.

It was at Orange that our third child, Stephen Alan, was born. While Patty and Jerry had been the model children, reading books, putting puzzles together, and listening to records, Stephen came home even from the hospital in an ornery mood. He absolutely refused to be entertained. And he cried day in and day out. I felt guilty going to the church and leaving him for Margie to take care of. At the same time, I couldn't wait to leave the house, to get away from his crying. He was slow to talk, and slow to walk. And he was the most hyperactive child I had ever known. But we all continued to love the little rascal, and it seems that Patty, always the little mother, could get him to do things that none of the rest of us could. Seven years later, the piano which I had finagled for myself would become Stephen's lifeline.

On to Richmond: The Capital of the Confederacy

After serving as minister of music and education for two years in Orange, I accepted a similar but higher-paying position with the Northside Baptist Church in Richmond, the second capital of the Confederacy (the first being in Montgomery, Alabama). In Richmond, I was able to join a ready reserve outfit at Richmond International Airport; the only problem was that I had to negotiate to be away from the unit to direct the church choir on Sunday for an hour. The rewards were unbelievable—a monthly check for four days' pay for only two days' duty. Not only that, I was able to use the military commissary at Fort Lee, near Petersburg, while on active duty.

With a portion of my active duty check from the summer of '64, we finally bought a stereo record player, which we had been wanting since stereos were first introduced while we were in the seminary. I would have bought one years earlier, but I knew Margie's principles. In the seminary, back in '59, one of the stereo salesmen at Sears, where I worked, wondered why the mechanism was so called. From having memorized Latin and Greek elements, I told him *stereo*, as in *stereotype*, meant "solid," and, of course, *phone* meant "sound." Beyond that, I wasn't much help until I learned that a player's components consisted of woofers and tweeters, thus giving a "solid sound."

There was absolutely nothing noteworthy at Northside Baptist Church, except directing six choirs and supervising an educational program for approximately 800 in Sunday School—and to have as the organist Barbara Cole, a truly talented musician with a gracious spirit. Some people may think working for a church is a glorious experience, being with beautiful people who always have other persons' interests at heart. Almost from the moment we arrived at the church, there were problems with the pastor that not even a sharecropper's son should have to contend with. The 16 months in Richmond were like the 40 years the Israelites wandered in the desert. When I didn't think I could take working for Northside any longer, I sent my college, university, and seminary transcripts to the State Board of Education and found that I was certified to teach English, music, history, and social studies. So, at least, I had an escape hatch from the church.

My short tenure at Northside Baptist was made slightly more tenable by our Saturday and Sunday afternoon excursions. We visited most of the James River plantation mansions, Jamestown, and Williamsburg. We were also able to go to the beach at Hampton, Virginia. So, the time in Richmond wasn't entirely wasted.

Though very sad for the whole nation, the only truly memorable event while we were in Richmond was President Kennedy's assassination, on November 22, 1963. I was having lunch with a church member at the Rotary Club in a downtown Richmond hotel, when the maître d' came into the dining room to make the somber announcement. I rushed home to tell Margie, but a neighbor had already come over to our house, crying, and telling her to turn on the television. For the rest of the day and evening, we listened and grieved, hearing Walter Cronkite, intoning that President Kennedy had been shot.

When I knew for certain that I would be leaving Northside on December 31, 1964, I reminded the church that I still hadn't been allowed to take vacation time. The pastor had said that inasmuch as I had taken off two weeks for reserve duty, I wasn't entitled to additional time off. Furthermore, he said that escorting and chaperoning 30 teenagers at the Baptist state convention center for a music retreat was my vacation, even though Margie and I had never worked so hard in all our lives as we did that week at Eagle Eyrie, in the Blue Ridge Mountains near Lynchburg. In addition to my teaching a music theory course at the convention,

Margie and I cooked for the kids in the church-owned cabin. So, to appease me, the church council overrode the pastor and gave me the month of December off with pay, and I immediately started working in the credit department at Sears on West Broad Street. It was such a relief to be away from the demands of the church and the pastor. Not only that, with the employee discount, I was able to buy clothes and shoes and presents that we could never have dreamed of on the church salary. We would have a decent Christmas after all.

Manassas Baptist Church and the Battle of Bull Run

On New Year's Day, 1965, after only 16 months in Richmond, I took a similar position with the Manassas Baptist Church, in Manassas, Virginia. Since I was from Alabama, and Margie, from New Hampshire, we thought it would be an ideal place to relocate. Manassas is the site of the first two major land battles of the Civil War, and ironically where the main thoroughfare is Grant Street, with Lee Street only a short side road in front of the courthouse.[23] On the grounds of the courthouse is a monument commemorating the 50th anniversary of the war's end, where both sides returned not as enemies, but as brothers and fellow countrymen.

Since we married, we had always lived in apartments, with the exception of the small house we rented while in Richmond. But Manassas Baptist allowed us to live in the parsonage inasmuch as the pastor wanted to buy a home of his own. We had never had so much room: four bedrooms, two baths, a spacious living room, dining room, and a full basement. The parsonage was on Longstreet Drive, named after a Confederate general.

I directed a number of choirs at Manassas Baptist, but the most rewarding was a children's choir of 56 voices, made up of an equal number of boys and girls. Robed in black and white, the choir sang from memory two-part anthems for the early service every Sunday. In addition to the anthems, the children's choir also sang a number of ariettas from oratorios. Two of the most popular ones were Mendelssohn's "O Rest in the Lord," from *Elijah,* and "But the Lord Is Mindful of His Own," from *St. Paul.* Both Patty and Jerry were in the choir. I couldn't have been nearly as

---

[23] Although General Grant's Union Army was victorious in the Civil War, I would have thought the main street would have been named for the Confederate commanding general, Robert E. Lee.

successful with this choir had it not been for the pianist, 14-year-old Becky Detwiler, who could sight read Bach, Beethoven, or any other classical composer I wished to use. In later years, after receiving her degree in music education, Becky became the organist and choral director at the church.

One of the highlights of directing the children's choir at Manassas was our being invited by Luray Caverns in the Shenandoah Valley to present a program at its outdoor religious service, preceded by a carillon concert. The Caverns granted passes to all the singers and chaperons. While at Orange several years before, we had also taken the children's choir to Luray on a tour but not to sing.

Not long after I began working at Manassas Baptist Church, I began taking some English courses at University of Virginia, Northern Center. While there, I also took structural and transformational linguistics, a particular interest of mine. I was the only student from the Deep South in the class, and I was embarrassed to join in discussion or ask the professor a question, lest I betray my Southern drawl. I had associated my accent with poverty and my meager upbringing. With some trepidation, one day after class, I approached Dr. Golden to discuss my problem. The professor was from New Jersey, and I thought he spoke perfectly, euphoniously in fact; there was simply a pleasantness about his voice. Telling him I was too embarrassed to speak out in class, I asked him if there was anything he could do to soften my Southern drawl, to help me smooth over the rough edges. I cannot begin to portray the look on his face, but he peered at me with a curious smile. He said, and I remember his exact words, "Mr. Danner, if I were omnipotent, I would not use any of my powers to change the way you speak. There is nothing wrong with your Southern accent. We all have accents—that's what makes our language so special. Just be thankful for your voice, and continue to cultivate it." It was one of the best pieces of advice I have ever received, permeating relations with my Northern Virginia Community College and University of Maryland students, who have diverse backgrounds, and come from every continent.

It is quite impossible to remember the names of the thousands of children and adults I have directed in choirs over the years. Sometimes, not being able to remember a name or face can be em-

As a 10-year-old choirboy

Mason Hollcroft

As an electrical engineer

barrassing, as the next incident relates. For the past several months, I have been working out in the gym with an engineer with the Rural Utilities Service, which as I have noted before, was originally Rural Electrification Administration. I told the engineer how I recalled poles being erected by hand when electricity first made it to the rural areas of southeastern Alabama. He said the spears the men used to upright the poles were called *pikes*. Over the months that we talked about various matters, I knew him only as Mason. Then, when I told him I would like to include his name in the memoir for his being so helpful, I asked him his last name, which he said was Hollcroft. I couldn't believe what I heard. I told him I had a Mason Hollcroft in my adult choir at Manassas Baptist Church 35 years ago when I first went there from Richmond. He said that was his dad, and that he, my friend, was in my children's choir. I simply had to ask him for a picture of himself when he was ten years old. And when he gave it to me, I then remembered him as one of the little boys I once directed in the junior choir.

There was no Air Force Reserve unit within a reasonable distance of Manassas, and I requested a transfer to the Virginia National Guard, an artillery outfit, in Manassas. As in Richmond, I needed to negotiate in order to direct the choir on Sunday. The company commander, Captain Lloyd Cowne, of Nokesville, Virginia, said he would agree to my time off, if in return I would deliver a sermon for the men in the field. I told him I would be glad to, except that I wasn't a preacher—I was a musician and an educator. This Army officer didn't negotiate on easy terms. "That may be," he said, "but just have a message ready for Sunday." I brought along the church's collapsible field organ, which had to be pumped with the feet. I was like a jumping jack, playing the organ and leading the singing, and then jumping up to lead the responsive reading, and back down again to play, and then up again to deliver the message. Finally, the battalion operations officer, a major, told me he would take charge of everything except playing the organ and delivering the message. When the artillery unit was later redesignated an infantry outfit, a position was created for a chaplain, and the new commander in Winchester requested that I be commissioned as a captain for the billet. I had met all the requirements of the Army; I was about to receive the commission and had already bought my captain's bars when my own denomination, at the last minute, wouldn't endorse me because I wasn't an ordained minister at the time.

For the four years at Manassas Baptist Church, almost every Sunday evening during the summer, we drove into Washington to the Watergate on the Potomac, directly opposite the Lincoln Memorial, to hear the President's Own, the United States Marine Band, play. Hearing the band was about the only recreation during this time, and it was free! Patty played the oboe and Jerry, the flute, in the band at school, and Stephen simply liked anything military, especially the colorful uniforms. Stephen would later play first chair tenor saxophone in the high school symphonic band.

Margie and I were once given tickets by the father of a young man to whom I was teaching piano, to attend the Washington Symphony Orchestra at Constitution Hall in Washington. Never had I seen a celebrity except for serving on a detail to guard President of the Philippines Magsaysay when he visited Clark Air Force Base in 1954, to thank us for helping him rid his country of the Huks. I had missed out on seeing President Eisenhower when he was inaugurated in 1953 because I was guarding an empty parking lot at Fort Myer, Virginia. But at Constitution Hall, sitting directly in front of us was a person who looked like Jack Benny. I nudged Margie and asked if she thought he might have brought his violin. She assured me that I was just seeing things. At the intermission, the maestro turned to the audience and announced that he was honored to have the "world-renowned" violinist Jack Benny in the audience. After Mr. Benny stood to a round of applause, the conductor remarked that he was "sorry" that Mr Benny didn't have his violin or he would have been asked to join the orchestra. Again, another round of applause. After the concert, I accidentally on purpose brushed up against him, just to say I had hobnobbed with a celebrity. "Oh," I said, "excuse me, Mr. Benny, I am sorry."

When Stephen was about six or seven years old, he informed me that he was going to be a Green Beret. He had memorized practically every one of Army Sergeant Barry Sadler's ballads of the Green Beret. I suggested that for now he concentrate on just being a boy. With a look of consternation that I should think such an absurdity, he said, "Don't be asinine, Dad; a boy can't start too early in life to know what he wants to do." Though he didn't become a Green Beret, he did become a paratrooper with the 82nd Airborne, and at this writing, is a Major in the US Army.

Shortly after President Carter was inaugurated in 1977, he made a television plea that households across America turn their thermostats down to 68 degrees to conserve the fuel supply. As soon as we heard the announcement, the kids and I pleaded with Margie to let us turn the thermostat *up* to 68 degrees. Her advice was that if you were chilly, put on a sweater, and if you were cold, put on a coat. Margie could have been appointed Secretary of Energy.

After taking Stephen to several specialists for his hyperactivity, our family pediatrician, Dr. Alvin Conner, recommended we get him involved in a hobby, and suggested piano lessons. I thought to myself that Stephen, now in the first grade, could never sit still long enough for a piano lesson, much less practice every day. But we were willing to try anything. So, we started Stephen in piano in the second grade with Mrs. Carper, the church organist and a dear friend of ours; and for eleven years straight, he won a superior rating in the Northern Virginia Piano Playing Festival. At the festivals, there were two judges; if one judge awarded a superior rating and the other, an excellent, the pianist was given the benefit and awarded a superior. In Stephen's case, he was always rated superior by both judges.

Even today, Stephen's three gold cups and his other awards decorate the piano. He would go on to play varsity football, teach wilderness survival skills, and climb mountains, but not once did he ever miss a piano lesson. To placate me, he even memorized

Schubert's *Marche Militaire*, one of the first pieces of classical music I had ever heard at Barbour County High. Not once did I miss one of his festivals or Christmas and spring recitals, and the only one missed by Margie was when she went to New Hampshire for her mother's funeral. However, the night he gave his se-

Stephen at piano

nior recital—and was chosen by the other 124 piano students Mrs. Carper taught, to present her with 125 yellow roses—would be the last time Stephen touched the piano. In fact, he had once asked me how he had been drawn into taking piano in the first place, especially since he was the outdoor type. I explained that we had done it for his own good, to control his hyperactivity, whereupon he promptly inquired of his mother if I was telling the truth or if it was just another one of my "war stories."

I simply must relate an incident concerning Stephen and the piano. In his senior year of high school, he was selected as one of the top 20 young musicians in Manassas by the Women's Music and Arts Guild. The guild scheduled a concert at the Methodist church where each of the musicians would perform. A junior fireman, Stephen promptly told his mother and me that polishing the ladder truck was a lot more important than playing the piano for "a bunch of old ladies." We tried to impress upon him that it wasn't every boy who was a budding concert pianist, and it would be a golden opportunity for him. Acquiescing, he said, "Dad, what time am I supposed to play?" whereupon I told him it was near the end of the program, that apparently the guild was saving the best for last. He said he would try to make it, and off he tramped to the fire station.

The musicians were all dressed in evening attire, and I said to Margie, "Oh no, Stephen left for the fire station wearing a plaid shirt, blue jeans, and sneakers." Margie told me not to worry, that she was sure he had gone back to the house to change. About five minutes before he was scheduled to play, in lumbered Stephen, plopping disgustedly on the pew beside us. And then, the dowager announced, "And now Stephen Alan Danner will play for us all "Variations on a Rachmaninoff Tune." In all his concerts and recitals, he had played with perfect aplomb and finesse. Now, it seemed that he was stuck to the pew; but finally, he plodded down front—still dressed in blue jeans, a plaid shirt, and tennis shoes—peered at the piano as though it was a completely foreign contraption, adjusted the piano bench, and absentmindedly surveyed the keyboard with a bored, nonchalant expression, like "What's this in front of me, a whole bunch of black and white keys?" My heart pounded, afraid that for once, he had stage fright. Then his fingers began to fly from one end of the keyboard to the other. I was never so proud in all my life—proud for him, but also proud for me. He was doing something that I had always wanted to do myself. And then everyone was applauding, and Stephen may have cracked a half smile, but which was more of a moue; then, he marched right out of the church, climbed into his old International Scout, and drove back to the fire station. As the artists and their parents and friends were sipping fruit punch and nibbling hors d'oeuvres, one of the overly refined ladies said to Margie and me, "Oh, I just know how you must be so very proud of Stephen. But I just didn't know a person so young could interpret Rachmaninoff so brilliantly. What a tour de force! By the way, where *is* Stephen?"

In telling of that incident, I'll have to relate just one more. Later in the spring, Stephen was also chosen as one of the top musicians in the state to play in a festival in Virginia Beach, slated for the Saturday before Mother's Day. This time, he made it definite—he wasn't going, no matter if his name had already been printed on the program and even if the governor himself might be the guest of honor. At the time, Stephen was working two jobs—as a handyman at a funeral home and as a delivery boy for a florist. He said that he had flowers to deliver, or a lot of mothers might otherwise be disappointed. Stephen always did have a soft spot for mothers, especially his own. What other mother would have stopped whatever she was doing to play *Battleship* with him when he was a little boy? I thought I had more important things to do than play games.

Though Stephen was the pianist in the family, Patty was the accomplished soloist. She sang the lead female roles in a number of musicals, including the role of Mary Magdalene in *Jesus Christ, Superstar*, which was presented at Trinity Episcopal Church in Manassas. Patty wanted to go to only one college—Virginia Tech, and that's where she went and from where she graduated. It was also where she sang alto in the Madrigals; it was in the Madrigals that she and one of the basses apparently were attracted to each other. She and Bill, now a pediatrician in private practice, are the parents of our first three grandchildren.

While Stephen was the pianist and Patty the soloist, Jerry was definitely the scholar of the family. In many ways, I felt he was my superior, for his intelligence far surpassed anything I had been blessed with. When he was in the fourth grade, he announced that he wanted no presents for Christmas, none at all. But, he said, if we could afford it, we could get the entire family a new set of *World Book Encyclopedia*. Jerry would actually read a volume from cover to cover. On family trips and vacations to Nags Head, North Carolina, he read novels by flashlight after dark in the back seat of the car. In high school alone, he read over 1,000 books from the Prince William County Library. Patty read about the same number, possibly more. When he was in high school, Northern Virginia Community College asked me to teach several courses in speed reading. I asked Jerry if he would like for me to share with him the secret of reading as fast as he could turn the pages. He asked me why, since he was already reading at least a book a night and watching television at the same time, not to mention being a straight A student, as well as playing on the basketball team. When in high school, he was the team captain of "It's Academic," a television program for high school scholars in the Washington area. In addition, he was selected to attend the Governor's School of Virginia one summer. In his senior year, he applied to University of Virginia, the College of William and Mary, and Wake Forest, and was accepted at all three. He chose Mr. Jefferson's university, in Charlottesville, which he had planned on attending since before he was even in the first grade at Orange.

The year after Jerry suggested we purchase the encyclopedias, he requested that we finally get a color television set—ostensibly for the family—but mainly, I am persuaded, for him to enjoy sports more vividly. His tastes became much more expensive as he got older. Just after he received his driver's license, he spotted an MGB on a lot in Fairfax. He said the only thing he really wanted for his birthday was that sports car. With the check I received from teaching two courses at Northern Virginia Community College, I bought his coveted convertible and had it delivered. It was parked in the driveway of our house when he woke up.

A highlight of our time in Manassas was the Prince William County Fair, the largest in the Commonwealth of Virginia. Of course, the Mennonites living on the farms outside Manassas generally won first place in the produce division. They had the largest tomatoes, onions, broccoli, and cauliflower, but Margie invariably won blue ribbons in several categories of sewing as well as for her apple and cherry pies. Two or three years, she also won the rosette, for best of the show in sewing. I won two or three times with my buttery peanut brittle with coconut.

As much a part of our family as our children and our grandchildren were Frisky and Collier. On a cold Thanksgiving afternoon, Margie and I went for our usual 2-mile walk. As we were walking, a forlorn, hungry-looking kitten kept following us. When it appeared that the kitten could go no farther, Margie picked it up, and we cut our walk short and took it home, fed it warm milk, and wrapped it in a cozy blanket. We later found that the kitten had been abandoned by a family on the block, who pleaded with us to keep it. The kitten grew into a cat quite soon and duly appointed herself the queen of the house. Her favorite place to stretch out and rest was on the guest room bed, especially if Margie had laid out material for a dress she was going to cut out. When that happened, Margie would find something else to do because Frisky would have dug her claws into the pattern. No one dared to bother Frisky while Frisky was taking her nap. Margie and Frisky could waste a good hour, playing hide and seek with each other.

Not long after Frisky came into our life, Stephen said he wanted a border collie. We had seen border collies at the Scottish fairs in Alexandria, Virginia, and at the sheep trials near Leesburg. We located a breeder near Front Royal, and Stephen picked out the cutest puppy of the litter. She was black all over except for her white nose, the tip of her tail, her lower legs and paws, and a ring around her neck. Stephen, who was studying French, said that with her regal manner, we would call her by the French word for collar. So Collier (pronounced cahl YER)

Lady Collier

she was, for the seventeen years we had the privilege of her company. She wanted to be a pal of Frisky, but Frisky would have nothing to do with her. She was the smartest dog imaginable. Our next-door neighbor shot Frisky with a BB gun, and said he would shoot Collier as well if she ever came on his property. So I walked the boundary line and told Collier that she must go no farther than our yard. Even when we threw the frisbee and it veered into the Chandlers' yard, Collier would stop almost in midair to avoid going into the forbidden yard. And I had only to pick up my car keys and Collier would bound for one of the cars, waiting impatiently until I said "red car" or "blue car." Once I told her the car color, she heeled at the indicated car until I opened the door.

The veterinarian called and said he had removed 35 pellets from Frisky's legs and rump, and gave her a fifty-fifty chance of surviving. He called the next day to say that he couldn't save her, and said he would dispose of her for us. I told him no, that we wanted her body. So I took Collier, who was only about six months old, with me. As always, she lay in the back seat, where she would stay until I opened the car door and told her to heel. Dr. Robins had put Frisky's body in a small cardboard box, taped securely, which I placed on the floor in front of the passenger seat. Collier whined and whined, practically pleading with me to let her come to the front. Finally, I patted the front seat, thinking she would lie on the passenger side and nuzzle up to me, as usual. As soon as I had given the okay, she moved to the front and then down on the floor, gently resting her head on Frisky's box until we arrived home. I buried Frisky out in the flower garden, placing a granite stone over the grave, and planting a red rose bush to commemorate the many years of joy she brought into our lives. Every time for the next month, when we let Collier out of the house, she would go to Frisky's grave and just lie there. But we knew how to change her mood. We only had to pick up the frisbee. Many times, I purposely tried to fool her. I would point that I was going to throw the frisbee in a certain direction, but suddenly throw it in a different direction. She was never fooled by my antics.

And finally, Collier couldn't run and catch frisbees any longer and even had to be helped into the car when we went for a ride. So, after 17 years of having Collier as part of the family, I had to take her to be euthanized. The veterinarian asked if I wanted a few minutes with her before she had to do the inevitable. I stroked Collier's glossy, silky, well-brushed fur and patted her foxlike head, and told her over and over what a friend she had been to Margie and me, the children, and our grandchildren. She looked up at me so trustingly, and then the veterinarian came in with the needle. I thought it would have taken longer, but in about ten seconds, her eyes closed gently, and I knew she was gone. I remembered to take off her leather collar with her name embroidered on it. Strangely, I didn't cry. I knew she had gone to where all faithful dogs go. There will never be another Collier. Since she died on a frigid day in December, with the ground too hard to dig a grave, I told the veterinarian to dispose of her body.

In early February 1973, I received a call from Vallie that Mama had had a stroke and wasn't expected to live much longer. By the time I got to the hospital, she was already in a coma, never recognizing me while I was there. The family knew that I had to get back to my job and said that they would understand if I couldn't make it back to Alabama when she passed away. With that assurance, I returned to Virginia.

Only two weeks later, on February 13, two weeks before her 84th birthday, Mama died, not having regained consciousness from the coma. Her funeral was to be held on February 15 in Ozark, Alabama.

I left Manassas, Virginia, early on the morning of the funeral, to catch a flight from Washington National Airport. I would connect in Atlanta with Southern Airways and land in Dothan, only 12 miles from Ozark. On the trip to the airport, I heard on the radio that a tornado was ravishing the southeastern United States, but I thought little more of it. I was scheduled for a one-hour lay-over in Atlanta, and would reach Ozark a full three hours before the funeral.

About an hour out of Atlanta, the pilot announced that we were in a holding pattern because of the weather. I sent word by the flight attendant to the pilot that I was due to connect with Southern in about an hour. He sent word back that we would arrive in plenty of time. He continued to reassure me that all was well, as we continued circling and circling.

As we were making our descent to land in Atlanta, I saw a Southern Airways plane taking off, and I knew then that I had missed my flight to Dothan. Frantic, I called Vallie and told her that Southern was putting me on a flight to Eglin Air Force Base, Florida, at least three hours' driving time from Ozark. I had planned on renting a car at Eglin and driving to the funeral, not realizing in my frenzy that it would be impossible to arrive for the funeral in time.

While I was enroute to Dothan, Vallie had called Shot Fleming, the husband of my long-time friend, Carolyn Davis, and asked him to meet me at the airport. He and Carolyn then drove me to a small airport where he had a small plane. We made the trip to Ozark in about 30 minutes, landing on a grassy airstrip, where Vallie was waiting for me. In anticipation of my arriving, the family delayed the funeral for an hour.

At the funeral, all ten children were present, and it would be last time that our entire family was together at one time.

After serving Manassas Baptist Church for four years, I resigned to take a job outside the church.

Teaching for Fairfax County Public Schools

After resigning my position with Manassas Baptist, I began, in January 1969, teaching music in the elementary grades for Fairfax County Public Schools, for the unheard-of sum of $10,000 a year. I was an itinerant teacher, teaching three days a week at Sleepy Hollow Elementary School, in Seven Corners, and then two days at

Braddock Elementary School, in Annandale. On Valentine's Day, I received around 500 cards from my little charges. About three weeks after beginning at Sleepy Hollow, the principal called me in. It was my first experience of learning that principals don't usually call teachers in to congratulate them on a doing a good job. But I was enjoying my job so much that I thought surely that was the reason for my session with her. Not only was I in love with the job, the classroom teachers were extremely appreciative of my teaching folksongs of the countries they were studying in geography. I was all geared up to be promoted as director of elementary music for the entire county. The principal had other ideas on my performance. She said that classroom teachers expect their students to return from the music session relaxed, but instead they were all keyed up and hyperactive. She informed me that the classroom teachers had said that after the students returned, the rest of the day was a lost cause. She further said two or three of the classroom teachers had observed me and that there was simply too much activity. The children were singing, clapping, dancing, and just having a merry time, and that I seemed to be enjoying the activities as much as, if not more than, the kids. She suggested that I just teach them to sing and tone it down. I asked her if it was possible for a leopard to lose its spots. In a few weeks, the sixth graders presented a program of folksongs from around the world, complete with native costumes, at the parent-teacher meeting. The parents were most receptive, and from then on, I never heard another negative word about our fun-filled activities.

I would probably still be teaching music in elementary school except that after playing the piano for six or seven hours a day, I developed bursitis. Eventually, even with medication, I could hardly lift my hands off the keyboard. Since I held multiple teacher certifications, I transferred to Herndon High School, where I taught English and reading for the next eleven years. At the same time I began public school teaching, I transferred from the Virginia National Guard back to a flying unit at Andrews Air Force Base, in Maryland, since I now had the weekends free.

In the summer after teaching music for Fairfax County, I needed to find a job in order to provide additional income. I learned that Fairfax County Public Library was looking for someone to go to library patrons' homes and pick up long-overdue books. This job

---

[24] Paine has often been described as "an Englishman by birth, a French citizen by decree, and an American by adoption." In *Common Sense*, he argued for the declaration of

proved to be more dangerous than anything I had ever done before, more dangerous even than guarding the perimeter of Clark Air Force Base in the Philippines from the Huks. Many patrons resented the county hiring someone to pick up books that they could very well have returned on their own. I had to remind them that they had had plenty of opportunity to do just that. At the end of the day, I would return to the central library and tell of my encounters. At one home, I found a ten-year-old boy whose parents had deserted him. He had some crackers and a half jar of peanut butter to live on. I contacted Social Services, who rescued the boy. One man came on the porch with a shotgun and told me to get off his property. By the time I was able to get a police escort, the man had moved out of the neighborhood, with thousands of dollars of the county's books. My supervisors thought I should write a book about my experiences.

It was during this time that the Disabled American Veterans appealed my case to the Veterans Administration, who then certified me a service-connected disabled veteran for injuries received in the Philippines while firing a quad50, which is really four 50-caliber machine guns actuated by one trigger. The VA encouraged me to take advantage of the rehabilitation program. Though I wasn't able to study at the seminary under the GI Bill, I was now able to continue my education while I taught English at Herndon High School.

I immediately began a doctoral program in American studies at George Washington University, Washington, D.C., with the idea of eventually teaching in that area. One of my professors was Mr. Mondale, the brother of Walter Mondale, Vice-President of the United States in 1968. The main emphases in his two courses were the growth of cities and the politics underlying them. My other professor was Mr. McCandlish, who taught the literary foundations of American government, and I was introduced to British-born Thomas Paine's *Common Sense*,[24] and Henry David Thoreau's *Walden* and *Civil Disobedience.* We also studied *The Federalist Papers* as well as the letters of John Adams and Thomas Jefferson after they reconciled their bitter differences, their cordial correspondence ending with their deaths, both on the same day, July 4, 1826.

Since Mr. McCandlish was quite aloof and erudite, I asked him

independence from England. One of his most famous sayings was "These are the times that try men's souls."

why, since he had two Ph.D.'s, he wasn't addressed as Doctor. He said that being a professor at George Washington should be all the status one needed. In Mr. McCandlish's class, I researched the beginnings of church music in the early days of the colonies. For my final project, I wrote a paper on the *Bay Psalm Book*, the psalter used by the Puritans on Massachusetts Bay Colony; I also brought in the church's field organ and played and sang two or three of the quaint psalms found in the psalter. Quite impressed with the originality of the work, Mr. McCandlish submitted the paper, "Whence the Bay Psalm Book?" to the *American Journal of History*, recommending that it be published. If it ever was, I was not informed of it.

It was in Mr. McCandlish's class that the dinner table discussions at Vallie's house paid off. I had never thought of "priesthood of the believer" being any more than a theological concept. Basically, the concept is that we don't need a priest to intercede for us before God, that the people, because of Jesus' death and resurrection, possess this as an inherent right. I found, however, that this concept undergirds both the Declaration of Independence and the United States Constitution. That is, we don't need a king or ruler to decree our actions, that we the people are fully capable of making sane and intelligent decisions. Even though Thomas Jefferson was a confirmed Deist, he openly acknowledged the influence of the Baptists in helping shape his views on the Declaration of Independence. And James Madison, the author of the United States Constitution, credited John Leland, a Baptist minister from Culpeper, Virginia, for helping develop the concept of the separation of church and state. Madison argued against Patrick Henry, who supported the idea of a state-supported religion.

The second semester, Mr. McCandlish assigned twelve novels, plus another 20-page research paper. I simply couldn't keep up on the readings, with teaching, raising a family, and attending Air Force Reserves; not only that, Mr. McCandlish said my final paper on the concept of nature in *Walden* lacked originality, and thus failed me for the entire semester. It was the first failing grade I had ever received, and I became utterly depressed. I appealed the grade to the dean of the graduate school, but by this time, Mr. McCandlish was in Maine for the summer, and couldn't attend the hearing. He wrote the dean and told him that even if he were in town, he wouldn't attend, for all his grades were final. The dean, however, advised me to "take the bull by the horns" if I felt justified in doing so, especially since Mr. McCandlish had given me an A the first semester and had recommended that my paper be published. I didn't have time to wait for the professor to return from Maine for the fall semester, and I chose to let the F stand without a fight. I went to see my counselor, Mr. I. W. Meade, at the Veterans Administration, and told him I was quitting my doctoral program. I was quite inconsolable, crying unabashedly as I told him I was an utter failure, that I didn't deserve to be using the government's money to attend school. The grade almost shattered the faith I had long held in my abilities.

Now, I know why the Veterans Administration employs counselors. After letting me pour out my story of failing the course, failing my family, failing even the 50 stars on the American flag—the flag I had practically worshipped since seeing it for the first time wafting in front of Barbour County High School when I was in first grade—Mr. Meade said while I may have failed the course, I myself was not a failure. He reminded me that I had served my country honorably, had been injured in a training accident that very well could have killed me, that I had a wife and three children, and that I still had the Veterans Administration and the United States Government behind me. He told me the 50 stars on the flag were still brightly shining and encouraged me to pick up the pieces and get back in the fight. When I received my doctorate three years later at American University at Constitution Hall, I sent Mr. Meade a special invitation to my graduation. Mr. Meade said that if he were to attend the graduations of all the veterans he counseled, he wouldn't have time for his family. He had given me such personal attention that I felt like I was his only counselee.

Since by now I had begun teaching at Herndon High School, I found that many of my ninth grade students couldn't read well, and I didn't know how to teach them. So, I transferred to American University, Washington, D.C., to study educational psychology, learning disabilities, and reading. It was without a doubt one of the best decisions I have ever made. One door was closed, another opened.

One of the highlights of my tenure at Herndon High School, in addition to obtaining my doctorate at Amerian University, was coaching the cross country track team. Over the summer, in 1977, a new athletic director, Coach Lou Pukal, was hired, and he had begun his duties in July, before football practice began. During the week before school actually started, I went to Lou's office to pick up an athletic calendar, since Margie and I went to many of the games. As soon as I walked into his office, Coach Pukal said, "Dr. Danner, I have a job for you. I want you to coach cross country." I was caught completely off guard, because I didn't think I had ever met him for him to call me by name, and was absolutely certain he didn't know of my athletic ineptitude. (He reminded me later that he had met Margie and me at a faculty party when he accompanied his wife Rosemary, who taught Spanish at the school.) I promptly told him I didn't have an athletic bone in my body, that I didn't play anything but the radio and the piano, whereupon he said the football coaches had told him that if anyone could motivate a group of boys, it was I.

When I told him I had never coached cross country—or any sport for that matter—he said I didn't need to know anything about the sport, other than give the runners a pat on the back and tell them to hurry back. In previous years, the school had fared rather poorly and often didn't have the full 7-man squad, although Herndon at that time was the largest high school in the state, with over 3,000 students. Already having lost almost two weeks of practice, I blitzed the school to recruit runners.

On the first day of practice, 63 boys and three girls showed up. Not knowing what else to do with a herd of kids, I assembled them by grades, with a grade for each row. I put one athletic-looking runner, Dave Hamilton, in charge of calisthenics, and just like in the military, we performed the exercises by the numbers. The only things missing were the rifles and bayonets. The football coaches and players often asked how I was able get the runners to exercise so sharply and enthusiastically.

After the calisthenics, Stuart Close, obviously the most experienced runner on the squad, rushed up to me, addressed me as "Coach," and queried me on my theory of long distance running. First of all, I was greatly embarrassed to be addressed as such, inasmuch as I had never been an athlete and had jokingly said I didn't even know where the boys' locker room was. Further, I hadn't the slightest idea as to what Stuart was referring. I was able to maintain some sense of decorum, however, and told him that we didn't have time right then for such an exhaustive subject, and suggested he come by my room the next day so that we could give the matter the full attention it deserved. I should have just quoted Coach Pukal and said, "Hurry back."

When Stuart came to my room the next morning, I confessed that I knew nothing of coaching cross country, much less about any theory of long distance running. I told him if he would tell me what to do each day, I would pretend to be the coach. We were probably halfway through the season before the squad learned that I was hardly more than an adult supervisor. But we had a full varsity squad, two junior varsity squads, and two freshman squads. We coaches of the Great Falls District came to an understanding: We could enter only one varsity team in a meet, but as many junior varsity and freshman teams as we could field. Our runners filled an entire school bus for the away meets, and some of the older boys drove their own cars as well.

Our first meet was at Chantilly High School, and as our runners dashed out of the bus and their cars to begin their stretching exercises, I overheard one of the Chantilly runners say despairingly, "I thought we were running against Herndon today; they've never had anything like this!" I told him, "You *are* running against Herndon today, and you haven't seen anything yet." Our varsity team won the meet, and from then on, I could hardly make it through the crowded hallways at school without the football players and other athletes addressing me as "Coach," and telling me how happy they were that the team had finally put Herndon High School on the state athletic map.

We won one meet after another, and were invited to a number of open events, at locations such as the College of William and Mary in Williamsburg; Georgetown University in Washington, D.C.; and the Georgetown Boys' School in Rockville, Maryland. For both of the two years I coached cross country, I was nominated as Coach of the Year for the Great Falls District.

As the Herndon runners crossed the finish line, they would immediately want to know their time. However, I often forgot to set the stopwatch, and even when I did remember, I often became confused with so many runners crossing the finish line at once, especially in the large meets when the uniform colors of some of the other schools were the same as Herndon's. Since Margie went with me to many of the meets, she took over the job of keeping time and did it superbly. To Margie, a job was a job, whether it was meeting dignitaries in the Pentagon, making ends meet on my meager salaries, or baking pies for the Prince William County Fair. It took only a few meets for a runner crossing the finish line to ask, "Mrs. Danner, what's my time, please?" without so much as acknowledging me as his coach.

Although I had started out quite ignorant of the sport, coaching was probably the highlight of my teaching experience, and I appreciate Coach Pukal giving me the opportunity. I even learned to wrap ankles, and I quickly learned that athletes are not unlike the rest of us. I saw them laugh, and I saw them cry. One strapping boy became quite teary-eyed on the way back from a meet we had lost, saying that it was his fault and that he had ruined "my" record. He had inadvertently missed a course marker, thus disqualifying himself, and causing us to place second. He was one of our best runners; even so, I told him there would be other meets and he would go on to bigger and better things. A year later when he asked for a letter of recommendation to the United States Naval Academy, I had no reservations about writing one. I still have on my office wall the plaque the first team gave me at the sports banquet, inscribed "Herndon High School's supercoach'—Cross-Country Team, 1977."

One day while I was waiting for the runners to return, I was sitting in the bleachers with Coach Pukal, observing the marching band practice for the upcoming football game on Friday night. When the band practiced the National Anthem, I stood and sang the words, simply out of force of habit. Coach Pukal handed me a microphone. After the band finished, Coach Pukal told the band director that I would be singing the Star-Spangled Banner at the game. So, we practiced it again, from start to finish. For the rest of the season, I sang the anthem at the home games of both football and basketball. As I was singing the anthem that day, a wild mixture of emotions overcame me. I began to think of all the colleges and universities I had attended and even graduated from. As I remembered Troy State, the college I cherished the most, I could say only that I had attended it. I couldn't say that I was an alumnus. I wrote the university and told them of my feelings. Portions of the letter were printed in the alumni magazine, and I received a letter from the alumni association that I had been made an honorary alumnus. And I received dozens of letters from other alumni who shared my feelings of our alma mater.

While at Herndon, I set up an experimental reading program for challenged students while working on my doctorate. Based upon my work at American University, I designed several word games for the students, games that I am now looking to have programmed in Visual Basic computer language for wider use. A church member who owned a carpet business installed brand-new carpeting in the reading room, making it a very pleasant and relaxing place. I installed magazine racks and book spindles, removed the desks, and brought in card tables on which to play the word games I had created, as well as oversized bean bags to lounge on. Word of the program reached the division office, and I was invited to join a team in setting up a model program for high-school students with learning disabilities, mandated by *Public Law 94-144, The Education of All Handicapped Children*. One of the requirements for being a member of the team was taking a course in *PL 94-144* at University of Virginia. After being a member of the team for a semester, I was sent back to Herndon High School to set up a program based on the model we developed. I continued to revise the model for three more years.

Working with teenage boys often created a turmoil in me. I could practically see myself in every troubled boy I worked with. In many instances, it was difficult to separate my teaching from the problems the boys were encountering at home and in their personal lives. I was in a constant state of anxiety. I thereupon resigned my teaching post to accept a position as an editor in the public relations office of the Department of Defense at the Pentagon. But before I could begin the job, President Nixon froze all hiring. The Air Force Intelligence Service then called me to indefinite active duty and assigned me to the Defense Intelligence Agency in Arlington, Virginia, where I plotted the coordinates of strategic bombing targets. Let me add that revealing this information is not *verboten*; only the target locations were classified.

American University: Reaching the End of the Row

Immediately after beginning teaching at Herndon High School, I embarked upon a program of studies at American University in

Washington, on my birthday, February 4, 1970. My goal was to receive a Ph.D. in education. Just as at Troy State University when World War II veterans received free tuition and books, my tuition statement was stamped "Paid in full by the Veterans Administration." The VA also issued me a voucher which I could use to buy books as well as any materials and supplies I needed from the bookstore. Not only that, the VA paid me a nice monthly stipend, which included the basic amount plus an allowance for each of my dependents. It was surely one of the greatest opportunities I had ever received. I shall always be grateful to the Veterans Administration for helping disabled veterans overcome some of life's greatest struggles.

All went well at American University throughout the spring semester; I was learning how to teach reading to high school students under Dr. Paul Leedy, a noted scholar and textbook author. However, troubles began to overwhelm me at the beginning of the summer session. Being on vacation from teaching at the high school, I had the entire summer to study. The professor of learning disabilities was preparing the class for a practicum in which we would work with disabled children at the Horace Mann Elementary School, just across the street from the university. The professor, Dr. Alice Rosenfeld, told me to stay after class. She then informed me that I had an extremely serious hearing problem and that I was to report to the registrar and drop the course, as well as the practicum. I was dumbfounded—never had a professor talked to me in such a manner. I didn't know what to say, other than ask "How could you possibly know?" She responded that she resented my questioning her professionalism, that she had training and a background in working with the hearing-impaired. She reminded me she held a Ph.D. and her word was final. She later told me that she could tell I had a problem by the way I cocked my head. Until other students reminded me, I wasn't even aware that I hardly ever took notes; rather, I kept my eyes riveted on the instructor.

The Veterans Administration, which was paying for my education, came to my rescue. I called Mr. Meade at the VA office, and was told to report to Dr. Wintercorn, the head audiologist at the VA Hospital in Washington. I poured out my story to Dr. Wintercorn, who immediately fitted me with a temporary hearing aid, and scheduled me for further testing for a custom-fitted aid. It came as no shock to see the walls of her office covered with plaques of appreciation from the major veterans' groups, such as the Disabled American Veterans, Veterans of Foreign Wars, American Legion, Catholic War Veterans, and Jewish War Veterans, praising her for her compassionate service to veterans. In later years, as my hearing deteriorated, she fitted me with double hearing aids. She would continue as my audiologist until she retired many years later.

After seeing Dr. Wintercorn, I went to the professor's office and told her that I was now using a hearing aid. Thinking I could now hear perfectly, she allowed me to continue in her class. If she had only known that the contraption caused more problems than it solved, she would probably have expelled me from the program. The hearing aid picked up every footstep, every crumpling of paper, every little sound. Whispers sounded like angry hisses. I got to the point of turning the hearing aid off while in her class and promptly taking it out as soon as I was out of her sight. But at least I was able to finish her course and complete the practicum. Since the professor felt I couldn't understand the soft voices of children, she assigned me to a 16-year-old mildly retarded boy, who was reading only on a third-grade level. He improved his reading somewhat, and toward the end of the practicum, Jerry, my older son, and I took him to a world-class soccer game at RFK Stadium in Washington.

My situation with the professor of learning disabilities was mitigated somewhat by two of the best and most learned professors that I ever had—Dr. Paul Leedy, and Dr. Franz Huber, professor of learning theories. They were both on my doctoral committee; and though we had mutual respect for each other, Dr. Huber questioned one of my statistical methods for testing the efficacy of inductive learning and required that the calculations be done by a computer program at University of California. The calculations done on the mainframe computer confirmed my original findings.

Dr. Leedy was instrumental in my working with Sidwell Friends School in Washington. I was assigned to give a battery of reading tests to one of its students and work with him for the summer. The student was a 12-year-old black boy from Southeast

Washington, who had been adopted by a prominent Jewish family in Northwest D.C., next to Embassy Row. Not only did I have the opportunity to put what I was learning to immediate use, I had the privilege of meeting and working with one of the nicest families in the city. Since I went to work with him directly after my midday class, Mrs. Feinstein always had lunch ready for my charge and me. She understood well the benefits of sharing a meal together.

There was one last hurdle to completing the requirements for my doctorate. I had already passed advanced statistics, which was like a foreign language to me, as well the foreign language proficiency test. The School of Education at American University required four comprehensives—three in one's own area of the education field, and one in another field, such as computers, linguistics, history. I chose as my outside comprehensive 18th-century American literature. This literary period was already familiar to me, having taken two semesters of American intellectual history at University of Virginia, as well as two semesters of American studies at George Washington University; I was also teaching literature in high school. Furthermore, the Department of Literature at American University gave me several study guides as well as examples of prior comprehensives.

This period of American literature embraces the movements of romanticism, realism, and transcendentalism. I thought I knew the characteristics of the movements quite thoroughly. But on the seven-hour exam, there was not, to my dismay, a single *ism* question. One of the instructions was to write an essay on the contribution of Mark Twain to local color, and how this, in turn, influenced humor in other writers' works of the period. I knew something about each of the ten questions, and in some of them, I could make what I thought were logical connections to romanticism, realism, and transcendentalism. Consequently, I filled ten blue books with gobbledegook, making tangential references to all the *isms* I had so clearly in my mind. If I failed the test, I would have to wait six months to retake it.

The university had integrated rigid measures to protect students from any bias of an individual grader. For example, two professors grade the comprehensive, neither knowing who the other is, and then the results are passed independently to the head of the department. If one grader fails the student, but the other passes him, the student is given the benefit of passing. The head of the department called me into his office to tell me both professors had failed me on the exam, leaving me no recourse; he then advised me to see Dr. Starr, one of the graders. I will never forget what the learned professor said: "Mr. Danner, I have no doubt that you are well-versed in 18th-century American literature, probably, in certain areas, as well as I. Although you related a lot of impressive information, you simply didn't answer the questions." I had thought I could impress the graders with my array of knowledge, even though I knew I had been quite sketchy on many of the questions. I should have learned my lesson when in Mrs. Hartzog's sixth-grade class at Elamville I was always spouting off information, only to be booted out of her class for being a smart-aleck know-it-all.

I wanted to graduate the following May, and it was now February 1973. If I had to wait six months to be retested, I wouldn't be able to graduate until May 1974. I couldn't wait that long. I thought I was depleting the national treasury by allowing the government to pay for my schooling and give me $600 a month besides for living expenses. Not only that, I wanted to show the Veterans Administration that I had no plans to go to school for the rest of my life. So, again I went to the Department of Literature to find out what other comprehensives I might be able to take. I chose Colonial and Revolutionary American Literature, both of which I had also studied at University of Virginia. At New Orleans Baptist Theological Seminary, I had also studied the works of Early American theologians. This period included the works of theologians and diarists, such as Cotton Mather, Jonathan Edwards, John Smith, William Bradford, Anne Bradstreet, Michael Wiggelsworth, and William Byrd. With only minimal preparation, and desperate to graduate in May, I took the test, sticking to the questions without giving any extraneous information, and passed it with little problem. I suppose the moral to that story is to simply answer the questions.

My quest for an education had come a long way from Clio Low School, Clio, Alabama, with Miss Andrews teaching us to read "See Spot run." I had gone on to Troy State for two years; graduated from University of the Philippines; studied Spanish at St.

Anselm's University in Manchester, New Hampshire; received degrees in church music and religious education from New Orleans Baptist Theological Seminary; studied educational philosophy, literature and linguistics at University of Virginia; and took American studies and the teaching of English at George Washington University. I also took courses in teaching the gifted at James Madison University, Harrisonburg, Virginia, and technical writing at George Mason University in Fairfax, Virginia. I was almost ready to receive the Ph.D. in education from American University.

Receiving the Degree of Doctor of Philosophy in Education

Sunday, May 13, 1973, at Constitution Hall in Washington, D.C., was a red-letter day in my educational experience. It had been 34 years since I entered first grade at Clio Low School, and Margie and the three children were there to help celebrate the occasion. It was one of the happiest days of my life, hearing my name— Horace Gerald Danner—called out to receive the degree of Doctor of Philosophy; being hooded with the red, white, and blue colors of American University; and receiving the gold tassel signi-

Receiving the Ph.D. at Constitution Hall, Washington, DC

fying the Ph.D. degree. I suppose I needed the Ph.D. to assure me that I was indeed out of the cotton fields.

I thought the graduation speaker must have been privy to my personal odyssey to obtain an education when she said that she knew there were those who had faced many struggles to obtain their degrees. Then, in an apostrophe to the doctoral candidates, she said we must not stop simply because we had reached the pinnacle of our formal education. She concluded by urging us to put what we had learned into practice, to pay back to society what our teachers and family had invested in us. Yes, for me, it had been a struggle—a long, hard row to hoe—but I must keep going. I must begin another row—I must attempt to invest in others. I must continue to teach, as others had taught me.

Having been immersed in the teachings of 18th-century Amos Bronson Alcott (the father of Louisa Mae Alcott, author of *Little Men* and *Little Women*), together with other transcendentalists, such as Nathaniel Hawthorne, Henry David Thoreau, Ralph Waldo Emerson, and Emily Dickinson, I began to exult in nature, the human spirit, and the meaning of life itself. One Saturday afternoon in the fall, after I had received my degree, my family and I were out for a drive, savoring the glorious autumnal splendor of Virginia's Shenandoah Valley. We had left the valley and were making our ascent to the crest of Skyline Drive in the Blue Ridge Mountains when we stopped, as was our wont by the mountainside, to fill our jugs with clear water gushing from a crevice in the rock. Looking up toward the haughty, undulating mountains with their array of gold, purple, orange, and red, tinted with evergreens, I opened my arms to the heights and declaimed, "I behold and embrace thee, Nature; let me take thee to my breast." After expending myself of my emotions, I glanced over to see Margie rolling her eyes and huddling our three children in her arms, whereupon she said to me, "Please get in the car, and I'll drive home." It's probably not necessary to say the family didn't always espouse my new-found ideas.

The Air Force Intelligence Service (AFIS)

In 1973, the year I received the doctorate, the Reserve flying unit to which I was assigned as a training superintendent at Andrews

Air Force Base, Maryland, was realigned, and I lost my position. I had enough years for retirement, but I loved the Air Force and wanted to continue serving. Hearing that a particular skill of mine might be useful for the Air Force Intelligence Service (AFIS), I applied for a billet with the outfit, with headquarters at Fort Belvoir, Virginia. I was rather peremptorily informed that my rank was too high and that I was too old. I was a 40-year-old Master Sergeant.

At the time, I was testing students for a special program in the Fairfax County Public Schools, and it was necessary to speak with the parents of one of the students I had tested. The father, Claude Watkins, came in; during the course of our conversation, I casually mentioned that I was in the Air Force Reserves. He then said he was a retired Senior Master Sergeant working as a civilian with the Air Force Intelligence Service, the same unit that had earlier turned me down for a job. Claude said, "My outfit could certainly use your services." The very next week, I received a call from the adjutant of AFIS, saying the unit had an opening for me.

My first writing assignment with AFIS was to research the attitudes of the American people toward the involvement of the United States in war from the time of the American Revolution to the present. What I learned surprised me. All wars, even World War II, were opposed by a significant number of American citizens. The title of the research paper was "Not with Swords Loud Clashing."

Not long after I finished the research paper, AFIS sent a black major and me to Patrick Air Force Base, Florida, near Cape Canaveral, to attend a 7-week course on race relations. While there, I brought the family down, and we were all able to visit Disney World. Although Patty and Jerry had to return to Virginia after a week on Cocoa Beach, Margie and Stephen stayed five weeks, for the remainder of the course. Toward the end of the course, I was invited to remain as an instructor. Though we all enjoyed our time in Florida, especially the beaches, we wanted to continue living in Northern Virginia. After the major and I returned to Fort Belvoir, we led weekend race-sensitivity seminars for Air Force intelligence officers—both field grade and general—throughout the Washington area for about a year at Bolling Air Force Base, DC.

I was then assigned to Operation Homecoming, the program that debriefed freed Southeast Asia prisoners of war. The debriefings were written up and compiled into classified papers that would be used in training pilots and others in high risk-of-capture assignments. Though I was a Master Sergeant when assigned, within two years, I had put on two additional stripes, to become Chief Master Sergeant. During my tenure with the intelligence community, I was designated the chief editor in the group; I was the only enlisted man in the editorial department. One of my papers, "Coping Strategies of Long-Term Prisoners of War," was published as a classified paper.[25]

Throughout my 35 years in the Reserves, I applied several times for a direct commission, but in each instance was disqualified because of having extremely poor hearing. Then, in 1974, my potentially big break came. I had received the Ph.D. and was an editor and writer for the Air Force Intelligence Service, when the Air Force initiated a commissioning program for those with advanced degrees, with no restrictions on hearing acuity, if keenness of hearing was not critical to the position one might hold. First of all, one needed to secure a billet before applying for the commission. I sought and obtained a position with the Defense Intelligence School (then headquartered at Anacostia Naval Station, D.C.). The billet approved for me was as an instructor with the rank of major. After all the paperwork was completed, the Air Force said it was restricting commissions to those with advanced degrees in the scientific and technological disciplines. After this, I resigned myself to enjoying the status of holding the highest enlisted rank.

During the summer of 1974, AFIS sponsored a family picnic, where the most outrageously delicious, barbecued chicken was served. It had a tangy, but sweet, garlicky taste. Not only I, but everyone, commented on its delicacy. I learned that the chef who prepared the chicken was a Chief Master Sergeant, originally from Taiwan. On the following workday, I called him and asked if he could scale down the recipe for a family of five, which he did, over the phone. In the years afterward, we have served the chicken at least 200 times and have shared the recipe with at least a hundred other persons. In fact, I have been asked by several organizations to prepare it at alfresco events. My daughter, who has pre-

[25] The title itself is not classified.

pared it on numerous occasions for her family and guests, calls it Pentagon chicken, but I told her it was more like Fort Belvoir chicken, since that is where the picnic was held. More properly, it could be called Chinese chicken, or, as the Chief said, Polynesian chicken.[26]

During the summer of 1976, I was stationed at the Pentagon, where I did some writing for the Secretary of the Air Force. By now, Stephen, at age 13, had changed his mind about being a Green Beret; his main goal now was to be a submariner and was interested in the Navy's Trident missile program. He said he wanted to have a talk with the Secretary of the Navy. I promptly told him that the Honorable J. William Middendorf didn't talk with young boys, he talked with the Secretary of the Army and the Secretary of the Air Force, even the President of the United States and foreign military attaches. That didn't satisfy Stephen. Again, I told him there was no way Mr. Middendorf could find time to talk to him. Stephen reassured me that I could get him an interview. Finally acquiescing, I said I would check with Mr.

With the Honorable Mr. Middendorf at the Pentagon

[26] If you would like the recipe, you can e-mail me at recipe@imprimis-books.com.

Middendorf's secretary, stifling my amusement at his presumptuousness. I went to the Secretary of the Navy's office and asked his secretary if she would do me a favor. I told her of Stephen's request and asked if she would please drop Stephen a line and tell him that Mr. Middendorf couldn't possibly speak with him. I assumed she would find Stephen's audacity as amusing as I had. She said she would be glad to write the letter after she had talked with Mr. Middendorf and let me know. I felt so satisfied that I had done my job, and that would be the end of it. In about an hour, she called and said that the Secretary of the Navy would be happy to see my son. Mr. Middendorf had called in an official Navy photographer, who took a picture of the three of us: the Honorable Secretary, Stephen, and me. Mr. Middendorf didn't appear that it was anything out of the ordinary to be talking with a 13-year-old boy about the Navy. He advised Stephen to live each day to the fullest and realize his dream of being a good soldier, whatever the service he might eventually choose. Mr. Middendorf could not have been a more perfect gentleman. Stephen was so awed by the 6-foot statesman that he forgot to ask about the Navy's missile program. In about a week, we received a framed autographed picture, dated August 18, 1976, two days after Stephen's birthday.

In 1977 and 1978, I was sent to Hickam Air Force Base, just outside Honolulu, for my two-week active duty reserve assignments. On one of those tours, I had the privilege of flying in a KC-135, an airborne refueling plane. I lay on my belly alongside the boom operator to witness the refueling operation. As the KC-135 lumbered along at around 400 miles per hour, its belly bloated with thousands of pounds of fuel, a jet fighter shot in behind us at about 1,000 miles per hour, impatiently slowing to our crawling speed. The boom from the refueler shot out, maneuvering to lock into the jet. The boom operator asked the pilot how much juice he wanted, to which he replied, "Oh, just a few pounds to get back to Hickam." The operator said, "Well, we're flying pretty heavy. Why don't you take some of this weight off us and go on a picnic?" As soon as the pilot had taken on about 2,000 pounds of fuel, the operator pulled in the boom, and the pilot banked sharply and was immediately out of sight.

While I was at Hickam that summer, two of my friends rented a car and asked me to ride with them around the island. After we left Honolulu and were inland, I couldn't believe what I saw: boarded-up shanties; stray, junkyard dogs; rusted automobiles and refrigerators sitting in the front yard or alongside the road; and dilapidated country stores. We then came upon expanses of pineapple plantations, owned by Dole on one side of the road, and DelMonte on the other. I told the other two fellows I wanted to look firsthand at a pineapple growing on the plant. One of them told me to make it worth my time and pick one. When ripe, a pineapple bends downward like an ear of corn ready to be picked. I didn't know it was ready to be harvested however; I cupped one of the pineapples in my hand, only for it to break off from the plant. I took the pineapple to the car and asked my friends what I was going to do with it. One of them said, "Eat it; you're the one who stole it." As I was about to get back in the car, I noticed a "No Trespassing" sign, which said that picking the fruit was forbidden and trespassers would be prosecuted. I took the pineapple back to my room, where it sat for almost a week. I couldn't bear to eat it, until another of my friends said if I didn't, it would dry up. I still would like to pay the owners of the pineapple ranch for the luscious fruit, but I can't remember if was Dole or DelMonte. I'm trying to atone for my error by eating a lot of pineapple.

In 1979, AFIS sent me to Korea for two weeks to observe the integration of the American and South Korean air forces in the air defense of the Republic of Korea. About 20 of us stationed at Osan Air Base were guests of the South Korean Government. Treated to an all-day affair in Seoul, we had a buffet of over 100 specialties of Korean Peninsula cuisine at the King David Hotel. No one warned me about the kimchi, a spicy pickled cabbage dish, seasoned with garlic, red-hot peppers, and onions. To assuage the burning, I drank not only my own glass of water, but also the glasses of two of my friends.

Being the highest-ranking member of the group, I was selected to lay the wreath at the Tomb of the Unknown Soldier of the Korean War. That evening, we were treated to a concert at the Walker Sheraton; one of the artists sang a Korean folk song, and then modulated into "Edelweiss" from *The Sound of Music*. She had announced that she was dedicating the song to the American servicemen who were so valiantly guarding her country. With the Demilitarized Zone (DMZ) only about 25 miles north of

Seoul, North Korea's artillery was at that moment aimed toward South Korea. When she got to the part about "Bless my homeland forever," I don't think there was a dry eye among us.

While in Korea, I bought Margie a jade necklace; I'm not good at picking out gifts, but I must have made a good choice, for Margie liked it tremendously and wears it often. In addition to the necklace, I bought several other gifts, which I chose to have sent by mail. At the wrapping station of the Base Exchange, a Korean employee had posted a sign with the caveat "No obcene publicans raped." At first taken aback, I soon figured out that they didn't wrap obscene publications.

Fauquier High School, Warrenton, Virginia

As mentioned previously, after leaving my teaching position at Fairfax County Public Schools, the Air Force Intelligence Service called me to temporary active duty. One day I took leave to take Margie to the dentist in Warrenton, about 15 miles west of Manassas, where we lived. While she was in the dentist's office, I walked across the street to the personnel office of the Fauquier County Public Schools and casually inquired about a teaching job since I didn't know how long the Air Force was going to keep me on active duty. Though it was the middle of the school year, I was given a contract almost on the spot. So, on February 1, 1981, I began teaching English and mathematics to high school students with learning disabilities—again! The director of personnel promised that he would place me on tenure at the end of the semester, inasmuch as I had been tenured when I left Fairfax County Public Schools.

Shortly after I began teaching at Fauquier High School, I was reminded by the principal that I had the dubious honor of being the only Ph.D. in the entire school system, including the superintendent. When I began checking the records of the students, I found that the school appeared to be flouting the mandates of *P.L. 94-144, The Education of All Handicapped Children*, which put me at odds with the administration immediately. The principal said that the school had been doing just fine before I arrived on the scene.

When I went to Fauquier, I had just written a vocabulary book, *Words from the Romance Languages*, which held considerable promise for students taking the verbals of the college boards. I asked the principal for permission to work with regular students after school, using the book. His words still ring in my ears: "Dr. Danner, I think you're on the same level as your special education students—you're not capable of very much." So, I bided my time, waiting for the opportune moment to broach the subject again.

Although I had never received anything less than a superior rating in Fairfax County, a more progressive school system than Fauquier's, the first evaluation of my classroom performance at Fauquier High School was anything but sterling. One of the assistant principals (and my immediate supervisor), called me into his office to share his assessment of me. He remarked that the jury was still out, and handed me my evaluation, saying when I was finished reading it over, I was to return it "to one of the other assistant principals or *I*." I simply couldn't resist telling him with utter indignation, "You mean to tell me I'm being evaluated on my teaching methods by a principal who obviously doesn't know to use the objective case of a pronoun after a preposition!" My fiery comment took me just one step closer toward leaving the Fauquier school system.

Toward the end of the school year, I was called out of my room to the office, where the principal and an assistant principal informed me they could not recommend my being tenured inasmuch as I hadn't been observed in the classroom. I told them that I had been there every day, and asked where they had been. When I reminded them of the personnel director's promise to place me on tenure, they said they ran the school, not the personnel director.

The school treated its football players as though they were gods, but the students in special education didn't even have a room where we teachers could display teaching aids the students needed for hands-on experience. I asked the new principal if we could clean out one of the empty trailers on the school grounds so that our students could have a permanent room. He said that he was reserving the trailer to put weight-training equipment in for the football players, reminding me that special education was the lowest of his priorities.

In my second year at Fauquier, I was finally permitted to hold an after-school class for college-bound students, using the book I had written. It was such a delight to balance my work with students with learning disabilities with those who were educationally aggressive and intellectually stimulated. It was very likely because of this class that the book received national as well as international recognition. One of the students went on to Howard University in Washington, D.C., and took the book with him, where his classics professor, Dr. Thomas J. Sienkewicz, ordered one to use in his classes, and then invited me to Howard to speak to his class. When Dr. Sienkewicz later accepted an endowed chair at Monmouth College in Illinois, he introduced Dr. Roger Noël to me, and we have been writing partners and collaborators ever since. While my field is educational psychology and English, Dr. Noël's is classical languages, thus making a synergetic relationship. In a recent letter, Dr. Sienkewicz related how he still uses the word-clustering technique I developed for using in *Words from the Romance Languages* (see endorsements at end of book).

Almost everything I tried to accomplish at Fauquier High School was negated by the administration. After two and a half years at the school, I was called to the office in April, where the principal said he was refusing to renew my contract—even though I was now tenured. I asked him had I done anything wrong, to which he replied, "Nothing. You're a very well-liked teacher, but you're just not a team player." After all I had tried to do, I was left with no one to turn to, and I felt utterly abandoned. Several of the parents of the students with whom I was working protested the principal's action, advising me to sue the school board to get my job back. I wanted nothing more to do with the system, feeling that if they didn't want me, I didn't want them.

With that, after fourteen years, I left high school teaching for good and immediately began teaching reading and literature at Northern Virginia Community College (NOVA), Manassas Campus. While teaching at NOVA, the Air Force Intelligence Service called me, requesting that I serve a special tour of active duty at the Pentagon to write a series of papers that were later presented at NATO headquarters in Brussels, Belgium.

Two years later when I escorted Margie to Blacksburg to receive her Master's from Virginia Tech, a male student rushed up to us and said that he would not be at Tech if it hadn't been for the after-school vocabulary class I had taught at Fauquier. It was a seeminly small gesture on his part, but it made me feel that my efforts at Fauquier High School had not been entirely wasted.

North Fork Baptist Church: A Civil War Field Hospital for both the North and the South

Shortly after leaving Manassas Baptist Church and while I was teaching at Herndon High School and attending American University, the North Fork Baptist Church, near Purcellville, Virginia, called, asking that I fill in for their pastor. By this time, I had been ordained by Manassas Baptist Church, and was approved to administer Communion, and officiate at baptisms, funerals, and weddings.

About an hour's drive north of Manassas, North Fork Baptist Church, as the name implies, was situated on the north fork of the Shenandoah River, and nestled in the higher foothills of Virginia's Piedmont. The soaring Blue Ridge Mountains could be seen in the distance. The church, over 200 years old, served as a military hospital for both Union and Confederate troops during the Civil War. There are still bloodstains on the solid oak planks of the floor, from the amputations performed by field surgeons during the war. Its gallery had been built to accommodate the seating of slaves. I encouraged the church to seek national historical site recognition, and before I left the pastorate at North Fork five years later, it had indeed been recognized as such, with a bronze plaque attached to the entrance of the stone structure.

One of the highlights at North Fork was to have Jen Lee, one of my students at Herndon High School, come and sing for us. When Jen was assigned to me as a ninth grader, the principal told me to teach him how to read. Jen was a fine, handsome young man, fresh out of South Korea, but he could speak only four or five words in English. I used all my free time, including lunchtime, to work with him. The toll on both of us was exasperating. One day I asked him if he had any hobbies, to which he replied he liked to sing. I learned that he had been in a school run by Presbyterians in Korea and that he liked to sing "How Great Thou Art." So, a part of his learning to read was learning the hymn in English. Every few days, we would go to the music room to practice. Then, I invited him to sing at the church. The church had a covered dish luncheon, the likes of which one can only find in Northern Virginia. He demonstrated eating with chopsticks and challenged the most daring to try their luck with them. My son Jerry picked them up and started using them as though he were an Oriental. The day was truly memorable. Three years later, Jen graduated from Herndon High School with honors and then joined the Air Force. He later served as a crewmember of Air Force One at Andrews Air Force Base. While I was teaching at Fauquier, he came by to see me, dressed in his Air Force blues.

On December 1, 1974, on a cold, blustery, snowy Sunday, we heard an awful boom during the worship service. We learned later that a TWA plane had crashed on Mount Weather, only a few miles west of the church, killing all 92 people on board. For some inexplicable reason, I was drawn like a magnet to the crash site, and Margie and I visited the scene the next week, noting the sturdy mountainside trees that had been sheared as the plane descended, finally hitting a massive, jutting rock, and flipping the plane over. Though the plane and the most of the débris had been cleared, we saw a baby's shoe lying on the ground. Only a few years later, we returned to Mount Weather, and except for the jutting rock, there was no evidence of the crash. It is surprising how Nature shows little regard for our human frailties and foibles. In spite of our manmade wars, automobile accidents, plane crashes, and train wrecks, Nature just keeps on doing its job, and I was reminded of Carl Sandburg's poem "Grass":

> *Pile the bodies high at Austerlitz and Waterloo.*
> *Shovel them under and let me work—*
> *I am the grass; I cover all.*

> *And pile them high at Gettysburg*
> *And pile them high at Ypres and Verdun.*
> *Shovel them under and let me work.*
> *Two years, ten years, and passengers ask the conductor:*
> *What place is this?*
> *Where are we now?*

> *I am the grass.*
> *Let me work.*

My Final Tour to Honolulu

In 1981, 30 years after my first visit to Honolulu aboard a Navy troop ship, the Air Force sent me there for the seventh time on a 13-week Reserve tour—this time, however, on a Boeing 747, and I was able to bring some of my family over for two weeks. My assignment was at Intelligence Center Pacific at Camp Smith, a Marine installation. On a reserve assignment, one isn't usually paid until the tour is complete, although on an extended tour, one can receive a pay advance. Since Margie, Patty, and her 4-year-old son, Nathan, were coming, I went to the finance office to ask for an advance. At home, we hardly ever ate in a restaurant, and our lives revolved around either going to school or teaching school. But while they were on the island, I wanted them to have the opportunity to eat in ethnic restaurants, visit and buy in Honolulu's shops, visit the Polynesian Cultural Center, and do all the other things vacationers like to do in Hawaii. The finance sergeant asked me how much I wanted to withdraw. Not used to spending money, I told him maybe a couple of hundred dollars. The sergeant informed me that once I returned to Bolling Air Force Base in Washington, D.C., I would be drawing over $3,000, and sug-

Margie and Patty arriving in Honolulu

gested that I might want to take a little more than a mere $200. So, I withdrew $500, the most money I had ever had in my pocket at one time. I didn't use any of the money to purchase leis to celebrate Margie and Patty's arrival; a friend and I picked orchid petals in her backyard and made the leis ourselves.

So, with my pocket bulging with money, we ate in Japanese and Polynesian restaurants, enjoyed Mongolian barbecue, took in the sights, including Punchbowl Crater National Cemetery, Diamond Head, the Polynesian Cultural Center, and enjoyed the private Air Force beach. With the catamarans and their brightly colored sails, the view was a perfect setting for "Red Sails in the Sunset," a popular song in earlier years.

I gave the advance to Margie and encouraged her to visit the shops and spend it on anything that fancied her, while I was at work. She and Patty toured the pineapple and macadamia nut factories—which had no admission fees—and bought some sewing material in Honolulu, but when we returned home, she still had most of the money.

For the two weeks they were in Honolulu, we housesat for a colonel, who was my boss. In fact, it was he who suggested that I bring the family over to take care of the house and walk the dog while he and his family were on the mainland. We had two cars— a BMW and a Volvo—to drive as we saw fit. Since the cars bore the colonel's insignia, I had to get used to returning the security guards' salutes when I entered a military installation. I felt so guilty returning the salute that I told one of the guards that I was a chief master sergeant, not a colonel, to which he replied that he was saluting the colonel's decal, not me personally. The only shadow in our two weeks together on the island was Margie's father dying; we simply couldn't arrange the logistics of her getting all the way back to New Hampshire in time for the funeral.

Of course, one of the sights at Pearl Harbor was the *USS Arizona*, the watery entombment of over a thousand sailors and officers. Oil still oozes to the surface, even after all these years. The day Margie and I paid our respects at the *Arizona* was also the occasion for around 200 Japanese Boy Scouts to do the same. It struck both Margie and me as a little strange that contemporary Japanese make visiting the *Arizona* an important pilgrimage. Our uneasiness was unfounded, however, for the scouts bowed and deferred to us at every turn. The young Japanese could not have been more polite.

Two of my dearest friends are Retired Navy Captain William M. Carpenter and his wife, Mary. They remark the surprise bomb-

The Carpenters as newlyweds

ing of Pearl Harbor and Hickam Air Force Base with their first-hand account. Fresh out of the U.S. Naval Academy, Bill was an ensign on the *USS Oklahoma*, which, along with 90 other warships, was docked at Pearl Harbor. On the night before the "date of infamy," as President Roosevelt called it, Ensign Carpenter had shore leave, and had gone into Honolulu to spend a honeymoon night with his new bride. They had been married two months earlier in Reno, Nevada, while the *Oklahoma* was docked in San Francisco. But Bill had to ship out the very night of their wedding. Mary followed Bill to Hawaii and then got a job as a private-duty nurse in Honolulu. Of course, the fate of the *Oklahoma* was that of the *Arizona* as well as dozens of other warships, and Bill would surely have been killed had he been on board awaiting his turn as officer-of-the-deck at noon on Sunday, December 7. Before it was time for him to return to the *Oklahoma* to stand watch, the ship was torpedoed. Bill and Mary were awakened by the sound of distant gunfire, which they then learned was from the Japanese attack on Pearl Harbor. Bill and a shipmate rushed to the naval base, but the *Oklahoma*, with many shipmates trapped below decks, had already rolled over.

Both stalwart members of Lake Ridge Baptist Church, Bill and Mary just celebrated 57 years of marriage. By their obvious love and devotion for each other, they appear still to be honeymooners. If Bill isn't attending a Pacific Rim economic conference in Tokyo or speaking at a high-level symposium in Honolulu, I can count on him and Mary every Sunday sitting in the second row of Lake Ridge Baptist Church for the second service.

I had other Reserve assignments at Hickam Air Force Base, where one can still see bullet holes in the Pacific Air Force headquarters building. The holes have been left as a sad reminder of our unpreparedness when the Japanese bombed and strafed the base. Another assignment was Scott Air Force Base, in Illinois. On one weekend at Scott, I caught a military hop to Denver, and then rented a car to drive down to Fort Carson to see my son Stephen, who was stationed there. We toured the Air Force Academy, shared a meal in one of those Western steak houses, and would have climbed to Pike's Peak, but the fog was too thick on that particular day.

End of an Air Force Career—in Panama

Even though I have been envied for my many tours to Honolulu, probably my most memorable military experience was my last tour, in 1985, at Howard Air Force Base, in Panama. There was a mix-up in my orders, and the people at Howard thought I would be coming a week later. Consequently, I arrived in Panama with no Air Force host to meet me. Before arriving, I didn't know that Howard was 40 miles from Panama City; anyway, the distance would not have been a concern if the Air Force provided the transportation. I saw three or four other Americans in the throngs, who happened to be headed for Fort Clayton, which was on the way to Howard. So we pooled our resources and hired a taxi. Once we arrived at Howard, I was in for another shock—I didn't have a place to sleep, since they weren't expecting me. But since I was traveling on official orders, they found a room for me—in the BOQ—bachelor officer quarters. And since the BOQ was so far from my office, the Air Force sent a military taxi for me each morning.

The word on a stop sign in most Latin American countries is PARA. But no so in Panama, where the traditional red octagonal sign has the word ALTO, which is the Spanish word for "high." At first, I didn't know quite what to make of it. However, because of the Americans' building of the Panama Canal, the Panamanians have adopted many English words. I surmised that they took our word *halt*, dropped the *h* which is silent in Spanish, and added the masculine *o* ending to get ALTO. If my rendition is not correct, at least it satisified my mind.

Amazingly, the sun rises in the Pacific and sets in the Atlantic in Panama. One only needs to look at a map of the Isthmus of Panama to see why. While at Howard, I saw the Panama Canal, and the ships gliding through the narrow channel, with only inches to spare on either side. In Panama, I was also able to use my Spanish. To confirm my return flight reservations, I went to the travel office at Howard, where the clerk was a Panamanian. He said he was unable to confirm my reservations, since the airline office in downtown Panama City was on siesta. I asked him what *siesta* meant, and he rolled his eyes and said, "Oh, you know, nappy nap time." I asked if he knew how we got the word. He replied that he hadn't the foggiest idea. I told him the word came from Latin *sexta hora*, or sixth hour, and was the sixth hour from sunrise, thus being the hottest part of the day. He said that sounded perfectly logical.

Two other experiences capped my two weeks in Panama. When the operations officer, a lieutenant colonel, told me he was from Oklahoma, memories of the Broadway musical *Oklahoma* came to mind. I told him that I had always wanted to visit his beautiful state, that I had images of it being a very exciting place. He drawled, "Well, Chief, I suggest you put Oklahoma sorta low on yur priority list, fer there ain't much ta see there." Back in Northern Virginia, I was working out with a rather distinguished gentleman at the gym. We were walking out to the parking lot when I noticed his car had an Oklahoma license plate, whereupon I related to him what the colonel in Panama had said. He said he begged to differ, that Oklahoma was indeed one of the best and most exciting places on Earth. When I asked him what made him so proud and possessive of such a barren and forbidding outpost—as the colonel had said—he asserted that he was the representative for the 4th Congressional District of Oklahoma. A little distraught, I left the miffed congressman without a handshake. Telling the incident to others, I was usually rewarded with at least a chuckle.

The other incident involves a very attractive and charming Panamanian señorita, who was a clerk in our office. She was wearing a jonquil-colored blouse, streaked with black lightning bolts; in my best Spanish, I asked her where I could buy such a blouse, that I wanted to buy one just like it for my wife. I thought surely the only place to buy one would be in one of the bustling international markets in Panama City. In flawless English, she replied she had bought it at Filene's Basement in Boston, where she was attending an IBM training seminar.

Working for The MITRE Corporation and Teaching at Northern Virginia Community College

About the same time I left high school teaching and had accepted a part-time job teaching reading and survey of literature at Northern Virginia Community College, I began working as an editor-analyst with The MITRE Corporation in McLean, Virginia, analyzing certain aspects of Third World countries' telecommunications capabilities. I also edited the engineers' contributions to the reports we produced on these countries. Once, while I was at MITRE, a director from another department borrowed me to work with one of his engineers in writing up a report on a computer configuration for the Air Force. It is simply not true of the old saying that engineers can't write, because I gained a lot of technical writing expertise in working with engineers who could also write well. But this particular engineer, considered one of the finest in his field, simply couldn't put a subject and verb together into a coherent sequence. My expertise is as a microeditor, rather than a macroeditor—I analyze individual sentences and try to make them into a logical paragraph. Consequently, I didn't think I could help him with his analysis. Then, I took a blank sheet of paper and asked him to tell me about the configuration, to go through it step by step. He related the process fluently, and as he did so, I jotted down the sequence. We followed this process throughout the document. After word spread that a literature and music teacher could take an engineer's findings and turn them into a document that flowed, I was declared a corporate-wide asset and made an editor-at-large for the corporation.

As already stated, I had just begun teaching English part-time at Northern Virginia Community College, at three of the five campuses—Alexandria, Annandale, and Manassas. Teaching there on a regular basis gave me the opportunity to test the ideas in *Discover It!*, a vocabulary book I had written in the inductive mode.

While at MITRE, I studied Russian with the idea of accepting an assignment as an arms inspector in the former Soviet Union. Russian was difficult for me, and I came to accept that I would never become fluent in the language, mainly because of Russian's unvoiced consonants, which I cannot hear, even with hearing aids. But I needed help with a translation—in particular, that of CCCP, which is Russian for USSR—for the vocabulary book I was writing. So, I went to a fellow MITRE technical staff member, Robert Garrow, a retired Marine colonel, and a Russian linguist. From Vermont, Bob was the type of Green Mountain fellow who didn't laugh much and who didn't put up with any foolishness. For instance, he was aware that I played the piano, though it wasn't something any self-respecting Marine would do, he said, even in the privacy of his own home. But, he said that was my business.

On this particular day, he deigned to ask how my weekend was shaping up. I told him I guessed I'd have to go to the Fort Belvoir commissary to buy a few groceries. In typical Vermont fashion, his response was short and quick, "And, may I ask, of all people, why would *you* be going to a commissary?" I told him I was retired military. He would have none of it, declaring that I was not the military type. I then told him I was an E-9, an Air Force Chief Master Sergeant. He said that he had known a lot of Navy chief petty officers, Army sergeant majors, Marine gunnery sergeants, as well as Air Force chief master sergeants, and that they were all pretty rough and tough men and that I simply didn't fit the bill. When I insisted I did not lie, he said that if I was military, I reminded him more of a lackluster captain relegated to some remote office of the Pentagon than a chief master sergeant with eight stripes on his sleeve and eleven ribbons on his chest. I took my military ID card from my billfold and showed it to him. His only response was, "How did you get it?"

Another of my colleagues at MITRE, Brigadier General William Tidwell, asked me what I was teaching at NOVA. I told him I was teaching English to international students. With a chuckle, he said that Northern Virginia would soon be inundated with foreigners speaking with an Alabama accent. Since we were both in the international program at MITRE, he came by my office nearly every day, however, to hear the anecdotes I told of the interchanges with my students. In the students' writings, I learned many heartbreaking stories of the Vietnamese boat people, Afghans displaced by the Soviet invasion, and the turmoil between Ethiopia and Somalia.

One day, not long after I had begun at MITRE, Charles Bradshaw, a sharp engineer, and I were discussing his technical article that he was going to present to Pentagon officials. He used the term *plesiochronous* (pronounced pleezy OCK rhu nus) as casually as he might discuss the weather. When I looked at Charles askance, he replied rather disdainfully that I must surely know the word, reminding me that not only was I the technical editor in a systems engineering division, I was also compiling a thesaurus of Latin and Greek word roots that would later be published. I had to confess that not only did I not know the word, I had never even heard of it before. Furthermore, the way that it was pronounced, I did not decipher the *chronos* part, which would indicated that it had to do with "time." I knew of *plesiosaurus*, but at the moment, I simply didn't make the connection.

Then Charles explained it to me. He said that in data systems the two timing devices do not operate at the same rate, that they are both asynchronous, not synchronous. Consequently, a buffer must be added that reconciles the two clocks. Such buffers are called plesiochronous timing devices. Charles said that the word was used quite often in data systems seminars. I said that surely the seminar leader must have explained the word. I figured that if I didn't know the word, surely engineers needed to have it explained to them in detail. After all, engineers already have their thing—number-crunching computers, formulae, and algorithms. Words are my turf! Charles said that the word didn't need explaining.

After Charles perceived my troubled countenance, he said that the word was quite easy, telling me that *plesio* means "near" and *chronos* means "time." Thus, the timing device brings the two clocks "nearer" in time. And, mind you, he was telling me! I thought that was my job.

Less than a week later, Bill Tidwell rushed into my office. The doyen of the office, Bill could discuss synthetic aperture radars and moving target indicators just as blithely as he could discuss the differences in the oratorical styles of Demosthenes and Cicero or Horace. There was a saying around the office that if Bill didn't know it, there was no need for us commoners to bother learning it, and very much like a saying heard across the country, "If you can't find it at Wal-Mart or Home Depot, you really don't need it." "Horace," he exclaimed, "I need to know what *plesiochronous* means. It's not in any of my technical and unabridged dictionaries." I calmly replied, "Come now, Bill. *Plesiochronous* simply describes a timing device to correct the difference in asynchronous clocks in data systems. In the business, we call it 'near time.' " Giving me a somewhat quizzical, yet satisfied, look, Bill only shook his head. I just said silently, "Thank you, Charles, for salvaging my credibility."

In one of the classes, I had a Somali young man and an Ethiopian young woman. I told the students that we were a microcosm of the United Nations, and that I hoped we wouldn't have any explosion of international tension in the class. I then directed the talk to the Somali and the Ethiopian, noting that their countries hadn't been the best of friends for 30 years, since the United Nations demarcated an arbitrary boundary between the two countries. The young lady smiled and said, "Only our countries are enemies." Before the term was over, the two were dating.

One day in class, a young lady from Peru appeared rather bored with the class exercise, probably from having worked all night before the early-morning class. Like Dr. Sterkx, who chided a young lady for clipping her nails in his American history class at Troy State, I turned to her and asked in Spanish, "Señorita Rodríguez, Usted no está interesada en la clase?" With a smile irradiating her entire face, she replied, "Sí, profesor; yo estoy muy interesada en su clase." I then turned to the student from Ethiopia, who also seemed to be lost at times, and said to him, "Now, if I only knew how to ask the same question in Amharic." I then nodded to each of the other international students and said respectively, "And Arabic, Chinese, Dari, Farsi, Hebrew, Hindi, Japanese, Korean, Pashto, Russian, Urdu." Finally, a student who was a plain ol' "Amurican," asked, "How about English?" The American student was in the class because he hadn't scored high enough on the entrance examination to take the basic courses in English composition.

On another occasion, a six-foot bronze-complexioned student opened the classroom door and peered inside as though he might have gone to the wrong room. From having taught international students for several years, I thought I could identify most nationalities merely by their physiognomies. However, I was at a loss to identify his country. Before he had a chance to take a seat, I said, "And which country are you from, may I ask?" He snapped to attention, and articulated very smartly, "Sir, I am from the Republic of Somalia." I then asked which city he was from—Mogadishu, Kisamayu, Bardera, or Erigavo. At the time, I was working at MITRE on technical overviews on Somalia and Djibouti, and consequently, knew the names of the major cities of both countries. Absolutely nonplused, he replied, "Sir, since I have been in this country, no one has even heard of my country, much less my hometown of Kisamayu." Of course, that was years before our country's involvement there. I might also add that I still can't tell the difference between a Somali and an Ethiopian, or either of them from an Eritrean. All three of the nationalities possess very pleasing features.

Usually, on the first day of class for international students, I ask them to write their equivalent of "Thank you" on the board. I felt that seeing the disparate ways of writing the expression would help bring them together as a community. While we had the usual expressions, such as *gracias*, *merci*, there were some, such as in Chinese, Korean, and Urdu, that can't be written in English. To my dismay, some of the students had no ready word for "Thank you." The highlight of teaching international students is to have them at my home for a cookout at the end of the semester, and it's especially fun to watch a non-Oriental try to beat a Korean, Vietnamese, or Chinese at ping-pong.

In January 1991, the dean of the English Department at NOVA called me at MITRE on the first day of class, saying that one of their reading teachers had fallen on the ice, breaking her leg, and asked if I could fill in for her until a permanent substitute could be found. MITRE gave me permission to teach two morning classes three days a week at the college, with the provision that I make up the time in the evenings. The teacher was out for the entire semester. At the end of the semester, the adjunct faculty was considerably reduced at the Annandale campus, and it was necessary for me to find other part-time employment.

Since MITRE had already given notice that my position would soon be abolished, I sought and received a position teaching freshman English composition at Montgomery College, Maryland, at the Germantown campus. I taught all morning at the college and then returned to MITRE in the afternoons, since I was now working only half time for MITRE. At the Germantown campus, I was selected as the adjunct professor making the most valued contribution to the college. My students had scored higher in a collegewide essay test than those of any other professor at the three campuses. I was also requested by the department head to make a presentation on the backgrounds of interesting words for the talented and gifted sixth graders of Montgomery County who would be visiting the campus on a particular Saturday. I made the presentation in one-hour blocks, as the students rotated all day. The eighth-grade daughter of one of my writing students illustrated the words on show cards, which I still use. For example, the student painted a Mexican boy (muchacho) sitting under an enormous hat (a sombrero) that cast a giant shadow. *Sombrero*, literally, means "under the shade." Since *atascadero* in Spanish means "mudhole," she illustrated Atascadero, California, a beautiful city I am told, with boys and girls playing in a puddle and making mud pies.

After teaching at Germantown for a semester, I was called to the main campus in Rockville, where I taught technical writing for four semesters. In one of those classes, I had a student, who was the son of the Ambassador of Myanmar, formerly known as Burma. I was invited to the Ambassador's home for a luncheon; it was through the ambassador that my vocabulary book was later used at the University of Mandalay. I was also invited to a reception given by the Embassy of Myanmar, in celebration of their Armed Forces Day. The reception area was surrounded by picketers who were protesting slave labor in Myanmar. At the reception, I met the ministers of defense from at least a hundred other countries, and was consequently invited to a number of other events. All this time, I was still working for MITRE half-time and teaching at the Manassas and Alexandria campuses of NOVA in the early mornings and in the evenings. It was a hectic schedule that I doubt I could handle again.

During my teaching at Montgomery College, I went home to Alabama for a Christmas vacation. While there, I had dinner with my brother James' extended family, including his and Ada's children, grandchildren, and greatgrandchildren. I was seated at a table with young men of late high school or college age. I told them at Montgomery College at least half the men were sporting at least one earring, and that not one of those at the table had one. Devin Danner, 18 years old at the time, a manager trainee at the John

Deere franchise in Troy and races motorcycles on Sunday, said, "I'm afraid if I came home with an earring in my ear, I'd be looking for a new place to live." Overhearing what his son said, Franklin said there was no doubt about it.

Teaching at the District of Columbia Prison

After working for MITRE for seven years and teaching part-time for ten years at NOVA and Montgomery College, I accepted a full-time position with Park College, Parkville, Missouri, which had a contract to conduct college classes at the District of Columbia Department of Corrections in Lorton, Virginia. I taught compositon at the prison for four years, until the program was discontinued. While there, I encouraged each of my students to write their story of how they chose a life of crime, that is, after I had gained their trust. A few of the students were never fully certain that I wasn't a government plant. I told them I was simply a white-haired old grandfather who liked to teach writing. "Yeah," they said, "but you're just the type of person the government likes. You're real nice to us, and in a weak moment, we might tell you something we shouldn't."

We were planning on combining several of the stories into a book titled "The Wrong Road Taken," a spin on Robert Frost's "The Road Not Taken." One of the prisoners designed a book cover depicting prison bars overlooking the two roads that diverged right outside the prison—one road to freedom, the other to incarceration. Despite many studies that show educating prisoners reduces recidivism, the program ended when Congress rescinded the provision of the Pell Grant that makes education free for prisoners. "The Wrong Road Taken" never became a reality, although I still have some of their stories on my computer.

Cover of
"The Wrong Road Taken"

Before beginning my assignment at the prison, one of the trusties who worked for the college asked me if I had ever taught

239

in a prison. When I told him I hadn't, he said I probably wouldn't last long. I told him that teaching was teaching, no matter where it was. He said, "Maybe so, but you've got two strikes against you already." I asked him what were the two strikes, but he hemmed and hawed that he didn't know if he should tell me, that he'd probably hurt my feelings. I then became quite adamant, reminding him that it was he who had brought up the subject. He said, "Well, you're white, and you've got a Southern accent—real Southern. All your students are black, and when they see your white face, they're gonna have doubts. And when they hear that accent, there ain't gonna be no doubt. They're gonna know you're one of the good-ole-boy white racists." When I told him I couldn't do anything about my being white or my accent, he wished me luck. In the four years I was there, race was never a factor in any of our relations.

On the first day of class, however, I did tell the students that the military had once sent me to a 7-week race relations instructor's school, where I learned much of the history of blacks in this country and many of the customs, attitudes, beliefs, games, etc. of the black male. I told them that I had also learned to be a black man, and that I could rap and dap with the best of them. I told this story at the beginning of each of the classes for four years. Invariably, a student would raise his hand, and say something to this effect: "Now, let me get this straight. I understand you went to a school for seven weeks to learn how to be a black man. Did I hear you correctly, or did I possibly miss something?" When I responded that he had heard me perfectly, he usually asked, "Did you graduate from this school? Did you get a certificate or a diploma of some kind?" Again, I replied in the affirmative. But the student usually had the last word: "Now, I'm 35 years old, and I've been black the whole time, living a life of crime on the mean streets of Washington. Now, when we start rapping and dapping, who do you think's going to have the upper hand?" The interchange between us was always good for a refreshing laugh.

Each week I gathered from church members books and magazines, such as *National Geographic*, *Reader's Digest*, *Time*, and *Newsweek*, and brought them to the prison. After I lugged two overfilled document bags through the checkpoint—after I and the bags were checked for contraband—one or two of the prisoners would meet me as far as the escape line to carry the bags into the classroom. Since the students were so eager to read something from the outside, trading the magazines back and forth as though they were baseball cards, they usually wanted to read them rather than get down to writing. After a few weeks, I waited until the last five or ten minutes of class for them to open the bags.

There are so many stories I could tell about teaching in the prison that it would fill a book. But two stand out. One involves a very handsome young man, one of the most knowledgeable persons I had ever met. In relating his story, he said that he had always been a good student, a good athlete, and a good son, and that he was often kidded by his older brothers for being such a good person. He didn't hang out in the streets, he didn't use drugs, and he didn't smoke or drink. He had an academic scholarship to attend George Washington University, and an athletic scholarship to attend Howard University. But one day, his brothers urged him to be one of the boys, to go into town with them and get stoned. And that is what he did. When they ran out of money, they attacked a young man, robbing him, and kicking him while he was on the ground. Left for dead, the victim not only didn't die, he later identified his main attacker—my student—before drifting into a coma. I heard him say so many times, "If I could only go back in time. I've got a brain, but I'm rotting away in prison for the best part of my life. And the man I attacked is locked up in his own prison. He will be in a vegetative state for as long as he lives. And my brothers are already back on the street."

In another incident a student asked if I knew how to protect my wallet when I was in a crowd, such as at a Redskins game. I said, "Certainly. I keep it in my front pocket." He then asked if I knew why he was in prison. Since I never asked students why they were incarcerated, I told him as such. He went on to say he was a professional pickpocket and shoplifter, employing the five-finger discount. And as a safety measure, he suggested I put my billfold in my front pocket, because the urge was coming on to do a little weightlifting. So I put my billfold in my front pocket. As we casually chatted, he related that he had taken billfolds out of men's front pockets and women's purses even while he was talking with them. He said he had bought diamonds, flown first-class, and stayed at some of the plushest hotels, all with lifted credit cards; further, he said there wasn't a thing in my billfold that he couldn't use, even as a prisoner. We were having quite a pleasant conversation, when all of a sudden, he handed me my billfold—intact, I might add. It was like a magician's trick, and he never told me how he did it.

One of my best experiences at the prison was having Victor Lugo as one of my younger students. Of Puerto Rican descent, Victor was the image of the boy next door. Articulate, intelligent, and well-mannered, he was the last person I would have ever expected in a high-security compound. On Father's Day he gave me a card that he had designed; he had calligraphically lettered "If only every boy could have a father like you, there would be no need for prisons." When the District's prison closed and its inmates transferred to Federal prisons, Victor was incarcerated at a number of institutions throughout the country. He continues to write me from the Federal prison in Cumberland, Maryland. He graduated as valedictorian of Allegheny Community College in Cumberland. He sent me a printed program of the graduation exercises; however, he was not allowed to attend the ceremony because of his incarceration.

Teaching for University of Maryland University College

Before beginning my teaching stint at the prison, I had begun teaching writing courses at University of Maryland University College, where I continue to teach. How I received an assistant professorship at University of Maryland could happen only once in a lifetime. The MITRE Corporation, whose sole client at the time was the Department of Defense, was forced to downsize because of a reduction in their allocation of the defense budget. Consequently, I was one of many who lost our jobs. Responding to a vacancy announcement from the Federal Government, I drove to Hyattsville, Maryland, to be interviewed for an editorial position in the Presidential Building. Since I would have preference for being a service-connected disabled veteran, I was almost certain that I would be hired for the job, as boring as it had appeared during the interview. When checking the building directory, I noticed that while the Federal Government rented two floors, University of Maryland University College also rented two floors. I had never heard of University College which, I later learned, provides both undergraduate and graduate courses for working students, not only in the Metropolitan Washington area, but across the country and on 39 American military bases in foreign countries. University College alone has slightly more than 1,500 professors.

As I was about to leave the building to return home, I noticed in the lobby several people with University of Maryland University College affiliation on their name tags. On a whim, I gave a copy of my résumé to one of them, asking that she please circulate it. I didn't take note of her name. When I arrived home in Reston, Virginia, 30 miles away, I had a call on my answering machine from Dr. Ruth Fagan, the head of the open learning department. She indicated I was the ideal candidate to be a professor in her department, noting that I was retired military, had a doctorate, had taught adults at the college level, had technical writing experience with the Air Force Intelligence Service and The MITRE Corporation, and was a published author. She said, however, that as a *pro forma* matter, I would need to come in for an interview. I asked her how she knew of me, only to find that I had given my résumé to her secretary, Wanda Santini. At the interview, I told Dr. Fagan that I had received an F while at George Washington University; she forthrightly disabused me of my anxiety, saying she was more interested in what I had done *after* receiving the failing grade.

I began teaching for UMUC in the fall of 1992, and have taught every semester since. I teach technical writing, business writing, and writing for managers. A recent workweek was as follows: Monday night, Annapolis; Tuesday night, College Park; Wednesday night, Fort Belvoir; and Friday night, Andrews Air Force Base. At least one of my classes each semester is a distance class, where I have students from all over the United States, and whom I never see, unless they live in the Washington metropolitan area. Occasionally, those outside the area send me pictures of themselves, and they can see my picture on my website: www.imprimis-books.com.

I got in a bit of trouble once by asking students to send me pictures of themselves. In my message to them, I said that I was usually a little more lenient when I was grading an assignment if I could put a face with the name. The next thing I knew, my department head called, telling me that a female student had lodged a complaint against me, that of invading her privacy. Sitting down with the department head, I asked her if I would be invading a student's privacy if the student was sitting in a classroom. The case was summarily dropped.

At University of Maryland, I regularly teach one class of international students, with the greatest number of them coming from Vietnam. But I also have an unusually large number from Israel. Because of them, I have been invited to the Embassy of Israel on a number of occasions. My first visit was enough to dampen my appetite for visiting embassies of any war-torn country. I knew the Embassy of Israel was on International Drive, but I was not further familiar with the area except I assumed there would be a problem parking, since it was next door to University of the District of Columbia. My student assured me that there would be no problem, that I could park in the Embassy's compound. Little did he know! I drove up the compound gate, and the armed guard wanted to know what my business was. Nonchalantly, I told them I was Dr. Danner, a professor at University of Maryland, and that I had come to visit three of my students. He said something that I didn't understand, and I continued waiting for the compound gates to open. What I didn't understand was his saying "I don't care who you are. Get the hell away from the gates." As I was waiting for the gate to open, two guards rushed out to my car, one with a .45 automatic raised in the air, and another with a shotgun pointed at me. Luckily, I had the names of my students, who were contacted and then escorted me into the Embassy where a sumptuous spread was waiting. I have returned to the Embassy a number of times, but now I know the protocol procedures, basically "don't park in front of the Embassy gate."

I hadn't worn my doctoral regalia since graduating almost twenty years before from American University. So when the university requested my presence at the graduation ceremony, I immediately responded that I would attend, inasmuch as the school paid for the outfit, with the red, white, and blue colors of American University and the gold and navy blue of University of Maryland. With all those colors, I would be one more proud peacock. When I went to the campus to pick up my gold-tasseled mortarboard, velvet robe, and the cape of many colors, I was dressed in cut-off shorts, an Alabama tee-shirt, and sandals. As I was rushing out of the campus store, one of the university employees congratulated me on "finally" getting my bachelor's degree, and wasn't it wonderful a dear senior citizen was getting the degree he had probably always wanted. I smiled and thanked her, but told her I already had two bachelor's degrees. "Oh, how simply marvelous, and now you're getting your master's?" I told her I already held a master's. She said, "I don't understand. University College doesn't confer a doctorate." I told her I already had a doctorate, that I was a professor of writing at the university. She was utterly embarrassed, but I found the whole incident quite amusing.

When my University of Maryland classes are held on military installations, I have a lot of fun. Before the first class, I arrive at least an hour early, and place the students' placecards and portfolios of syllabi, assignments, and handouts on the tables or desks; under the lectern, I also place my baseball-type Retired U.S. Air Force cap, complete with my Chief Master Sergeant's insignia. I sit in the back of the room with a fictitious placecard. And since I am in my late sixties, many students assume I'm simply a senior citizen taking advantage of a free class. Some strike up conversations with me, asking what I do and where I work. I tell them I'm a writer and do a little consulting, and that I try to take advantage of a writing course from time to time to hone my skills.

After a couple of minutes past the prescribed time for the beginning of class, I saunter to the front and ask in mock indignation, "Does anyone know who's going to teach this class? I'm getting tired of waiting." Though two or three students have usually figured out the masquerade, I say, "Well, I guess I'll have to teach it." I usually ask them if they might think it unusual that a guy from Alabama, living in Virginia, teaches for University of Maryland. I tell them since Alabama is a state of professed grammarians, but possessing few historical markers, I was traded to Virginia for a couple of dozen Civil War signs. And the ultimate is that Virginia traded me to Maryland for undisclosed rights to Chesapeake Bay blue crab harvests.

After a few other prefatory remarks, I say that students usually want to know what the instructor wants to be called. I tell them that the civilians have a choice: They can call me Dr.

Danner, since I *do* have a Ph.D.; they can call me Professor Danner, Mr. Danner, or even by my first name if they desire. Then, I pull myself up to my full five feet, ten inches, don my Chief's cap, and say, "You military personnel, just call me Chief, 'cause I'm a retired Air Force Chief Master Sergeant." Breaking the ice somewhat, the little routine gives me an opportunity to be the center of attention—if only for a few minutes.

In my twelve years at University College, I have found that the students can be divided into two types: those who take an upper-level writing course first, to get it out of the way, and those who wait until the last minute because they dread writing. Most of the students fit into the second category and are desperate to finish the course in order to graduate. In this state of urgency, I tell the class that a certain number of them will have to drop the class, that the university's computerized enrollment system made a mistake. I tell them that we can't allow more than two persons with the same last name to enroll in a class. In my international classes, where most of the students are Vietnamese, I have had as many as ten with the name of Nguyen, pronounced nu WEN.

One of my methods of teaching is to excerpt offending sentences from students' papers, typing them on a separate sheet, which I then pass out to the class to see if they can spot the errors. My rationale for this method is that students seem to pay little attention to my corrections, but if they can see that their peers have problems with the sentence, they will take my criticism more seriously. Just last week in Waldorf, Maryland, one of the sites where I am now teaching, John Stine wrote in his autobiography the following sentence: *I grew up on Cobb Island which is at the intersection of the Potomac and Wicomico Rivers.* None of the students could see any problem with the sentence. I told the class there were three errors. I immediately had them lower case the capital of *Rivers*, and told them to put a comma after *island* inasmuch as a *which* clause is nonrestrictive. Finally, I asked John if the Potomac and Wicomico rivers took turns letting the other flow through. I finally led them to see that Cobb Island is at the *confluence* of the Potomac and Wicomico rivers.

Two or three years ago, in a class at Fort Belvoir, Virginia, I instructed a student to put semicolons outside a quotation mark. He begged to disagree, saying that he had gone to a Jesuit Brothers school in New Jersey, and that the brothers taught him to put the semicolon just where he had placed it. I told him that I was sure the brothers had taught him correctly, but he had probably forgot the rule. This young Army sergeant said, "Well, I work for the Army's radio and television service, and we have a lot of writers with Ph.D.s on the staff. I'll just have to check with them, and I'll let you know." At the next class, when I entered the room, he was helping two of our Vietnamese students, but he didn't speak to me as he usually did. I said, "Larry, what did all those Ph.D.s say about the semicolon?" In a barely audible voice, he said, "You were right."

One day just a few months ago, I was getting ready to go to class at Andrews Air Force Base when I received a call from Jim Gillin, my supervisor at College Park. I don't usually receive calls from the university except when I am being offered a class, when requesting my permission to enroll an extra student in the class, or when there is a problem. I knew there must be a problem because it was too late in the semester to be offering me a class or asking my permission for a student to enroll late. Jim started out pleasantly enough, asking me about my health and how my swimming was coming along. He said that I had been with the university for ten years, and he had never had a complaint about me, but said he needed to ask me a question. He then asked if I had been drinking before or during my last class at Andrews. I asked, "Like what?" He said it had been reported that someone had smelled either vodka or gin on my breath. It was just too good an opportunity to pass up. I said, "Well, Jim, to tell you the truth, I DID have a drink before coming to class." Waiting a moment for that little morsel to sink in, I continued, "It was in 1954, when our military police unit in the Philippines was invited to the San Miguel Brewery in Manila for an all-day affair of Filipino cuisine and San Miguel beer. Though my buddies knew I didn't drink, some of them kept urging me to have just a sip. I tasted it and couldn't wait to spit it out." I never did find out who made the accusation, whether it was a student, a fellow faculty member, or the administrative staff. But Jim said he knew me well enough that he knew I didn't drink, and that was the end of it.

I have never received a rating from a student or a colleague other than that of superior, and receive a letter every semester from the dean that I have been rated in the top five or ten percent of the 1,500 instructors at the university. But it takes only an occasional complaint to keep me vigilant about my dress, decorum, and relationships with students, as the next incident indicates. I was teaching a "brown bag" special at Andrews Air Force Base, from 11 a.m. to 1:30 p.m., twice a week. I usually went to class directly from the gym, wearing whatever I had been working out in, sometimes cut-off shorts with sandals or sweatpants with tennis shoes. The assistant dean called me after class one day and inquired about what I was wearing in class. I had to think for a moment and told her I couldn't remember—it was either cut-offs or sweats. Rather peremptorily, she said, "Dr. Danner, please take a moment and look around the room at what the other men are wearing, and dress accordingly." I told her that I could tell her right then, that most of them were wearing fatigues, while a few of them were wearing Class A's. I later learned from the Andrews Superintendent of Education, Master Sergeant Wright, that a major general had passed my room and seen me in bare feet, since I had slipped off my sandals. The general inquired of Sergeant Wright, "Who is this guy, and what's he doing on a military base, dressed like a hippie?" Sergeant Wright said, "Oh, that's Dr. Danner, professor of writing at University of Maryland, and retired Air Force Chief Master Sergeant. He's got it together. He's a free spirit, General." The general wasn't at all amused, telling Sergeant Wright to take care of the situation. While I still go the College Park campus in varying states of dishabille with whatever I happen to pull out of the closet, I make sure that I at least wear shoes when I teach on a military installation.

The Grand Finale: *Discover It!:*
A Better Vocabulary, the Better Way

In 1972, while studying at American University, Dr. Huber, professor of learning theories, made a statement that was to become the inspiration for *Discover It!*, the vocabulary book that Dr. Roger Noël and I co-authored. "What we discover for ourselves," Dr. Huber said, "we learn faster and retain longer," which is one of

Plato's laws of learning. I conceived that a program might be developed whereby a student *discovered* the meanings of a host of words rather than first memorizing individual meanings of words or roots, thereby adding excitement to learning and saving the student hundreds of hours of time. Inductive, or discovery, learning has proved to enable more efficient assimilation of material, but the method had never been applied to building an academic vocabulary.

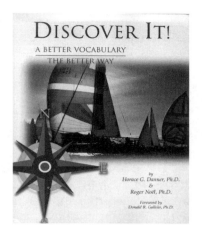

For several months, I toyed with developing a schema that would make optimal use of inductive learning. Finally, I clustered words that shared a common element or root, such as *fugue*, *fugitive*, *refugee*, *centrifugal*, and *nidifugous*, listing the words in a column aligned on the common element, *fug*. I ask the student to select two words whose meanings are known, and then define them. Usually, *fugitive* and *refugee* are selected, with variations of the following definitions given: a fugitive flees from the law, and a refugee flees from his or her country. Since "to flee" is the common meaning, the student logically assumes it's the shared meaning of all the words.

In the design, the student simply turns the page to confirm the answer, finding that "fug" is the root of Latin *fugere*, meaning "to flee." This step is called "immediate reinforcement," an important concept in learning. Psychologists have shown that when students feel good about the progress of their learning, they have more incentive to continue.

The next step is called "associative bonding," and is found under the *Clavis*, Latin for "key," which has come to mean "a key to 'opening' the meaning of words," or a glossary. When we can associate something already learned with something new, there is a more permanent bond of learning of a new concept, and is analogous to mortar holding bricks together. Consequently, in the *Clavis*, Dr. Noël and I have written notes on selected words listed in the word cluster; for example, *centrifugal* literally means "fleeing from the center," which reinforces the fleeing aspect of a fugitive and a refugee.

Now the student is ready to tackle words such as *nidifugous*, which could possibly be found on a college entrance board examination. With *nidi* meaning "nest," *nidifugous* describes a bird, such as a chicken, turkey, grouse, or pheasant that can "flee" the nest shortly after being hatched, as opposed to a robin or wren (described as *nidicolous*), which must remain in the nest until it's mature enough to fly.

I first began using the discovery approach with my students at Herndon High School. After taking an after-school course in which I used this approach, David McGowan, a football player with a learning disability, scored appreciably better on the verbals of the college boards. He exclaimed, "If *I* can score higher, just think what other students can do with this approach. In fact, Coach, why don't you put this in a book?" Taking Dave's suggestion, I set out to put the discovery approach into a book.

The first version of *Discover It!* was titled *Words from the Romance Languages*; I started writing the manuscript on Thanksgiving Day 1979, and finished it before school was out the following spring. Then I received a two-week tour to Hickam Air Force Base, Honolulu, where I typed the book on an IBM Selectric II on my off-duty time. I didn't know if I would be able to use an Air Force typewriter, and I thought of renting one to use in my room. But on my first day at Hickam, I was in the snack bar, when someone called out "Danner!" from somewhere in the canteen. I knew of no one on the entire island of Oahu who might know me, so I assumed I must have been mistaken and reached for my carton of orange juice. Then I heard my name called again, and I looked up to see a full colonel, saying "Clark Air Force Base, 1953." It was Colonel Edward E. Johnson, whom I had served with at Clark from 1953-1955, only when we were there 25 years before, I wore three stripes and he wore only two. We were best friends and often rode patrol together. But in 1980, he was the director of all Air Force security forces in the Pacific. So, I had both a home and an office for the next two weeks, eating dinner with him and his family just about every night on the lanai, and then using his IBM Selectric II in his office to finish the book.

After our chance meeting in the snack bar, Ed escorted me

Clark AFB Police

to his office, called the staff together, and then pointing to a framed picture of our police unit taken in the Philippines, challenged them to identify me. In the picture, I weighed a mere 125 pounds and was only 21 years old; however, every person in the office picked me out. *The Hickam Flyer*, the base newspaper, did a rather nice article on our meeting after 25 years, he in his colonel's uniform, and I in my Chief's. [I am the second from the right on the last row. Ed is the second person from the left on the back row. Gerald Hertzfeldt is second standing from the left, with Anthony Bachigalupo—with the scrunched-up face next to him. Gerald and Anthony are mentioned elsewhere in the memoir.]

Ed had gone to Officer Candidate School (OCS), and then rose rapidly to full colonel. He retired during my last Hawaii assignment, and I was invited to "roast" him during the retirement ceremony for once having been his superior—if only by one stripe.

Finding so much interesting information about words as I was doing research for the book, I approached Bennie Scarton, Editor of *The Journal Messenger* (Manassas, Virginia), to see if he would be interested in my writing a column on words, patterned after Frank Colby's newspaper column, "Take My Word for It," that I had first read in *The Montgomery Advertiser*. For several years, I wrote "Take My Word," and later switched to *The Potomac News*, of Woodbridge, Virginia, to write "A Way with Words," reported to have a readership of 75,000. I wrote the column for seven years, and my best-received column was titled, "Let the Arabs Keep Their Oil, We'll Keep Their Words."

In 1982, while I was still teaching at Fauquier High School, Edward Greene, chairman of the English Department of the American Embassy School in New Delhi, India, and editor of *IQ: International Quarterly*, became aware of the vocabulary book as well as the column I was writing for the newspaper. He thereupon asked me to write a column on words, with the audience being the teachers in American Embassy schools around the globe. With a byline, this one column opened up an international market for the vocabulary book. It's amazing how news travels among educators. Not long after the book was used in New Delhi and other American Embassy schools, the overseas military dependents schools heard of the book, which opened up still another market.

And then, I was interviewed on Northern Virginia Community College's television program as well as its radio program. The college sends its educational interviews to be broadcast over local radio and television stations, in order for the broadcasters to fulfill one of the licensing requirements of the Federal Communications Commission. People I hardly knew would tell me they saw me on television the night before. Not knowing that the college had sent out the tapes, I responded that they must be mistaken, that I was in bed asleep. Later, I was interviewed on WAMU, American University's National Public Radio affiliate. Every time a program was replayed, I received a flood of orders. A listener from Estonia living in nearby Maryland ordered 100 of the books to be used in the two universities in his native country. I was later invited to go to Estonia.

In the course of the whirlwind surrounding the book, I was invited to give a lecture to the students of Northern Virginia's Thomas Jefferson High School for Science and Technology on the integration of Latin and Greek within a science curriculum. This magnet school continues to produce the highest number of National Merit Scholars in the country. While at Thomas Jefferson, I presented the backgrounds of some words used in science and mathematics. One of them was "mile," which comes from Latin *milia passuum*, or 1,000 paces. To this group of young scholars, who also win more science awards each year than any other high school in the country, I remarked that we now measure a mile by feet rather than paces—something, of course, they already knew. So, I asked them rather nonchalantly how many feet were in a mile, promising to give a copy of *Discover It! A Better Vocabulary the Better Way* to the first person who gave the correct answer. Not a single hand was raised. I chided them that surely of all these young scientists, there had to be just one student who could answer my question. Finally, a young man timidly asked, "Five thousand two hundred eighty?" Of course, he was right, but I was expecting 300 hands to go up at once and was wondering how I would choose a winner.

In 1993, when I first came on-line and was able to access the Internet, I searched for "Toastmasters," because two Toastmasters organizations had already invited me to speak to their groups, where I was able to sell a number of my books. What I found on the Toastmasters home page astounded me: listings of hundreds of individual groups across the country. I searched for the ones in Northern Virginia and the Metropolitan Washington area, sending emails to several organizations and "inviting" myself to demonstrate the book. In the first week alone, I spoke to groups at Fort Belvoir, Virginia; Office of Naval Intelligence, Suitland, Maryland; and Census Bureau, also at Suitland, always bringing back fewer books than I took.

Before leaving this section of my life, I want to relate how Dr. Noël and I became collaborators, especially since we have met only once, and that was two years after the book was published. One of my former students at Fauquier High, who had taken an after-school college board preparation course I was teaching, enrolled at Howard University in Washington, D.C. He took with him the book *Words from the Romance Languages* that I used in the course. His classics professor, Dr. Thomas J. Sienkewicz, was impressed with the content and format of the book and suggested that instead of publishing it myself, I should submit it to University Press of America. Dr. Sienkewicz also purchased a copy for himself. I revised the book, adding to it considerably, and titled it *An Introduction to an Academic Vocabulary.*

Dr. Sienkewicz then left Howard to become the chairman of classics at Monmouth College in Illinois, where Dr. Noël was the chairman of the Department of Modern Foreign Languages. Dr. Sienkewicz showed *Words from the Romance Languages* to Dr. Noël, who also liked the book, but being an astute scholar of the Romance languages as well as Greek, noted areas in which the book could be improved. When Dr. Noël wrote me of his interest, I asked him to work with me on the revision. We worked for three or four years, writing, rewriting, critiquing each other, until finally we felt we had the ultimate product. Then about fifty of my colleagues of scientists, engineers, and linguists from The MITRE Corporation critiqued the manuscript. After all this, I then asked three of my classes at Northern Virginia Community College at Annandale to use the book for a semester. The final book is therefore the work of Dr. Noël and me, my colleagues at MITRE, my students, a Methodist minister, and a Catholic priest, who was head of the English Department at Paul VI High School in Fairfax, Virginia. Dr. Noël is now Chairperson of the Department of Modern Foreign Languages, Georgia College and State

University, Milledgeville, Georgia. I should also thank Margie, as I got up each morning at 3:30 for two years in order to work on the book at the office before the day crew began arriving. She never complained, bless her New England heart, about my pursuing rather quixotic dreams.

Dr. Noël was a boon in working with me on the vocabulary book. From Belgium, he was fluent in French and German and possessed invaluable expertise in Italian, Portuguese, and Spanish as well, not to mention Flemish. However, he had no knowledge of Romanian, the other main Romance language—the others being Catalan and Provençal. Not wanting to depend entirely on a Romanian-English dictionary, I sought out the services of the Romanian Embassy, which was then under Communist control. Since I was working at MITRE on a classified Government contract, I had to follow strict security protocols in obtaining permission to visit the Embassy. I was advised to seek entry as an educator, which I was, not as a MITRE employee. I was also advised not to accept anything from Embassy personnel, no matter how innocently offered, nor was I to give anything to the Embassy staff.

When I went to the Embassy of Romania, it was a hot, sultry day in July. Thirsty and perspiring profusely, I could hardly wait to enter an air-conditioned building and get a drink of water. I was ushered into the receiving room where I met with the Honorable Dumitri Aldea, First Secretary for Cultural Affairs. Mr. Aldea apologized that there was no air conditioning, saying that the Embassy was strapped for funds, but he did ask if I would like a soda. I had been told not to accept anything, but I was at the point of collapse from thirst and the heat and told him I would be glad to have one. He rang for the maid, and in about half an hour, she brought in a can of soda that hadn't recently seen the inside of a refrigerator. The can was so hot I was afraid it might explode in my hands.

About halfway through checking the Romanian elements of the book, Mr. Aldea abruptly stopped and said he would like to make a proposal. I broke out in a nervous sweat when he said, "I help you. You help me." I thought surely he was suggesting that I compromise myself by giving him classified information, inasmuch as I had already been briefed by Security that the Embassy most likely knew more about me than I knew about myself. Mr. Aldea said that since I was an educator, and already working with international students, he would like to invite me to the Embassy to practice English conversations with the staff. I told him I would try to work it into my schedule, and suggested that in the meantime, the staff listen to one of the network newscasters, such as Dan Rather, Tom Brokaw, or Peter Jennings.

I was not aware that while I was inside, an agent of the Federal Government had taken note of my license plate number; nor was I aware that I had been photographed by a remote camera as I entered and left the Embassy. In a few days, an agent visited me, wanting to know the purpose of my visit and the details of everything that transpired. I am not at liberty to reveal any further relations with either the agency or the Embassy. Suffice it to say that if the Romanian elements in *Discover It!* are needed, be assured that the information did not come easily or without personal sacrifice, the details of which again I am not at liberty to disclose.

On the very day I planned to take the revised vocabulary book to University Press of America, Craig Prall, a young computer scientist at The MITRE Corporation, whom I had met only a week before, came into my office to renew our acquaintance. So proud of the *magnum opus* Roger and I had just completed, I showed the manuscript to Craig, expecting him to share my enthusiasm and stamp it with his own imprimatur. Craig, from Ohio State University, and by all accounts, an A student from the time he first started nursery school, wasn't greatly impressed. With a voice as flat as his native Ohio cornfields, he merely glanced at it and droned, "If I'd put that much work in it, I'd want it to look it." Quite frankly, I was taken aback that a computer scientist would have any knowledge of book writing or design, and asked what could possibly be wrong with it. "Everything," he said.

The "everything" turned out to be the printing, even though it was done on a state-of-the-art Hewlett-Packard laser printer. He said that I should have done proportional print, rather than monospaced. At the time, I wasn't even aware of the difference. He thereupon set out to reformat the entire book, which required his having to encode special printer fonts for the monospaced characters where I had aligned the common roots of words. He also designed the musical *segno* symbol on page 174 of the book, since we were not able to find the symbol in any of MITRE's fonts. Alas, after printing out the book, we found that the proportional print reduced the amount of page print by at least a third. It was, therefore, necessary to do additional research to fill in the blank space on each page. After six months of reworking the format and adding material, it was then submitted to UPA, where it went through five large printings. After several years, the book was declared out of print; since I had always held the copyright, I republished the book under the imprint of my own company, Imprimis Books, and titled it *Discover It! A Better Vocabulary, the Better Way*.

Not long after Roger and I completed the vocabulary book, I had the opportunity to prove its effectiveness in raising the verbal score of a student taking the college entrance board examinations. The young man was the son of a colonel stationed at nearby Quantico Marine Base. After working with him and showing how the book worked, he raised his verbal score from 630 to 745, out of a perfect 800. Already a super athlete, he received a number of offers of scholarships as both an athlete and a scholar.

Pleased with my work with his son, the colonel invited me to dinner at the family's home in Quantico. As he and I talked after dinner, he appeared impressed with my credentials in the military and in the academics. He offered me a job in one of the professional military colleges on base, but said I would need to fill out the application. When the application arrived, there was a listing of duties, such as supervising the writing of lesson plans and visiting classes to insure compliance with the plans. The individual duties of the job were quantified as to the percentage of time to be allotted to each task. I considered myself well qualified in each of the areas until I came to the very last one, where it was indicated that I would spend 5 percent of my time marching with the troops with a 65-pound backpack every six weeks. I called the colonel and told him "No, thank you," adding that in the Air Force, I had never even worn a knapsack, much less a 65-pound backpack.

Last year, a mother in Woodbridge, Virginia, called and asked if I could work with her son on improving his verbals on the college boards.On one particular day, we were discussing the Latin root *nov*, and I told Robbie that it had two meanings: new (from *novus*), as in *novice* and *renovate*, and nine (from *novem*), as in *November*. Looking puzzled, I told him that *November* was the ninth month in the Roman calendar when there were only ten months. He still looks puzzled. Since he is Catholic, I suggested that he associate *November* with *novena*. He wanted to know what *November* had to do with a prayer. Instead of answering him directly, I ask him what kind of prayer was a novena. He said he had no idea. So this Baptist had to tell this young Catholic fellow that a novena was a prayer for a special request for nine consecutive days.

Recently, I received a call from the secretary of the McGuffey[27] Reading Center at University of Virginia, wishing to order a copy each of the vocabulary book, the general thesaurus, and the medical thesaurus Roger and I had written. The secretary also said that the director of the center, who was also a professor of education at the university, wanted to invite me out to lunch. Generally free during the day—since I teach at night at University of Maryland—I made the two-hour trip to Charlottesville to meet with the director. Dr. Thomas Estes approved the vocabulary book as a text and had the university bookstore order 50 copies for his students. The book had already been ordered by Barnes & Noble college bookstores, Books-a-Million, and Borders bookstores, mainly in the Washington, D.C., area.

Because of the vocabulary book, I have been invited to give talks on inductive learning and vocabulary development at a number of educational association conventions in Virginia. I have made presentations at the state home school convention, the Virginia Association of Teachers of English, the state association for parents of the learning disabled, and the southeastern division of the National Reading Association. I also give presentations on the book to local chapters of Toastmasters, who are always looking for innovative ways to increase their members' public speaking vocabulary.

One day while living in Reston, Virginia, which is the headquarters of dozens of national educational associations—so that they can be close to the halls of Congress—the executive secretary of the Council for Exceptional Children, Mr. Jeptha Greer, invited me to his office to discuss the book's implications for

[27] William Holmes McGuffey (1800-1873), an American educator and clergyman, compiled *Eclectic Reader*, from which many American children learned to read. He held various

youngsters with learning disabilities. In the course of our meetings over the next several weeks, I related to him something of my background. He practically commissioned me to write an account of how a fellow from the cotton fields of Alabama came to write such a "splendid" book. Although I had been economically deprived during my childhood, I had been most fortunate in receiving a first-rate education in my native state, and the thoughts of Miss Andrews, Mrs. Moore and Mrs. Carter, Mr. Palmer, and Mrs. Baxter began to take focus. I immediately set out to write this memoir, the first edition of which was used by the council's lobbyists to help influence members of Congress to appropriate more funds for educationally deprived youngsters throughout the country.

After finishing the vocabulary book, I started on a project that would take five years for Dr. Noël and me to complete. Had it not been for Craig Prall setting up the computer program, completing the thesaurus would have taken much longer. Since The MITRE Corporation encouraged its staff to publish, I began assembling the first comprehensive thesaurus of word roots in the English language. I had learned dBaseIII database programming, and I put the resources at my disposal to use. As I finished portions of the thesaurus, I sent them to Dr. Noël, who with his background of Latin and Greek, helped make the thesaurus a standard for years to come. Comprising almost 800 pages of Latin and Greek roots and examples, *A Thesaurus of Word Roots of the English Language* was published by University Press of America (UPA), Lanham, Maryland, in 1992. Covering roots used in archeology through zoology, the thesaurus is now in its fourth printing. It continues to sell worldwide, through both Roman and Littlefield and my own company, here in Occoquan, Virginia. Via the Internet, Imprimis has sold books all over the world, including Belgium, Germany, South Africa, South Korea, and Australia. The books are also listed on the Amazon.com website as well as others.

Originally, I had thought of including all major Latin and Greek roots in the thesaurus, but found that the medical roots alone would require a book in itself. Therefore, Imprimis Books published *A Thesaurus of Medical Word Roots*. Completed in 1995, the 505-page book has sold 200 copies to date. I am grateful to Dr.

Presbyterian pastorates as well as professorships, the last of which was at University of Virginia.

Medical Thesaurus

Joseph A. Procaccino, Jr., a University of Maryland University College colleague and chief legal counsel for the Air Force Surgeon General's Office, and to Brian E. Steyskal, B.S., one of my writing students at University of Maryland University College, for editing the medical thesaurus. My biggest order for the thesaurus was from the Walter Reed Army Hospital in Washington, D.C.

If it hadn't been for caring teachers; several of my brothers and sisters; a black lady who gave me kerosene; a dean who gave me a job as well as encouragement; a professor who astutely enunciated my paucity of words; a pastor who opened up a vista of learning; a professor who would lead me to see the advantages of discovery learning; the student who suggested the book; and students who responded to untested ideas, the vocabulary book and the thesauri might never have become a reality.

Teaching Piano

Earlier, I mentioned that I taught neighborhood kids while living in

Jason Young & I

Orange to pay for the piano I had surreptitiously bought. In the 35 years since, I have not thought of teaching piano. However, at the fitness and aquatics center, where I work out and swim almost every day, one of my whirlpool buddies, Jim Young, wanted to know when I was going to start teaching his son, Jason, piano. I suppose that Jim thought that anyone who plays also teaches, or at least, *can* teach. I told him I hadn't taught in quite a number of years, that I was not the best keyboardist in the world, and that there were a lot of piano teachers out there, all to which he replied, "But Jason wants *you* to teach him piano." I had met Jason only the week before when he was working out in the weight room, and I immediately began to have my doubts. I asked Jim how big his son's fingers were. Jim said that Jason had normal fingers. I figured if Jason was 6 feet 4 inches tall and weighed in at 265 pounds, his fingers might be just a tad large to fit between the keys.

Finally, I acquiesced to teach him, and his mother brought him for his first lesson. Jason didn't have his driver's license yet; at the time, he was only 15. The first thing he said when he came for his first lesson was that he wanted to be able to play the song that the band was playing when the *Titanic* went down. I hadn't yet seen the current movie, but I remembered Margie and my seeing *A Night to Remember* almost fifty years ago. In that movie, the band played "Nearer My God to Thee." I sat down and played the hymn with all the finesse I could muster, with full right-hand chords and left-hand octaves.

With the unabashed exuberance of the boy still lurking in his man-size frame, he exploded, "That's it! It's the same song that was played in the movie. And that's just the way I want to play it." I thought that if he liked hymns so much, I would play another one, so I played "Amazing Grace," saying that both Catholics and Protestants liked that particular hymn. Jason replied, "That's really nice. You probably didn't know, but I'm Jewish." His mother, Cindy, promptly said I could teach her son anything I felt like. But I told Jason to bring some music pieces from his synagogue, and we would concentrate on those. So, we both began to learn Hanukkah and Purim songs, Israeli folk songs, and the national anthem of Israel. And I might say, his fingers are not too big; they are just right, not only for playing the piano but for blocking for the defense in football. He just graduated from Osbourn Park High School, Manassas, Virginia, where he played left defensive tackle.

I've Been "Laying Down"

Two or three years ago, while I was in Alabama for a visit, Vallie misused the intransitive verb "to lie," as in "to lie down to rest."

She said that she had been "laying down for a while." Now, it was my turn. I asked what she had been "laying down." A little annoyed that her baby brother had the chutzpah to correct her, she said that she had been laying herself down. Since she had been so diligent in correcting me when I was younger, I thought she would appreciate my enlightening her. I delved into explaining that *lay* is a transitive verb and must have an object, and *lie* being intransitive, doesn't have objects. I told her the principal parts of *lie* were *lie, lay, lain*, as in "I *lie* down every day for a nap; I *lay* down yesterday; I *have lain* down in the past." I then told her she should have said, "I was *lying* down." I reminded her of the verse from the Nativity story, "And ye shall find the babe lying in a manger." She would hear none of it, declaring that *lying* so used was probably old-fashioned just as "ye" and "manger." I said, "Vallie, this is what I do for a living. I teach this type of thing to budding writers at University of Maryland." "Well," she said in a quick riposte, "you can just teach all you want, to those budding writers in Maryland. We've got our own way of talking down here in South Alabama."

National Defense University, Fort McNair, Washington, D.C.

Just recently, I received a call from the National Defense University at Fort McNair, Washington, D.C., wanting to know if I could lead a writing seminar for the high-ranking officers studying there for a year. One of my former students at University of Maryland was on the academic staff there, and he had recommended me. I went to Fort McNair to be interviewed by the academic dean for the university, as well as by the two instructional deans from National War College and Industrial College of the Armed Forces. The three colonels, all holding Ph.D.s themselves, addressed me as Dr. Danner or Professor Danner during the course of the interview until finally I said to the dean, "Colonel, since I will be teaching on a military post, I'd just as soon be called by my military title—just call me *Chief*." Regardless of my request, they continued to address me by my academic title. Then, the dean said, "Dr. Danner, not all your students volunteered for this course; we actually told some of them to register for it. What will be your response if some colonel or Navy captain complains about being "put" in your class?"

Not knowing exactly how to respond, I lapsed into my good ole boy Alabama mode, saying "Well, Colonel, I'm not exactly sure how I'll handle it, but I guess I'll think of something. But, there's one thing for sure—I won't tell them I'm a Chief Master Sergeant!" Even the rather austere female Army colonel laughed at my response. But once I got the contract, I told the dean that since I practically exuded a "lifer" military career, I was afraid I might slip up and tell the class inadvertently. Or, a student might see the military decal indicating my rank. The colonel told me I was free to handle it any way I liked. So, I told the students on the first day of class. Not one student indicated any surprise; so, I told them I was expecting some reaction. A marine colonel with a chest full of ribbons said, "Dr. Danner, if you've got something to bring to the table, we're ready to eat." And I was never addressed by my first name—as students were encouraged to do when addressing each other—for the entire 16 weeks of the seminar, not even after I invited them to do so. Toward the end of the course, I reminded them that not once had any of them called me by first name, whereupon a full colonel stood, snapped to attention, and saluted me—mind you—an officer saluting an enlisted man, and said, "Professor, from now on, I shall address you by your first name—Chief!"

Puerto Rico: Emerald of the Caribbean

In late December 2000 and early January 2001, I traveled for the first time—except for a one-day trip to Quebec—outside the continental United States as a civilian. In my travels to the Philippines, Japan, Korea, and Panama, I had always gone on military orders. I had a month off from teaching at University of Maryland, I could travel for free on military aircraft, and the temperature was in the low digits in Northern Virginia. So, I saw no reason not to bask in the 80-degree temperature of Puerto Rico.

My son Stephen was stationed at Fort Buchanan, just outside San Juan. I certainly planned on visiting him and his wife and my three beautiful granddaughters, but my main purpose was to relax on the beaches and return with a nice tan. Consequently, my main base of operations was Roosevelt Roads Naval Station on the eastern tip of the island, where the Atlantic and Caribbean meet, and where I planned to stay in the Navy Lodge. However, Stephen called and said that he and the girls were coming to take me to Fort Buchanan. Before we left for San Juan, however, we had a nice picnic on one of the pristine beaches at Roosevelt Roads.

I had planned on renting a car and crisscrossing the island, which is only about 100 miles long and 35 miles wide. But while I was in San Juan, Stephen adamantly forbade that I rent a car, saying that I would be killed, that the Puerto Ricans would pass me on the shoulder, even on the median. So, I contented myself with lying in the hammock at his house, seeing the sights of San Juan, and taking Stephen and Mary to Ruth's Chris Steakhouse in San Juan.

After the dinner, Mary said we could either go dancing or go to the casino, which was right next door to the restaurant. Well, I couldn't dance, and I would never have thought of setting foot in a casino.What would my church people back home say if they knew I had gone to one? So I told Stephen and Mary I would simply watch them play blackjack. But Stephen said I would be safe with the slot machines, and told me get a twenty-dollar bill changed into quarters. He advised me not to leave the casino with less money than when I entered. He then showed me how to pull the lever of the one-armed bandit. After that, he and Mary played blackjack, but he would return from time to time to see how I was doing.

For the first four or five tries, I may have won five or six quarters. And then the impossible happened. My coin tray filled up with more than $400 worth of quarters. Stephen and Mary heard my tray jingling, and they came by to check on me, promptly telling me to cash them in and get out while I was ahead. But no, I had to try for the grand slam. I kept putting my quarters back in, until Mary thought she would try for the same luck. Immediately, she won a sizable number of quarters and promptly converted them to paper money. It was at that point that I decided to cash in my remaining quarters, and to my dismay, received only a twenty- and a ten-dollar bill. I ended up with ten dollars more than when I came in, and I declare that is the last time I will ever sit in front of a slot machine.

Stephen had to begin packing for a five-month expedition to Guatemala where his outfit would rebuild roads, dig wells, and build schools. Consequently, he took me back to Roosevelt Roads, where I remained for the rest of my vacation.

As Stephen was taking me back to Roosevelt Roads, I remarked that I could describe Puerto Rico in two words: mountains and sea. He told me to add concrete and asphalt. Puerto Rico is indeed a crowded island, with more people per square mile than any state in the United States, except New Jersey. And they have to have highways to get to where they're going. While the island is a tropical paradise, its backroads and beaches are an environmental and ecological disaster. They are not only a disaster, they are a disgrace. The only beach that I visited in Puerto Rico that was free of debris was at Roosevelt Roads. The others are a mishmash of flotsam and jetsam of the sea, together with styrofoam containers, tin cans, discarded tires, junked automobiles and refrigerators, and every other type of rubbish one could imagine. Except for the flotsam and jetsam, the same goes for the backroads. The island has no recycling program whatsoever. If I were the governor of Puerto Rico, I would begin a massive clean-up program.

As soon as Stephen left me off and showed me to my room at Roosevelt Roads Navy Lodge, I promptly rented a car, and started my delayed tour of Puerto Rico. I drove from one end of the island to the other, stopping to chat in the marketplaces and eating in small roadside restaurants. I drove to the top of El Junco, the rain forest mountains. I purposely used Spanish to see if I could survive in a Hispanic environment. I may not have Spanish down perfect, but I had no problems communicating with the people. And I might add, no one ran me off the road, as Stephen had predicted. The only problem I experienced was driving back from San Juan through Carolina on Three Kings' Day, the day of gift-giving. There were hordes of people and thousands of cars, not to mention men riding horses up and down the highway— sometimes *on* the highway. A trip that would have normally taken me no more than an hour took me almost three hours.

All in all, the excursion to Puerto Rico was most enjoyable, but I was ready to return to the frigid temperature of Northern Virginia. I had to get back to work, teaching another class, writing another book.

Full Circle: A Rip Van Winkle Journey to the Past

I made a pilgrimage of sorts to Elamville and Clio, and to Troy State—now a full-fledged university offering master's degrees—in 1990. It had been over forty years since I had seen some of these places! I had returned on occasion for a funeral, taking a quick flight in and a quick flight out, but never staying long enough to reflect on my formative years. I longed to revisit the scenes of my childhood, such as Clio Low School, where I had been nurtured by Miss Andrews, Miss Pullen, Mrs. Chandler, Mrs. Wilkinson, and Mrs. Carter. The school had been converted into a medical garments factory, and a new one had been erected across the street in the field where the prisoner of war camp used to be during World War II. Old Barbour County High School is now the George C. Wallace Museum. Area students are now bused to the high school in Louisville.

To my utter dismay and sadness, the place I loved so well—the once-proud and classical town of Clio—is in a regrettable state of disrepair. Many Southern towns are thriving, with new homes, new schools, new businesses. Even with a population of twice that when I was growing up—it's now around 2,000 (mainly because of those moving in to staff the new state prison)—Clio's days appear to be as numbered as those of ancient Athens, Sparta, and Carthage. Indeed, it is not the town I remember. It is not the energetic commercial and agricultural center of cotton gins, peanut warehouses, and beautiful, palatial homes. Instead of beautiful homes, there now seems to be a mobile home on every other block. There is no longer a cotton gin, and the peanut warehouses are rusting shells of tin. There is no longer a hotel. There is neither a doctor nor a dentist with an office in Clio. And the flags of the United States and the State of Alabama no longer fly in front of the high school, for as I said, the high school is gone. The rose gardens that Loyce and Olon and the NYA planted are now choked with weeds as well as discarded soda cans and beer and soft drink bottles.

Several years ago, a tornado wreaked havoc throughout this once-classical town. What remains shows the signs of gross neglect. What has happened to you, the town that spawned the likes of Governor George C. Wallace; Dr. T. Stroud Jackson; Dr. Reynolds; Dr. Tillman; State Senator MacDowell Lee; Lee Hunt, a retired scientist with the National Academy of Sciences in Washington, D.C., and the author of *A Town Called Clio*; Alto Jackson, Esquire; Sam Jackson; the incomparable Shellye Louise Jackson Moore, my angelic teacher; and so many other important and influential people? What happened to the town of well-stocked stores and clean streets, colonnaded homes bedecked with the showy camellia and japonica? What happened to the classical town that was the center of my boyhood universe? What forces could bring a town so worthy to dilapidation? Where is the local pride that once possessed the Clionian citizen? I can only wish for a bright new day in the place I loved so well. Like the phoenix of old, may it again rise from the ashes to take its rightful place among the flourishing towns of Alabama, the South, the Nation.

I also wanted to see Elamville, home to Slawson's and Wilkinson's grocery stores and the beer halls. There are now no stores and no beer halls in Elamville. Slawson's store has been turned into makeshift living quarters, and Wilkinson's store is all boarded up. The whistles of the Central of Georgia railroad are now silent, as the train hasn't sped through Elamville in 30 years or more; even the rails have been taken up—it's difficult to see where the tracks once lay. I also wanted to see Elamville School, where I had studied under Mrs. Botts, Mrs. Moore, Mrs. Hartzog, Mrs. Tyler, and Mr. Palmer. There is no physical evidence that the school building ever existed. After 50 years, the old gymnasium on the hillock stands like a lone sentinel. I understand it is used as a senior citizens' center, one that I would be eligible to use if I still lived in Elamville.

I wanted to see again the tin-roofed shacks where I once lived, but they had long been torn down or had deteriorated and been overtaken by kudzu vines. I took a picture of what's left of the house on the Robinet Place, but I am too ashamed to include it in the memoir. I was amazed and pleasantly surprised to find that there are no more sharecroppers' tin-roofed shacks—not even one. Where sharecroppers' shacks once stood are now pastures with grazing cattle, tree farms of loblollies and slash pine, and vast cotton and peanut farms. Moreover, as reported in *The Washington Post*, there are no more sharecroppers! Not in the United States— not even in Southeast Alabama!

I didn't see a single mule. And no one picks cotton by dragging a sack between two rows and pulling the cotton from the opened bolls. Instead, a motorized picker eases along the rows, pulling the cotton with mechanical fingers, eight rows at a time. And the operator sits in an air-conditioned cab listening to the radio, watching television, or talking on a wireless phone. And no one shakes peanuts by hand and stacks them with pitchforks anymore. A combine plows eight rows at a time, shakes the dirt from the peanuts, tosses the peanut vines into a windrow, where they are left to dry. Then a machine picks the peanuts from the vines and bales the hay in a single operation.

The old Barbour County High School was just as grand and stately as ever, but its two-storied, brick walls once covered with ivy were now denuded and aged. As I drove slowly past it, I could visualize Mr. Botts, Doc Chandler, Coach Price, Miss Hixon, Mrs. Ard, Mrs. Laird, and Mrs. Baxter; I could hear echoes of the speechmaking, the quartet singing, the piano in the auditorium on which I practiced. I could revisit in my mind the library where I was introduced to the classics, in both books and music; the old athletic house where we dressed for cross country; the football field where I was a cheerleader. What a flood of memories!

I yearned to see again Mrs. Moore's home, the site of the Easter egg hunt and where I had run through the blinding rain for help, and to visit her brother, Dr. Jackson, who until his retirement had been Clio's town doctor since the end of World War II. He lives in one of the few palatial homes left in the town, and he graciously received and entertained me. For years the pianist at Clio Baptist Church, he demonstrated his unique style of piano playing after I pleaded with him to do so.

I wanted to stroll the grounds of Troy State, still studded with flowering magnolias; to visit Bibb Graves Hall and to reflect on Miss Goodwin's advice on speaking and on Dr. Ervin's substantial contribution to my mastery of the piano. The small liberal arts college had grown into a campus so complex that I had difficulty orienting myself.

Hallelujah! You've Come Home!

During my stay in Alabama, I also visited my childhood friend Lomax. On that particular Sunday, Elam Baptist Church, where

With Lomax Robinet and Royce Abercrombie
(I'm in the middle)

I had practiced and played the piano as a teenager, asked me to play for the morning service. After another Sunday dinner at Ruth's—just as when I was a boy—Lomax, now a successful businessman, and I went for a jaunt in his 4-wheel-drive pickup truck. We drove through fields, woods, and on some rather rough roads to get to some of the places where I had once lived and to visit some of my old friends and relatives. When I stopped by to see Royce and Becky, their son Carl took a picture of Royce, Lomax, and me.

Only the house on the Evans Place on Pea River Road is still intact; it's where we lived when Mrs. Moore drove me home from school in the fourth grade. I also wanted to linger along the road on which I had once hobbled with a swollen foot to catch the school bus; I found the road, but couldn't distinguish where the house used to be because of a stand of loblollies that had been planted. I especially wanted to see again the house where I lived when I borrowed the kerosene from Miss Eva, and to reminisce about my visits with her. Even with the extra traction, we couldn't get back to the old place, for beavers had dammed up the stream I once forded to get to school.

As we drove by the place where Mrs. Griffin's house once stood, Lomax asked, "Horace, you remember Miss Eva, don't you?" *Did I remember Miss Eva!* I told him about borrowing the

Miss Eva

kerosene and her words of encouragement, which had been Miss Eva's and my secret. He asked, "Did you ever tell her you have a Ph.D. and that you are a college professor and a published author?" Reluctantly I admitted that I hadn't seen, called, or heard from Miss Eva since leaving Alabama, and that surely she must be dead by now.

Lomax exclaimed, "No, Miss Eva's not dead! She lives in a trailer just outside Elamville." As we pulled into her front yard, there she was—Miss Eva, 87 years old and leaning on her walker, slowly hobbling out onto the front porch to meet us. Greeting Lomax with a hug, she wondered, I am quite sure, who the white-haired old man was. Lomax said, "Miss Eva, I brought someone to see you."

The old lady peered at me as if I were an alien. I said, "I am Horace, Nelson Danner's youngest son." Seeing not the faintest glimmer of recognition, I added, "Miss Eva, do you remember giving a skinny teenage boy kerosene so that he could study, and encouraging him to stay in school and study hard, 'cause there's room at the top"?

Finally, the light of recognition dawned. "Hallelujah, it's Horace! It's really you. You've come home."

It was now Lomax' turn. "Yes, Miss Eva, he has come home, and he came home with the education you wanted him to have. He's an English professor, and an author."

Thank you again, Miss Eva; and thank you, Miss Andrews (see below); Miss Pullen, who still lives in Clio; Mr. Chandler, who died December 2000, and his widow, Mrs. Chandler, who lives in Auburn, Alabama; Mr. and Mrs. Botts, both deceased; Mrs. Moore, who, until her death in May 2001, lived in Clanton, Alabama; Mrs. Wilkinson, assumed to be deceased; Mrs. Carter, deceased; Mrs. Hartzog, who lives in Ariton, Alabama; Mrs. Tyler, deceased; and Mrs. Baxter, who now lives in an assisted living home in Montgomery. On one of my recent visits to Alabama, when Mrs. Baxter was still living at home, I played her piano, the one Mary Ann and I took lessons on during the summer of 1949.

And thank you, Miss Hixon, deceased, but until recently afflicted with Alzheimer's disease, residing in a nursing home in North Alabama, unable to speak a word or respond in any way); and Mrs. Laird, deceased.

I must add a special note on Miss Andrews, my first-grade teacher. I learned from Mr. Alto Jackson that she is 94 and lives in the same house as where she grew up, in Louisville, Alabama. I called Miss Andrews right away to tell her how she had played such an important part in my education. Miss Andrews was a little out of breath by the time she got to the phone, as she said she had to run into the house because she was outside raking leaves, and that she had forgotten her cell phone! Alas, she didn't remember me.

The status of my brothers and sisters in order from oldest to youngest is as follows: Lovick: died in 1974; his widow and my wart remover, Lessie, lives in Skipperville, Alabama; Lalar: the story book reader, died in 1993; Vallie: lives with her husband in Midland City, Alabama, and volunteers at a hospital in Dothan, Alabama; James: died December 15, 1998; his widow, Ada, who still loves to fish, lives in Brundidge, Alabama; Ellie Mae: who prayed for my soul, died in 1988; Olon: died in 1987; his guitarist widow, Estelle, lives in Ozark, Alabama; Loyce: died in 1992; his widow, Betty, still lives in Lipsomb, Alabama; Ralph: died June 1, 2001, at the Central Alabama Veterans Administration Medical Facility, Tuskegee, Alabama; his widow, Alcie, lives in Prattville, Alabama; and Bennie: with his wife, Alberta, now retired from missionary service in Guatemala, live in a retirement home in Nashville, Tennessee.

Charles Brock, my cousin Ruth's son, is now retired from the Navy and is helping write a book on the heritage of Clio and Barbour County. Ruth, crippled with arthritis, and now in her 80's, isn't able to go to church much anymore. But each time I return to Alabama, I make it a point to eat with her and Charles, especially when they're having the catfish Charles has caught at Pea River. After we've eaten, she ushers me into the living room, where she asks me to play the piano again, and we sing "Whispering Hope," "Amazing Grace," and "What a Friend We Have in Jesus."

The status of those professors and others named in the memoir is as follows: Dean Boyd: deceased; Dr. Ervin: my piano teacher, deceased; Miss Goodwin, deceased; Dr. Sterkx: deceased; Dr. Ammerman: deceased; Dr. Huber: still professor at American University; and David McGowan: the student with learning disabilities, who gave me the idea for the vocabulary book, is now a syndicated cartoonist, living in Herndon, Virginia. Dave and I are now working on a children's book of words, for which he will draw the illustrations. Finally, thanks to the thousands of students, both in high school and in college, who helped me over the years test and retest the inductive—or discovery—concept of amassing an academic vocabulary.

Epilogue

Our three children are college graduates and Patty and Stephen have married college graduates. At this writing, Jerry, the scholar, prefers the single life.

Out of the cotton fields (and the peanut fields), I am now semi-retired and able to do what I enjoy most—teaching at University of Maryland University College, continuing to write books exploring the delights and treasures of the English language, swimming and working out in the gym, singing bass in my church choir, and playing the piano for my church. And, I might add, playing my very own piano, with a lamp to read and play by, and with a number of pairs of shoes to choose from. And I drive a new Saturn with a CD player so that I can listen to classical music—as well as Irish love songs—as I commute to the university and its satellite campuses. I couldn't have made it without the help of a lot of kind and caring people, including Margie and the children. I love you all.

Thank you for letting me share my memoir, if not my entire life's story, at least, the parts that can be told. If it will encourage a teacher to listen and help a student even more, or a student to overcome any obstacle to obtain an education, it will have been worth the effort.

In the words of Booker T. Washington, "I have learned that success is to be measured not so much by the position that one has reached in life as by the obstacles which he has overcome while trying to succeed."

End Notes

I returned again to Alabama for Christmas in 1991, to see my family, relatives, friends, and teachers. I visited Miss Eva on Christmas Day; this time, she called me by name as I entered her home. I asked her how many times or how often had I borrowed kerosene. She replied, "Horace, honey, I don't remember. Lots of times. What I remember more than your borrowing kerosene was that you were always singing to the top of your lungs as you passed my house." After we had chatted for a few minutes, I gave her a sum of money that paid for the kerosene and possibly some of the interest that had accumulated over the years. Although reluctant to take the money, Mrs. Griffin acknowledged that as a widow with mounting medical bills, she could surely use it. I assured her, however, that no amount of money could pay her for her support and encouragement. As a small token of my appreciation, I autographed a copy of my book for her. I was grateful for that opportunity to express my thanks to Miss Eva, because she died in January 1996.

In January 1992, I traveled to Savannah, Georgia, to visit Mrs. Laird, the teacher who started the boys' quartet. In an advanced stage of emphysema, Mrs. Laird's labored breathing was rapid and shallow. However, she was alert, and I had the opportunity to play the piano for her and her friends. She said, "Horace, you remember I smoked. I've quit, but not soon enough." She hadn't lost the lilt in her voice and the twinkle in her eyes. I have just learned that Mrs. Laird died recently.

And now a note on some of my high school and college classmates. Chris Green received a Master's degree in Spanish from the *Instituto Tecnológico y de Estudios Superiores de Monterrey*, Monterrey, Mexico, and taught Spanish for 30 years at Robert E. Lee High School in Montgomery—all in the same classroom. John McRae Hart earned a BEE (bachelor of electrical engineering) from Auburn University and is now retired, living in Florida. Ila Mizelle became a high school biology teacher, and died in 1996. Carolyn Davis, a mother of four boys, lives with her husband in Florida. Royce Abercrombie just retired from DynaCorp as a balance and weight technician at Fort Rucker, Alabama; he lives with his wife Becky about a mile from where he grew up outside Clio.

Robert (Bobby) Anderson, my tutor in algebra at Troy State, received his Ph.D. from University of Alabama and became a distinguished professor there. Wade Hall received his Ph.D. in English, and is now retired after a brilliant career as a professor of English and the author of at least a dozen books on the South. Robert DeLoach, a member of the quartet, graduated from Auburn and became an engineer. Now retired, he lives in Anniston, Alabama. It has been difficult to contact him, since he is always on the golf course. I have not been able to establish contact with David Clark, from Fort Myer, and Paul Merritt, my best friend in military police school at Camp Gordon, Georgia.

Besides my brothers and their wives and my sisters, there are three persons who have helped me tremendously. One is Lee Hunt, who was born and raised in Clio, and who wrote *A Town Called Clio*. Now living in Alexandria, Virginia, after retiring as a geologist from the National Academy of Sciences, he has given me the benefit of his vast repertoire of facts and figures. Lee also received his graduate degree in geology from American University. On his back porch overlooking the Potomac, Lee and I have sat and talked for hours, while Anne, his wife, served us refreshments. It was he who corrected my information on the width of the Milky Way and gave me permission to use his icy description of Blue Springs. Lee also suggested that I go into more detail about my going to American University.

While Lee Hunt suggested that I give more details about my academic work at American University, one of my University of Maryland students, Chief Master Sergeant Jean D. Delancy (Retired), suggested I fill in the blank spaces of my military career. So, J. D., thanks for wanting to know.[28]

And then there's the grand patriarch of Clio, the owner of *Jacksons'*, Alto Lofton Jackson, Esquire. Mr. Jackson has just retired after practicing law for 60 or more years, operating his store, and doing a little farming, he said. It was Alto who sold Mama my new pair of overalls when I entered first grade (see first grade picture). Mr. Jackson first wrote me after one of his sons downloaded the old electronic version of this memoir from my website. He then made copies of it and distributed it to just about everyone, especially my teachers who were still living. He writes in the classical manner, using gerundial possessives as deftly as a skilled

---

[28] J. D. is with Booz, Allen, Hamilton, a consulting firm in McLean, Virginia.

surgeon uses a scalpel. He knows everyone who has ever lived in Clio, and informed me that Miss Andrews, my first grade teacher, was not only still living, but taking care of her house and garden. In an earlier version, I had assumed that she was deceased. I was greatly saddened to learn from him that Mrs. Laird and Miss Hixon had died just recently. He also informed me that the Coca-Cola pencils and tablets were distributed by the Nu-Icey Bottling Plant, in Clio. And he reminded me of something I had completely forgotten—Clio even had a hotel. Or was it Lee Hunt who told me that?

Mr. Jackson wrote, using a manual typewriter. I asked him if the typewriter might possibly be the same one on which he typed my recommendation to Troy State almost 50 years ago. He said, "Not quite, but almost."

I invite your comments concerning the memoir. I would also encourage you to write your own, regardless if you choose to publish it. If writing your memoir does for you what it has done for me, you will come to appreciate more the many positive influences on your life, quite apart from any setbacks along the way. Your offspring may also appreciate the opportunity of reading your story.

Additional Credits

Just about all my students at Northern Virginia Community College, Montgomery College, and University of Maryland University College, as well as those at the District of Columbia Prison, have read the memoir and have made numerous suggestions. For instance, a prisoner student from Puerto Rico questioned why I would do such a thing as "stick a nail in my foot," as originally recounted in the memoir. While this is the usual expression in Alabama, I thought his suggestion was quite constructive, so I changed the phrase to "I stepped on a nail which pierced my foot." One student at Montgomery College wanted to know if the semicolon key had worn out yet on my word processor, inasmuch as I overused semicolons—according to him. I might add that Dr. Noël agreed with him.

I also want to express my appreciation to Charles Dawson of Wedowee, Alabama, for his sending me maps of Barbour County, showing in detail all the roads on which I used to live. Charles and his brother Eddie were two of my special friends while we were living on the Lee Place.

The first edition of the memoir was funded by Ms. Zelma Darden of Manassas, Virginia. After reading the online version, Ms. Darden felt that the memoir should be made available to high school students and their parents and teachers. Her gift made it possible to produce the memoir originally in booklet form, and a copy was included free with the purchase of a copy of *Discover It! A Better Vocabulary, the Better Way.*

I would also like to pay tribute to Dr. Chalmers Archer, originally from Tchula, Mississippi, and author of *Growing Up Black in Rural Mississippi*. Dr. Archer is also the author of *Green Berets in the Vanguard*, published in 2001 by Naval Institute Press. One of the first Green Berets, Dr. Archer is a professor at Northern Virginia Community College, Manassas Campus. His experiences, so poignantly related, parallel many of the incidents related in *Out of the Cotton Fields*.

Though I haven't seen James Chiodo, with whom I was stationed at Fort Myer, Virginia, since July 1953—almost fifty years ago—he sent me the complete roster of fellow trainees at Camp Gordon, Georgia, where we were in military police school. He also sent copies of promotion and assignment orders involving both of us, as well as of David Clark, John Bawsel, and Fredy Faust, three other friends who figure prominently in the memoir.

Finally, I want to pay tribute to my young friend, Angelo Segui. He is the light of my life and the hope of the future. Because of a series of unsettling circumstances, Angelo and his Colombian mother ended up in the homeless shelter of Prince William County, Virginia. A friend of mine married the mother and adopted the boy. Angelo is beautiful, as can be seen in the dedication picture; he is also exuberantly happy, extremely intelligent, and remarkably funny. He calls me Abuelo, Spanish for grandfather. The shirt he is wearing in the picture was purchased at the Salvation Army thrift shop in Woodbridge, Virginia. I am setting up a fund for him, to which readers may contribute. I want to make sure he gets the education that a person of his caliber and circumstances deserves. Since he was born in Miami, he is an American citizen. And I wouldn't be surprised that one day he will be sitting in the Oval Office as Angelo Segui, President of the United States of America.

Major occurrences since last printing:

Ms. Josephine Baxter, my piano teacher, died.

Ms. Becky Abercrombie, wife of my good friend Royce, died.

Ms. Virginia Carper, the piano teacher of my son Stephen, died.

Ms. Zelma Darden, who funded the first printing of the memoir, died.

Clio, the town I loved so well, has made major improvements. It now has a new town hall and fire station. Most of the homes on Elamville Street have been restored and are a beauty to behold. In addition, the town has a new enlarged post office.

Outside the town, there is a new chicken processing plant, where most of the employees are Mexicans, which the town has abopted as friends and neighbors. To accommodate them, there are now two Mexican stores and a bakery. Many of the Clionians are learning a few words in spanish.

The rusting tin shells of the peanut warehouses have been razed.

In May 2005, I returned to Alabama for a whirlwind of events:

On May 11, The Clayton Record, the weekly newspaper of Barbour County, interviewed me concerning the memoir. The article appeared May 20, 2005. I learned that there are plans to make the memoir into a play.

On May 13, a literary ladies' club in Enterprise, Alabama, entertained me at a luncheon; the ladies bought all the copies of *Discover It! A Better Vocabulary, a Better Way,* that I had brought. Each of them placed an order for a copy of the memoir as well.

On May 14, members of the classroom improvement staff of the Alabama State Department of Education held a luncheon for me in Montgomery. We discussed the use of *Discover It! A Better Vocabulary, a Better Way,* in the schools of Alabama.

Of course, while I was in Alabama, I visited my 93-year-old sister, Vallie, who is in a managed-care facility in Dothan. She is extremly feeble, but I managed to take her out to a steakhouse. I also visited my cousin Ruth, who was a surrogate mother during my teenage years. She just celebrated her 90th birthday.

Testimonials and Endorsements

Dr. Thomas J. Sienkewicz
Minnie Billings Capron Professor of Classics
Monmouth College
700 East Broadway
Monmouth, Illinois 61462
(309) 457-2371 OFFICE
(309) 457-2310 FAX
toms@monm.edu
http://www.monm.edu/academic/classics

February 18, 1999

Horace G. Danner, President
Imprimis Books
PO Box 614
Occoquan, VA 22125

Dear Horace:

I am writing to thank you for sending me complimentary copies of *A Thesaurus of Word Roots of the English Language* and *Discover It! A Better Vocabulary*. I will treasure both books not only for their intrinsic value but because of my long association with both of the authors.

As you know, I have continued to make use of your word clustering technique in my vocabulary building courses for many years, first at Howard University and now at Monmouth College. I find this technique to be especially valuable in administering diagnostic tests to my students at the beginning and at the end of the semester.

Thank you again for the books.

Sincerely,

Tom

Thomas J. Sienkewicz

461-1 Lambeth Field
Station 1
Charlottesville, VA 22904

September 6, 1999

To Whom It May Concern,

As a student, I have witnessed firsthand the value of a complete and extensive vocabulary. Truly, it is imperative that educators instill in their students a respect and passion for expanding their language skills early in the educational process. It is a shame that the tools necessary to aid in this development are either not up to the appropriate standards or are simply not available. The unique approach to building a better vocabulary presented in Dr. Horace Danner's *Discover It!* is the remedy to this problem. The simple and intuitive method of learning in the *Discover It!* system is the key to overcoming the kind of frustration that accompanies the mere word memorization presented in traditional learning styles. Dr. Danner presents word families with common elements, encouraging the reader to ascertain new vocabulary words based on known root meanings. I have found that this is the most effective way to absorb new vocabulary words, as the stress is on the ability to discover the meanings in a useful way, and not to simply commit them to memory. This approach eliminates the feelings of disappointment and frustration that often prevent young students from building and mastering their vocabularies. *Discover It* presents a new paradigm of learning that I am eager to embrace and recommend.

Sincerely,

Jason Sebranek

Jason Sebranek
University of Virginia

**FAIRFAX COUNTY
PUBLIC SCHOOLS**

Department of Instructional Services
Walnut Hill Center
7423 Camp Alger Avenue
Falls Church, Virginia 22042

October 3, 1997

Horace G. Danner, Ph.D.
Imprimis Books
P.O. Box 614
Occoquan, VA 22125-0614

Dear Dr. Danner:

After reviewing *Discover It! A Better Vocabulary, The Better Way,* I am pleased to recommend it for use as supplementary material to support vocabulary and language study in Fairfax County Public Schools.

I will inform the English department chairpersons about the text and ask them to add it to their list of supplementary materials.

Sincerely,

Donald C. Humbertson, Ph.D.
Coordinator, Secondary Language Arts

SPELL
Society for the Preservation of English Language and Literature

10034 Mesa Madera Dr. ● San Diego CA 92131 ● (619) 549-6788; Fax (619) 549-2276
● E-Mail: richard.lederer@pobox.com ● URL: http://www.pobox.com/~verbivore

Richard Lederer
Vice President

August 8, 2001

Dear Drs. Danner and Noël:

The pirates of long ago protected their treasure by constructing chests that possessed several locks, each lock with its own key. So it is with vocabulary. To unlock the trove of words that is the treasure of our tongue, a speaker and writer must possess many keys. Only then will he or she be able to unlock the varying shades of meanings of thousands of words.

I am impressed with the many keys to the power and the romance of words that you share with your readers in *Discover It! A Better Vocabulary -- The Better Way*. The etymologies, root clusters, word lore, quotations, and quizzes all serve to increase the student's adventure as a learner – a life-long learner, because the book encourages a love of words that will not diminish with the passing years. That is in part of a reflection of the authors' own passion for language, which lights the entire book.

May students and teachers around our planet discover *Discover It!*,

Richard Lederer
Richard Lederer
author of *The Miracle of Language*
usage editor of *The Random House Webster's Unabridged Dictionary of the English Language, Third Edition*

SPELL National Office: P.O. Box 118, Waleska GA 30183
E-mail: spellorg@mindspring.com — URL: http://www.mindspring.com/~spellorg/

Attention High School Seniors
Memoir Contest

Occoquan Books, which published Dr. Danner's memoir, announces a contest for high school seniors, who themselves faced and overcame extreme obstacles in acquiring their education. Occoquan Books, through the sales of this memoir as well as through donations, will award a cash prize to the senior writing the winning essay.

Essays will be judged on the severity of the obstacles, efforts to overcome them, and grammatical correctness. The number of awards will depend on the amount accrued from memoir sales up to the cut-off date, April 30, plus any amounts received from corporate and individual gifts. The maximum amount to be awarded is $1,000. If more than that amount has accumulated, a second, third, fourth, etc. prize will be awarded.

Essays shall be of 1,000 to 1,500 words, word-processed, accompanied by a recent photograph, a cover sheet, and mailed to Occoquan Memoir Contest, P. O. Box 614, Occoquan, Virginia 22125. The cover sheet will include the student's name, address, phone number where the student can be reached, parent's name, and name and address of school. Students must not write their names on the essay itself, as the essays will be checked by a committee of educators, and it is possible that a paper might be written by a student of the committee member. Each paper will be coded so that only the contest administrator knows the identity of the student.

Those corporations and individuals wishing to contribute to the fund which will award the prizes are encouraged to write for details.

The Occoquan Fund
P. O. Box 614
Occoquan, Virginia 22125

Questions concerning the contest may be sent to Dr. Danner by email at imprints5283@comcast.net. The telephone number is 703-491-5283.